July '03

RUSSIAN ODYSSEY

For Ika,

With appreciation
for your efforts
toward Aquarius, and
with love,

Nancy

RUSSIAN
ODYSSEY

Trials and Triumphs of an
Aquarian Seeker

∿

Nancy Seifer

Library of Congress Number: 2003091628
ISBN :   Hardcover   1-4134-0082-5
               Softcover   1-4134-0081-7

This book was printed in the United States of America.

Author's Notes about the Cover

The work of art on the cover is *Kitezh Transformed* by Ivan Yakovlevich Bilibin (1876-1942). It was created in 1929 as a set design for the Rimsky-Korsakov opera *The Tale of the Invisible City of Kitezh and the Maiden Fevronia.*

The tale of Kitezh emerged after the catastrophic demise of Kiev, "the Mother of all Russian Cities," in 1240. Orthodox Russia was born in Kiev in 988, and the Christ spirit flourished there until its destruction by Mongol invaders. A legend later arose that a holy city, *Kitezh*, had been submerged at the bottom of a lake to escape annihilation. One day it would reemerge resplendent, like the New Jerusalem, the city and its people transfigured.

The cover layout was designed by Matt McArdle *(mattm@mattmcardle.co.uk)* of Bath, England. Graphic art, also by Bilibin, frames *Kitezh Transformed.*

To order additional copies of this book, contact:
Xlibris Corporation
1-888-795-4274
www.Xlibris.com
Orders@Xlibris.com
18374

CONTENTS

To spiritual seekers everywhere.

"Paradise . . . is hidden in each one of us . . . (E)ach man (is) guilty for all before all, besides his own sins . . . (W)hen people understand this thought, the Kingdom of Heaven will come to them, no longer in a dream but in reality . . . (E)very action has its law. This is a matter of the soul, a psychological matter. In order to make the world over anew, people themselves must turn onto a different path psychically. Until one has indeed become the brother of all, there will be no brotherhood."

Fyodor Dostoyevsky
The Brothers Karamazov

The Law of Rebirth is a great natural law upon our planet. It is a process, instituted and carried forward under the Law of Evolution. It is closely related to and conditioned by the Law of Cause and Effect. It is a process of progressive development, enabling men to move forward from the grossest forms of unthinking materialism to a spiritual perfection and an intelligent perception which will enable a man to become a member of the Kingdom of God.

Alice A. Bailey
The Reappearance of the Christ

ACKNOWLEDGMENTS

Russian Odyssey went through many stages before arriving at this final one. Throughout its long evolution, I received support from individuals in ways that ranged from the concrete and tangible to the moral and spiritual. My heartfelt thanks to all: Rufus Crown, Judi Dean, Daniel Entin, Jackie Halpern, Betty Hart, Alice Kossoff, Harold Leich, Laraine Lippe, Patricia Lynden, Laraine Mai, Barbara Valocore, Margaret Vann and Robin Zeamer.

I also want to extend my special thanks to the Lifebridge Foundation for its generous assistance.

Finally, I am profoundly grateful to my husband, my companion on the Way. Without his continued support, encouragement, and assistance, this book would not have come into being.

FOREWORD

*R*ussian Odyssey is a book for everyone interested in spirituality, Russia, and the Aquarian Age. But in its essence, *Russian Odyssey* is for seekers facing the challenges of the Spiritual Path in a difficult world. It is for all of us who are growing spiritually and moving toward the ultimate choice of relinquishing our narrow interests to serve the Greater Good. In this sense, it is a story for everyone awakening to the soul's journey through the school of life.

The author writes in the introduction: *My travels to Russia began in the 1980s when I found myself on the spiritual path, having left my professional life a decade earlier.* She made a decision, under the promptings of her soul, to leave a career path and discover her life purpose. Many who read this book will share a similar urge to "find themselves" in order to give greater meaning and substance to their lives.

The remarkable image on the cover of the book, by the Russian artist Ivan Bilibin, symbolizes the "narrow razor-edge path" that forms the way of approach from the material world into the realms of spirit. The pathway, constructed of blocks of light and darkness, moves toward a red doorway evocative of the "Gates of Heaven" in the icon screens of Russian Orthodox churches. Bilibin seems to suggest that the heavenly city, under the blazing rainbow sun, must be entered through that narrow passageway.

To take the imagery further, the blocks of light and darkness in the pathway can be seen as the checkered pattern of our lifetimes. The Way of Return is born of the struggles we face in balancing, fusing and blending the light and shadow sides of our nature. From the crucible of our experience, we craft the steps along the way. Over time, each perfect stepping stone is created from the quarry of our own souls. Through lifetimes of trial and testing, we achieve balance and integration. Finally, perfected and made whole, we enter through the doorway into the realms of light and soul awareness.

As you read this *Odyssey*, you will discover that the soul of Russia is engaged in an archetypal struggle between polar opposites: darkness and light, cruelty and kindness, profound suffering and great spiritual aspiration. The contradictions of mystical thinking and bloody earthly struggle, earmarks of the Russian experience, form the essential conflicts of a nation that yearns to enter the heavenly city. The struggle must ultimately be resolved and transcended if Russia is to fulfill her prophesied spiritual destiny.

The triumphant experience of the author provides a living example to this end. Her trials upon the path and her eventual passage through the doorway of light serve as an inspiration. Her struggles, described so honestly and openly in *Russian Odyssey*, are a living example for all who wrestle with the polarities and contradictions reflected in the Russian experience — a magnification of the human experience. Her story illustrates how harmony is wrought from conflict through lifetimes of testing, and how trial and tribulation always precede ultimate triumph.

Russian Odyssey is also a story of Aquarius, the constellation into which our sun is now entering. Aquarius is the sign of Service to the One Life. Service is the fruit of many lives of purification and testing. For the author, and for all triumphant seekers, serving others is natural. It is the nature of the Path Itself. Having turned within to find understanding, having grasped and registered a sense of true interconnectedness with all souls, the natural (one could rightly say supernatural) urge is to share the light found within with others. The radiance born in the inner recesses of being must be given freely to all, as giving without wanting in return is the nature of the Way.

The way is the same for each of us. It is not easy. We start out identified with the body in which we dwell. Our consciousness is imprisoned in the form. We are asleep, but in time, we are jostled awake by the barbs and prods of life and we begin to seek something higher. We seek inner guidance to become integrated and illumined, to feel a living urge to serve and give. We must each somehow discover the meta-physical realities within our own being and bring them into living demonstration.

In *Russian Odyssey*, the author shares her search for truth and the inner guidance that led her to Russia. There she faced, and finally released, a karmic pattern first encountered in her difficult early life. As you enter into her spiritual quest, you may be touched deeply, as I have been, by a new reality. Hopefully, you will come in touch with the light of your own higher self. In this light you may begin to see a greater light revealing the requirements of the Way of Return for all of us.

You may see, for example, how necessary it is to let go, to relinquish that which is lesser for that which is greater. You may begin to see the role that clear sight and discrimination must play in revealing to each of us how certain patterns of behavior have plagued our lives. You may see, in a new light, karmic residues that must be relinquished if we are to enter into fuller life. You may sense, as well, how important, how essential, it is to learn detachment from the things of this world before the worlds of light and Spirit can be truly known.

Above all, God willing, as you read this real-life story of a fellow traveler on the path to the inner city of light, you may begin to sense the beauty of the play of light and shadow that paints the pathway of return. You may grasp more clearly the reality of the journey that we each must travel if we, too, are to discover our place in the scheme of things, and make our unique and self-created contribution to the world.

Russian Odyssey can open our eyes if we read it with an open mind and a loving heart. It is written in the spirit of Truth and brings new light to the nature of the One Life and the journey of lifetimes that we all share in this schoolhouse of life on planet Earth.

M. K.Vieweg
February 2003

INTRODUCTION

In truth, this is a story of two odysseys, one born of another. It began as a search for the enigmatic Russian soul at a time when spirituality was reemerging in that country, with the fall of communism. I set out on this quest as a writer, an observer, at a distance from my subject. But I ended up on a life-changing journey, full of alluring adventures and tortuous trials, which was to culminate in a personal metamorphosis.

My travels to Russia began in the 1980s when I found myself on the spiritual path, having left my professional life a decade earlier. I went there first as a "citizen diplomat," during the Cold War, unexpectedly encountering fellow seekers along the way. It was their thirst for spiritual knowledge that sparked the idea of writing a book. In the course of my initial interviews, I came upon a "spiritual family," magnetic individuals who led me to the sacred soil of Old Russia, where renewal was underway. They also led me into a labyrinth, from which finding my way out posed the ultimate challenge for my soul.

Before embarking on my journey, I discovered a series of prophecies about Russia that further fueled my quest. They appeared in disparate metaphysical texts and Russian writings, yet all concerned the flowering of Russia's soul, the expression of its highest potential. At their core was the notion that Russia had a significant role to play — at an unspecified time in the future — in fostering a new, universal spirituality. One prophetic source linked the soul of Russia, alone among the souls of nations, with the Aquarian Age.

By 1990, there were abundant signs of spiritual awakening among Russians. Some were consonant with experiences of Aquarian seekers around the world, while others were uniquely Russian, born of its soul's urge — traceable back a thousand years — to unite heaven and earth. While exploring these developments and interviewing people who had once seemed utterly foreign, I gradually, mysteriously, found myself becoming absorbed into their midst.

Much of what happened to me in Russia bore the unmistakable imprint of Destiny. Encounters took place that could not have happened merely by chance. Yet I discovered, only belatedly, that their purpose was altogether different from what I had originally supposed. Instead of furthering my book about Russia's soul, they had been intended to free my own soul from a karmic pattern rooted in previous lifetimes. And thus one odyssey gave way to another: a journey through Russia from the vantage point of the soul.

Because my story reaches back to past-life experiences that influenced the circumstances of this lifetime, it became necessary to offer the reader some personal history. Thus the book begins with impressionistic sketches of my early years and the events that impelled me toward the spiritual path. Part One of the book, *Starting Out*, serves as the foundation for the rest, bringing the reader to the place where my Russian odyssey begins — Part Two, *The USSR*. Part Three, *Mother Russia*, traces my deepening involvement with people and places in the Russian heartland. Part Four, *Heading Home*, describes the trials I endured and the ultimate triumphs, the spiritual harvest of this odyssey.

In telling this story, it is my sincere hope that the reader will come away from it with a deeper understanding of the reality of reincarnation, or the Law of Rebirth, and of karma, also known as the Law of Cause and Effect. Discovering these spiritual laws helped me to make sense of the early part of my life. Living the rest of it in light of these laws has given me incontrovertible proof that what we normally view as "life" is merely one chapter in an ongoing Book of Life, recorded in the depths of our immortal souls.

NOTE TO READERS

The story you are about to read is true
in every way but one.

The names of the Russian figures have
been changed and their identities altered slightly.
The same is true of the Russian town where
much of the story takes place.

Part One

Starting Out

Losses and Acquisitions

The first journey of my life took place when I was four years old. A harbinger of things to come, it formed my first set of memories, striking chords that lingered over time. In the winter of 1947, our family doctor advised my mother to take me to a warm climate to cure a rasping bronchial cough. On the train trip south, I had my first experience of a broken heart. It was an omen, though I was too young, mercifully, to know about omens.

The object of my affection was a tall man with skin like ebony and a smile that beamed like the sun. Throughout the day he stopped by our compartment to ask if we needed anything; at night he brought fresh linens, turning our sitting area into sleeping quarters. His presence radiated warmth and joy. On each visit he asked, in a voice that sounded like music, *An' how's miz Nansah feelin'? Is there anythin' I can bring her?* For three days and nights I inhabited a perfect universe.

As the train approached our destination, I made the shattering discovery that this man, a Pullman Car porter, was not getting off with us. He was already part of my world. I pleaded with him to come, not comprehending why he laughed, gently, in response to my pleas. When he left our luggage on the platform and returned to the train, I ran toward him. He stood there motionless, his smile concealing the chasm between our worlds — revealed in the harsh glare of my mother's eyes.

The main reason for this voyage was to soak up the Florida sunshine, but my mother couldn't abide the frittering away of time. In the mornings we sat on a shaded veranda of the hotel where she taught me how to write. On afternoon excursions she taught me the words of her favorite song. Over and over we sang, *The girl that I marry will have to be, as soft and as pink as a nursery. The girl I call my own, will wear satins and laces and smell of cologne. Her nails will be polished and in her hair, she'll wear a gardenia . . .*

Long after I had committed the words to memory, they remained mysterious to me. Over time I discovered what a nursery was, and a gardenia, and *satinsandlaces*. But I recall singing this song while waiting at the bus stop across from our hotel, holding my mother's hand, and watching a crowd of strangers gather. They would ooh and aah at my blond ringlets, blue eyes, and dimples, telling my mother that I was "another Shirley Temple." She would smile proudly, but was not one to utter words of approval.

My father was the opposite. Full of love and affection, he called me his "little ray of sunshine." The high point of my day was being scooped up in his arms when he arrived home from work. As far back as I can remember, there were hard angles, rough edges, and fixed boundaries with my mother. With my father there were none. In Florida, as the weeks passed by, I anxiously awaited his arrival. He and my two older brothers were to come down during winter school break.

Hours after their arrival, there was another separation. My father, determined to have the boys take full advantage of their brief stay in Florida, promised to take them night-fishing on day one. All five of us walked out to the end of a long pier. The boys boarded the boat and I tried to follow, but my father turned me back, warning that it was too dangerous. I cried my heart out but the more I cried, the more sternly he refused to allow me to go. Feeling utterly abandoned, I stood on the pier with my mother watching the boat vanish into the darkness.

A year or so later, another life thread became visible. Before most families had their own television sets, a neighboring town on Long Island held an event to promote the new medium. It was a so-called beauty pageant for five-year-old girls: we were to walk across the stage of our local movie theater in front of a TV camera. I became paralyzed by fear, refusing to budge despite the coaxing of a battery of adults. Decades later, upon discovering reincarnation, I puzzled over the possible past-life origins of that event. It, too, was to have many echoes over time.

Otherwise, during those early years, life was more pleasant than not. In addition to my brothers and a sleep-in maid, our household usually included a grandparent. My father's father, who lost his sight, lived with us before moving to a home for the blind. My mother's mother moved in next. Grandma's arrival was a blessing for me. She was a constant source of affection, as well as a safe harbor from periodic attacks by the younger of my two brothers, for whom my existence was a constant source of irritation. It was his misfortune to be the middle child in a family where the eldest was deemed to be near-perfect, and where the youngest, a long-awaited baby girl, was often doted upon.

I remember sitting on Grandma's lap and feeling as though I were floating on an ocean of love. The soft, undulating flesh of her bosom, arms and belly melded into a warm, protective cocoon in which I could remain happily ensconced for hours. To be near her, I also spent long periods of time on her bedroom floor next to her sewing machine table. I would curl up on the rug watching her feet pump the treadle, like a pet lying near the feet of its human companion.

When it came to verbal communication, however, Grandma and I were greatly limited. She had immigrated to America from Poland as an adult, a mother of four small children, and had never learned much English. I was a curious child, always wanting to know the reasons for things, forever asking *why*. Grandma had a pet phrase that was guaranteed to foil my questioning, as it left me thoroughly mystified. *Y is a crooked letter*, she would say, which sounded like *Vy ees ah krookit litter*.

In our kitchen, there was a special cabinet reserved for Grandma's dishes, or dishes used when she lived with us. An observant Jew, she observed kosher dietary rules. I remember her being at the major Jewish event of my childhood: the Bar Mitzvah of the younger of my brothers. Yet the person I remembered best from that occasion was our black housekeeper, Perry. She had on a new dress, instead of her uniform, and she wore a beautiful white flower in her hair. It was a gardenia, the first I ever saw.

In a photo taken that day, Perry was holding me in her arms. I was six, almost seven. On my face was a look of sublime contentment. Perry was another pillar in my life, another source of affection, another surrogate mother, like Grandma. Although my mother did not hold a job in those years, she was always busy, unavailable, preoccupied with projects ranging from decorating our house to finding apartments for Grandma's relatives — refugees from Hitler's concentration camps arriving in the US.

In the summer, "the children" were sent to camp. My brothers went to sleep-away camps while I attended a local day camp. The year I turned eight, I was allowed to go away to camp for one month. At the end of two weeks, my parents came to visit me. Two weeks later I returned home, and within a matter of days my world came crashing down. The lights went out, the pillars collapsed, the roof caved in.

My father killed himself. I knew nothing except that he was gone, forever. Policemen roamed our house, along with weeping relatives and neighbors. My mother lay on her bed sobbing, encircled by female relatives. Grandma enfolded me in her arms, saying, "Don't cry, don't cry." No one knew the psychological cost of not grieving, least of all an elderly woman from the old country. I stopped crying, pushing the pain underground. To keep it there would require inordinate emotional energy, for decades.

Perry left shortly thereafter. She was unable to go down to the basement, the scene of my father's final act. Since it was also the place where canned food was stored and laundry was dried, my mother felt obliged to let her go. Grandma went to live with one of my aunts and died two years later. My older brother went off to college, and soon the younger one. My mother went to work, leaving me in the care of an Irish maid with a fondness for whisky.

I survived largely with the support of friends, whom I would eventually be forced to leave.

Five years after my father's death, everything changed once again. I acquired a new father, a new last name, and a new home in a different part of the country. The name and the home belonged to a man from a big Midwestern city whom my mother decided to marry. At a court appearance shortly before the wedding, I was asked to raise my right hand and swear under oath that I voluntarily agreed to be legally adopted by this man, still a stranger. At barely thirteen, nothing about my life was voluntary.

And yet, the story of my mother's encounter with her second husband made this new life seem conspicuously fated. It had a touch of kismet that made it all the more romantic to my stepfather, a natural storyteller, who loved to regale listeners with the tale. He had been widowed for a year when his golfing partners convinced him to join them on a round-the-world cruise leaving from New York Harbor. One of them knew a widow who lived in the city and invited her to the ship's bon voyage party. She, in turn, invited my mother, an old friend, to accompany her.

After accepting the invitation, my mother was stricken with a migraine headache the day before the party and declined. But her friend was insistent and the next day she felt well enough to go. On board the ship, my stepfather caught a glimpse of her from the far end of a large, crowded reception hall and "made a beeline for her," as he used to say. It was right out of the song *Some Enchanted Evening . . . You will meet a stranger, You will see (her) standing, Across a crowded room . . .*

When the ship returned to New York three months later, they met again. Shortly thereafter they took a brief trip together, and then my mother's new beau came to our home to meet my brothers and me. On his second visit, they announced their plans to marry. Thus it was that I was pried away from my friends and catapulted into a new life in a strange city. The "sweetener" offered me was the promise of my own telephone, in a place where I didn't know a soul.

I attended an excellent high school connected with a university, but my attention lay elsewhere. The summer after freshman year I lost a good deal of weight, which transformed my social life. It was flattering to suddenly find myself the object of male attention, but also confusing. I was aware that only my external appearance had changed, nothing else. That made me wonder who or what was being sought after — the superficial image or the *real* me. This was my first brush with the dual nature of reality, though I was light-years away from comprehending it.

My parents enrolled me in a class on Judaism, but I found the ancient history and practices difficult to relate to. Unlike some classmates who assimilated the material quite readily, I seemed to lack the mental hooks on which to hang it. Curiously, it was Christian Science, in which my mother had found solace as a grieving widow, which had piqued my interest. Testimonials to faith healings, like that of an elderly man who rose from his wheelchair in defiance of physicians who said that he never would, had left an indelible impression.

Nevertheless, I was an avowed atheist by age thirteen. It seemed to me that if there was a god, he was cruel and unjust. I adopted as my credo the little ditty that went: *If God is good there is no God, if good is God there is no good.* I believed, or assumed, that we all lived on this earth for a given time and then passed away. It never occurred to me that life might have a deeper purpose. I simply tried to adapt to the hand that was dealt me and keep the pain submerged.

Home, during my high school years, was a place I preferred not to be. My stepfather, a likeable, jovial man, was unwittingly swept into battle between mother and daughter. My mother tried to cope with life by controlling it. She demanded that I *obey* her, unquestioningly. But I was born with a curious mind and a rebellious spirit. I bridled at what seemed to be arbitrary authority. It was a useful trait for a future seeker of truth, but trying, needless to say, for my mother. My stepfather, retired from a long business career, wanted to enjoy the good life with his younger wife. They traveled a lot, wintered in the south, attended fancy balls, and still his spouse was unhappy. The stated reason: her rebellious teenage daughter.

Going away to college loomed large on the horizon. When I finally arrived there, on my own at last, I was less interested in the intrinsic rewards of learning than fulfilling the requirements for independence. In those years, many girls were sent off to college mainly to obtain "Mrs." degrees. Long before graduation, my sorority sisters began delving into bridal magazines, visualizing their futures as suburban housewives. I had no idea where I was headed, but I knew it was somewhere else.

Out in the World

After college, things unfolded seamlessly. In any given situation, there was one conspicuously open door. My experience of life was walking through a series of such doors. It actually began before graduation, during the spring of my senior year when I traveled to Washington, D.C. with friends in search of a summer job. Lacking any sense of vocation or direction, I was drawn there merely by the aura of John F. Kennedy that lingered over the capital in the months after his assassination.

For a week in April of '64 my friends and I pounded the pavements, hunting for summer intern slots in competition with thousands of students from around the country. With only hours to go before leaving for the airport to return to school, I visited the office of a senator from my home state. As expected, summer jobs had long since been parceled out to the politically well-connected. But a lovely woman there went out of her way to help me, placing a call to someone she knew elsewhere.

I found myself sitting in a plush, wood-paneled office with all the trappings of power. The man who occupied it graciously looked over my résumé, but didn't know of an appropriate job for me. I returned to school empty-handed, having assumed it was *pro forma* when this man asked to keep a copy of my résumé. But a month later he called to say that a summer job tailor-made for a French major had come across his desk. When I hung up the phone, dizzied by the news, life suddenly began to hum with possibility. It was as if an invisible force had swooped down and plucked me out of the narrow confines of my world.

I entered the *real* world during a sweltering Washington summer, in the days when air-conditioning was still considered a luxury. My job was to translate papers written by French-speaking West Africans — participants in an international economics colloquium sponsored by the Labor Department. As an intern, I also attended a series of "White House Seminars," weekly talks given by Johnson Administration officials to two or three thousand of us packed into a hotel ballroom on Wednesday mornings.

The speakers who inspired me were the spiritual heirs of John F. Kennedy: his brother, Robert, and his brother-in-law, Sargent Shriver, the first Peace Corps director. They reignited the feeling I'd had four years earlier when I happened to hear JFK giving a campaign speech on the steps of my student union, while I was registering for freshman classes. That was his public unveiling of the Peace Corps idea. Something new came alive in me when I heard it. That feeling resurfaced during my summer in Washington. A year later I was in Peace Corps training, headed for French-speaking West Africa.

In my African town, the third largest in the Ivory Coast, two hundred foreigners — mostly Caucasians — were sprinkled among the forty thousand residents. Peace Corps volunteers were treated as welcome guests, yet it was eye-opening to find myself part of a tiny minority. There were times, during visits to remote villages, when babies burst out crying at the sight of me, frightened by my abnormal appearance. At the end of a stay in such a village, where I was the only white person, I had the odd experience of looking down at my own limbs with a jolt, surprised to recall their color.

Sitting around a cooking fire at sunset in an Ivoirian village was unimaginably peaceful. In the cities, things had already changed. Crime was still rare, and usually of the petty variety, but it was on the rise. An acquisitive, materialistic Western culture was being foisted upon traditional, communal societies. The entire country, a former French colony, was being inundated by a wave of change that appeared inevitable, though not necessarily in the best interest of Africans. While the part played by Peace Corps volunteers was small and seemingly benign, it raised for me, for the first time in my life, the question of responsibility for the consequences of one's actions.

My main assignment was teaching in a program called *Foyer Feminin*, hearth for women. It offered everything from literacy in French, which had become the national language, to sewing and nutrition. The ability to read and write was especially coveted by women and girls, as formal schooling was largely reserved for boys. A problem arose around the slowness of my method for teaching reading. I began with the alphabet and moved on to syllables, whereas my African counterparts, minimally educated themselves, taught their students to recite by memory, sending them home to "read" for their families almost immediately.

Apart from the friction caused by my teaching style, I felt completely at home in Africa. The people, especially the women, were warm, open, and full of goodwill toward American volunteers. They viewed us almost as a different species of white people, living as we did without air-conditioning, cars, big houses or other European "necessities." More importantly, the spirit of JFK had preceded us. In the simplest mud dwellings, there was often a poster of him hanging next to one of the Ivoirian president. The name Kennedy, with which babies were being christened, had become synonymous with America, and with goodwill.

For two years we lived on a tiny stipend, feeling richly rewarded by the notion, however illusory, that the world was a slightly better place for our efforts. We also had incredible opportunities to grow personally, to discover the range of our inner resources. As the end approached, however, I again faced a void. Nothing called to me. One day a newsletter arrived from Peace Corps headquarters in Washington. At the back was a listing of resources, including jobs for returning volunteers. One item caught my attention. I sent off a résumé, but received no response.

When I returned to the States months later, I called the organization, located in New York. The reason I hadn't heard from them was that the person then holding the job listed couldn't decide whether she wanted to return to school or stay at the job. The day before I called, she had finally decided to leave. The director complimented me on my good timing. I was hired to direct a summer program for African women, which combined studies in community development with travel in the US.

The State Department, which funded the program, decided to invite participants from the Ivory Coast for the coming year. That was a joyful coincidence for me, but proved distressing for my African-American assistant. Her French was rudimentary, which made it difficult for her to communicate at all with the Ivoirian women, while I had an easy rapport with them. That was 1968 — the summer when black rage, which had dramatically escalated during my two years in Africa, erupted in violence. My assistant's frustration erupted in anger. I was traumatized, she was fired, and the program's funding dried up soon thereafter.

Searching for a new job, sitting on a New York City bus, I noticed a sign that read: "Get Involved. Call the Mayor's Volunteer Coordinating Council." The charismatic mayor, John V. Lindsay, had miraculously pulled the city through that fiery summer without major incident. Elsewhere, inner cities had gone up in flames, cauldrons of seething anger in the wake of the King and Kennedy assassinations. In New York, Lindsay courageously walked the streets of black ghettos and managed to keep the peace.

I called the number on the sign. The story was similar: someone was just leaving. I was hired to match volunteers with public and private agencies seeking their help — straightforward, practical work, useful for learning about government. Six months later I found myself in politics, organizing volunteers for the mayor's reelection campaign. There I encountered two separate, parallel realities. One was an exhilarating crusade to reelect a man who stood for higher, better human instincts. The other was a dog-eat-dog contest for top dog, a political jungle strewn with corpses. The stakes were exceptionally high that year, as some envisioned Lindsay, and themselves, in the White House.

In the midst of this mayhem, I finally discovered a profession that called to me. I applied to journalism school, but did so almost as a lark, believing the odds were stacked against my acceptance at the most prestigious school of its kind. When I was accepted, I faced a major dilemma. In order to enroll, I would have had to leave the campaign months before Election Day. In the end, I couldn't do it. Despite what I already knew of the dark side of politics, the mayor's main opponent was an avowed racist, and he was well ahead in the polls.

When Lindsay won, I looked for a job in journalism, but lacking a degree and experience, my best offer was the night beat in a suburban backwater. At that point, I reminded myself that I still believed in "good government," and that campaign workers had job priority in the new administration. I wound up in the Mayor's Press Office with the task of creating a "neighborhood press office"— a link between City Hall and hundreds of neighborhood, ethnic, and foreign language newspapers. Many were the local papers of working-class communities, the very communities that had nearly defeated the mayor's reelection bid. And now the presidency was on the radar screen.

What began as an effort with a large public relations component evolved, over time, into an initiative with teeth. In the course of meetings with newspaper editors scattered across the city's five boroughs, I discovered that racist slogans in the election of '69 had masked some legitimate grievances. The people in white ethnic, blue collar neighborhoods had felt roundly ignored by the mayor and were letting their frustrations out on ethnic minorities. They saw themselves as hard-working taxpayers who received nothing from government, while inner city Black and Puerto Rican communities "got everything."

During a conversation with a friend in a government agency, I stumbled upon a fact that had somehow been overlooked at City Hall. By then, working-class communities were entitled to some of Johnson's "Great Society" programs, like day care and senior citizens centers. As a result of numerous memos on this and related subjects, I ended up as Aide to the Mayor for Ethnic Affairs, a position where, among other things, I helped working-class communities organize to apply for federal funds. Previously, whatever help they received had come in the form of political favors from local party bosses who in turn demanded their allegiance. This was a new era, superseding the old spoils system, or so I believed.

Reality, as in *realpolitik*, proved otherwise. The Mayor's operatives had tried to replace the old political clubhouses with John V. Lindsay Associations, but had failed. Unable to fight the bosses, they had decided to join them. When new programs for children and the elderly began to materialize — along with new community centers and jobs — the power brokers saw them as choice plums for the old patronage system. They wanted to pluck them out of the hands of the community people whose labors had produced them, and feed them into the political machines whose support they needed for a presidential race.

In a last-ditch attempt to salvage what rightfully belonged to the people, I asked for a meeting with the mayor, who had backed my efforts. I wanted to know for certain that *he* knew what was going on, hoping, naturally, that he would intervene on my side. But the moral divide appeared not to register with him. He told me that he saw no essential disagreement between his senior staff and me (the lowest on the totem pole), and advised me to try to see things more as they did. I was dumbfounded. It was one thing to watch ambitious young men wrestle over access to power; it was another to sacrifice my own integrity. Thus at age 29, powerless and defeated, I left the world of politics.

I ended up at a think-tank on the problems of white ethnic America, where I happened to be attending a conference during my final weeks at City Hall. The director had heard that I was leaving and invited me to join his staff. The work was a natural extension of what I had been doing, and learning, at a comfortable distance from the battlefield of politics. The goal was decreasing urban tensions between white ethnic groups and racial minorities through social policy initiatives.

The main challenge I faced there was altogether different. I was assigned to write a monograph on white ethnic working-class women in America, based on my New York experience and a growing body of research. Awaiting me upon its completion was a conference at which I would have to speak. For a full year I lived with the terror that had first surfaced when I was five. Somehow, I managed to survive the actual event. As a result, public appearances became a part of my job. And that led to yet another kind of dilemma. I found myself in the incongruous position of being viewed as the spokesperson for a huge segment of American women, of which I was not a part.

The solution came through a suggestion from a writer who kept urging me to write "a real book." I began thinking about compiling oral histories of working-class women, authentic voices of women around the country who could speak for themselves. The idea was barely formulated when a friend invited me to a dinner party. Seated next to me was a vice-president of a major publishing house. I mentioned my new idea. He said it sounded like a book they would be happy to add to their list. The next thing I knew, I had an agent, an advance, and a book deadline, in addition to my job.

The book evolved into an escape route from a role that felt increasingly inauthentic. When it was published, I left that job, and that world. Passing through open doors had taught me a lot, but hadn't led me to a place that I could comfortably call my own. At age thirty-three, I decided to give myself a few months to reflect on what I really wanted to do with my life.

As the months flew by, the nature of my questions became transformed. "What should I do with my life?" was replaced by "Who am I?" And then, "Why am I here?" "What is the purpose of my life?" "What is the purpose of human existence?" The questions that haunt all spiritual seekers had become mine, though at the time I still firmly believed that I was an atheist.

The Couch and the Cosmos

During my so-called career, people had expected big things from me. Opportunities seemed to fall into my lap and I managed to get up to the plate for them — until there came the line I could not cross and the role I could not play. During most of those years, however, my personal life was languishing. When the lights went down on the small stage of my daily life, I was alone with an unhappy self — not all the time, but enough of the time to make me realize that I needed more help than my closest friends could provide over dinner.

Once before, many years earlier, I had briefly visited a psychiatrist. The summer after my junior year in college, I had suffered from intense anxiety. In order to graduate, I had to take a course in public speaking. I'd postponed that dreaded requirement until there was nowhere to hide. During summer school, while my classmates were at the beach, I was in the library, obsessively preparing my talks in an effort to camouflage the fear. My professor nicknamed me "stone face" and gave me a B+ for effort, the toughest grade I ever earned.

Also that summer, I was living at home for the first time in two years, encountering a withering stream of criticism from my mother. My coping mechanisms collapsed under the assault, often leaving me in tears for no *apparent* reason. My mother decided that psychiatry, the profession of my older brother, was the solution. I didn't object in theory, but the psychiatrist I saw had a strange habit. He closed his eyes when I spoke. At first I assumed it was his way of listening intently, but then I noticed his head bobbing. It took me several weeks to comprehend that he was actually soundly asleep.

The next time I needed help to cope with life was nearly a decade later, not long after my departure from City Hall. Having left there with the feeling that right was on my side, it was unsettling to be reminded daily, in the newspapers, that my opponents remained deeply entrenched in power. But that was a tiny splinter compared to the demon of public speaking that hovered, again, at my think-tank job. Compounding that anxiety was the matter of my social life.

My relationships with men appeared to follow a pattern. They would start with a splash, with the glamour of true romance, then eventually fizzle, leaving me with echoes of the pain of abandonment following my father's death. It made little difference who brought about the end. The suffering was in the loss, the emptiness. One springtime it was so acute that I cried out — to the Being in whom I did not believe — "Why is this happening to me?" Shortly thereafter, I found myself in the office of a New York psychiatrist.

I liked him immediately. He broke the rules of Freudian psychiatry by offering personal information about himself in place of the proverbial blank screen. Some of it was disconcerting; as his own history of relationships left a lot to be desired. But that seemed to level the playing field. Having a real human being sitting across from me, one whose insights were of blinding clarity, was all that mattered. By the end of my first session I learned that I had a fear of emotional intimacy. That may not sound like much in the 21st century, but it came as a bolt of lightening in 1972.

Every week I had a private session with him and a group therapy session. In the private session, he was an empathic healer, always "on my side." The group situation, intended to be a microcosm of society, was entirely different. There I saw the lengths to which I went to be viewed in the most favorable light, to keep my shadow side hidden, even from myself. I also saw how many of us "walking wounded" there were on the streets of New York City, appearing as successful young professionals, devoting untold energy to creating images, appearances, impressions, while living unsatisfying, inauthentic lives.

It struck me later that the costs to society were enormous. Our obsession with the appearances of success had produced an unspoken ban on emotional truth. Moreover, the gap between inner and outer lives, private and public personas, was widening. As the drive for success intensified, the inner voice, the voice of conscience, was increasingly silenced. At the time, I didn't fully grasp the dangers inherent in suppressing parts of oneself to fit into the prevailing American culture. I was simply unable to live that way.

My psychiatrist maintained that the best-adjusted people were those whose mothers adored them, from infancy, as if they were the Christ child. In his view, that kind of mother-love could compensate for any inherent limitation. At the same time, a child born with tremendous gifts, but deprived of nurturing love, might never develop his or her innate potential. A condemning parent could cripple a child's motivation; a toxic one could undermine the sense of self-worth needed for *genuinely* successful living.

He worked hard to strengthen my inner core. Without him, I may never have risen to the challenges of writing or speaking that loomed so large at my think-tank job. Many irrational fears evaporated in the clear light of his insights. But his crowning achievement was to help me see my mother, and myself, through *his* eyes. He urged me to sever ties with her, though that was impossible for me at the time; it would have meant separating from my entire family. And something else was keeping me tied to her, something I would not be able to identify for a long time.

After four years, my therapy seemed to have run its course. I still had no mate, the main reason I had originally presented for entering psychotherapy. But somewhere along the way, my objective had changed from finding a partner to finding the disparate parts of myself. I left with a greater sense of wholeness than I had experienced since childhood, but I knew there was more to be uncovered, and that I was going to have to look elsewhere.

A sign of where to look came, unexpectedly, from a young woman in my therapy group. Over dinner after one of our weekly sessions, she mentioned a visit she'd had with an astrologer. What she told me was fascinating, even though I had always found the occult, about which I had no firsthand knowledge, slightly repugnant. Once I'd gone to see a palmist with friends as a form of entertainment. But astrology somehow seemed darker, more threatening. When I called the astrologer to make an appointment, I became aware of crossing a threshold into a world that was, at the very least, utterly foreign.

For my reading, I sat in a chair facing the astrologer. On a table just behind her were two large Siamese cats, positioned like book-ends, staring at me. I was prepared to answer questions from her, but she inquired about nothing beyond the time and place of my birth, which I'd provided to her when I made the appointment. On the basis of that alone, she proceeded to tell me about myself with an air of authority. She described my interests, talents, occupations; my difficulties and sorrows; the nature of my relationships. Occasionally she stopped to ask if she were correct, but mainly proceeded as if she had all the facts. Eerily, it seemed as if she did.

After telling me, for example, that writing would come easily to me and would likely be part of any work I did, she stated that I would be concerned with "women of the underclass." In a general sense, nearly all of the jobs I'd had, starting with my Peace Corps assignment, fit under that rubric. What made her statement even more astonishing was the timing of it. I had just completed the monograph on working-class women in America and had begun contemplating the book of oral histories.

My head was spinning. There was no place for cosmic mystery in the scaffolding of my mind. The astrologer seemed to know more about me than I knew, or that I could consciously articulate, about myself. And she knew things *before* I did. While I was living my life, moving through sequential experiences that appeared randomly linked, she had the tools to see the grand design. She knew the kind of work I would be led to do, the issues I would be concerned with. She knew of my father's sudden death when I was young, the nature of my relationship with my mother. And she foresaw what I was heading toward.

When I first went to see her, my career commitment had begun wavering; I was having pangs of inauthenticity. When I returned a few years later, in my early thirties, my questions had a greater sense of urgency, in part because of the ticking biological clock. Her conclusions about marriage and motherhood were more tentative than about occupation, but she made several observations. It appeared to her that I would get married, later rather than sooner. As for motherhood, she said, "Whether you have children of your own or not, you will do your nurturing primarily out in the world."

There was another issue that concerned me. I was sensing something new in the depths of my soul about "the world" and my place in it. It was a mysterious feeling, beyond my comprehension, yet increasingly powerful. The astrologer told me, quite matter-of-factly, that over the next few years my life would be completely transformed. The "reason" was that Pluto, the planet that represents transformation, was reaching a sensitive point in my natal horoscope. It would make me feel impelled to let go of the past while having no clear sense of the future, as if I were out in the middle of an ocean with no land in sight.

Her description of what I had begun to feel was awesome in its accuracy. It left me both exhilarated, for the affirmation it contained, and bewildered. I had grown up in a universe ruled by science. If a thing was not measurable, provable, or explainable, it could not be real. By that yardstick, astrology was not real. Yet its capacity to reveal who I was and describe my inner state of being surpassed the capacities of scientifically-trained professionals. I would sit and listen to the astrologer tell me about myself, silently affirming, "Yes, that's true." Yet I could not have articulated much of what she said; I simply lacked sufficient conscious awareness.

When I finally left the "real" world, astrology became my compass. It helped me locate myself in time and space. Initially I had planned to unwind for six months and see where the spirit led me. As the months flew by, the world I knew slipped further and further into the distance. There I was, in the middle of the ocean, with no land in sight. Astrology, which I had begun to study, helped me make peace with the timing of things, and with the nature of my evolving, transforming, life.

It revealed what I would call the "signature of my soul." By then it was obvious that my life was going to be different from the lives of most people I knew. The reason was a mystery beyond the scope of astrology. But the positions of the planets at the moment of my birth illustrated, in black and white, *how* I would experience life. My natal chart indicated that I would inevitably be concerned with issues of life, death, and transformation. This went beyond the physical deaths that shaped my childhood. It seemed I was destined to undergo a personal transformation — an inner experience of death and rebirth.

By the 1970s, the term "transformation of consciousness" had become commonplace in new age circles. It was used frequently, offhandedly, yet its actual meaning had always been obscure to me. Paradoxically, it continued to elude my intellectual grasp even after becoming the dominant force in my life. During the early stages of this transformation, I still could not define precisely what I was feeling. The only thing I knew for certain was that I was not going through "a phase" after which I would be "my old self" again.

I was undergoing a tidal wave of change that wreaked havoc with my perceptions of reality and my sense of identity. Astrology was the only language I knew whose vocabulary made sense of my experience. Its symbols offered such precise descriptions of my inner life that eventually I stopped asking how it could work, and simply accepted the fact that it did. Without this new language, the stresses of those years would have taken a far greater toll.

I was under enormous pressure, internal and external, to explain myself. People who cared about me perceived my choices as off the mark, over the edge. I had left a promising career immediately after the publication of a book that was quite well received, without having any alternative pursuit. Or any rational explanation for my actions. As months turned into years, rumors occasionally came back to me about the state of my mental health, including the possibility that I'd had a nervous breakdown.

With only my old language, it was impossible to counter such misperceptions. After awhile, I simply gave up trying. Mysterious forces were at work in my life, offering glimpses of other planes of awareness. Incredibly, my main ballast, the preserver of my sanity, was the knowledge that Pluto was transforming my basic sense of identity — who I was, and how I related to the world. Understandably, almost no one I knew from the life I left behind could possibly comprehend.

Higher Justice

When I began my job at the think-tank on ethnic diversity, a secretary named Paula was assigned to work with me. She was eccentric, but in a way that was endearing. It was impossible to know how old she was, since one of her shibboleths had to do with age, something she would not reveal on pain of death. At most she was ten or twelve years older than I was, yet she took me under her wing like a mother hen.

Paula liked to counsel me about various things. Nutrition was one of them. She believed in it passionately, almost fanatically. One of her more unorthodox prescriptions was eating three raw almonds a day to prevent cancer. Periodically, she went out to a nearby health food store at lunchtime to replenish her stock of raw almonds. Before taking them home, she would leave some on my desk. With each offering came a heartfelt plea that I consider adopting this daily practice.

At the time, I scoffed at such things. It sounded like quackery. One day Paula arrived at work with a book, the source of this bizarre-sounding prescription. She marked the pages concerning raw almonds and asked me to take a few minutes to read those few pages. The twinkle in her eye suggested that she foresaw the outcome: that I would become a fellow convert. But she could never have imagined the impact which that book would have on my life.

It was a biography of Edgar Cayce, "the sleeping prophet," once America's most highly acclaimed psychic. I became engrossed by his story. A simple man from rural Kentucky with almost no education, he was a commercial photographer by trade, and a fundamentalist Christian. He read the Bible from beginning to end every year and taught Sunday school. In his early twenties, he was stricken with an illness that doctors were unable to diagnose. In searching for a cure, Cayce uncovered a new universe.

The cure resulted from hypnotic suggestion administered by a trained practitioner. But Cayce soon discovered that he could put himself under hypnosis through auto-suggestion. Moreover, when he entered a sleep-like trance, he was able to gain access to a wealth of medical information. When carefully applied, this information resulted in seemingly miraculous cures. As word of his cures spread, desperately ill people from across the country and around the world sought his help.

Cayce was a phenomenon that modern science could not explain. A man with an eighth grade education and no cognizance of medical terminology in his normal waking state, he could enter a realm of consciousness where information unknown to modern physicians was given to him. That information provided cures for illnesses that were deemed incurable. I read well past the pages marked by Paula, unable to put the book down.

At a certain point, Cayce's readings moved beyond the purely medical into another sphere entirely. He himself found some of their contents, which his secretary read back to him when he awoke, extremely troubling. While in trance, receiving guidance for a sick person, he indicated that the cause of the person's illness could be traced to a previous life, and went on to describe the circumstances of that life. Cayce wrestled with the notion of reincarnation, as it went totally against his Christian beliefs, yet over time he gave many such readings in trance. In the end, the proven validity of the medical information helped him make peace with the rest.

Cayce died during World War II from illness exacerbated by exhaustion. Along with the normal flood of healing requests, he was deluged with pleas from people desperate to know if their loved ones who had gone off to war were still alive. He had given more than 14,000 transcribed readings. They formed the basis of countless books on topics ranging from dream interpretation and extrasensory perception to Egyptology, astrology, and reincarnation, in addition to medical subjects and Cayce's own story.

While reading the book that Paula loaned me, about Cayce's life, I had an epiphany. A light went on when I read about the theory of reincarnation. I'd always wondered why some people were born on the right side of the railroad tracks and others were not. And why some were born into loving families and others were not. The existence of such disparities *from the moment of birth* had fueled my atheism. It seemed irrational to believe that the luck of the draw or the roll of the dice shaped a person's entire existence on earth. Yet if an all-powerful being was assigning some of us to heaven and others to hell, what kind of being was it?

Cayce provided the answer that had been eluding me. His readings offered evidence that our current lifetimes were fragments of a greater life experience. The readings suggested that those fragments could not be fully understood in isolation from the lives preceding the present one. Each soul evidently had a unique succession of lifetimes, chapters comprising the soul's Book of Life, the composite record. The idea that we arrived here as blank slates was merely an illusion.

All of a sudden, the questions I had been asking for as long as I could remember had answers. It came as a relief to discover that this was not a random universe. But that sense of relief was short-lived, replaced by the disturbing implications of reincarnation. The question of responsibility immediately presented itself. It appeared that the seeds of our present struggles had been sown in previous lifetimes, *by us*. If we were suffering, we were reaping what we sowed, in accordance with a Higher Law. The purpose of that law, which operated over the course of our many lifetimes, was to bring the scales of divine justice into balance.

The light of truth dawned on me in a life-changing way. If nothing happened randomly, if we are merely reaping what we sow, then we are not, despite all appearances, hapless victims of circumstance. This awareness shook the foundations of my reality like an earthquake. Everything turned upside down and inside out. It meant that I was not, as I had always supposed, an innocent victim of an unloving mother, or of a cruel and whimsical fate that took my father from me; there were reasons for everything.

With this shattering realization, the curtain slowly rose on a new act in the play called life. In the first "act," I had been pitied by others for the circumstances of my early years, and in truth I pitied myself to a degree. "Family" and "home" meant abandonment and suffering. Healing had begun with my psychiatrist. He held my hand, metaphorically, as I revisited past traumas and reopened old wounds. He had also played the role of "good mother," providing me with an experience of the kind of mother-love that produces healthy children with a solid sense of self-worth.

By the end of my psychotherapy, the blinds had been opened and the sunlight had begun to filter in. I felt more comfortable in my own skin. A lot of negative conditioning had fallen by the wayside. I had arrived in therapy having internalized, to a large extent, my mother's condemnation of me as being "all wrong." I left having been convinced by my psychiatrist, who taught me to see life through his eyes, that it was *she* who was "all wrong."

From that perspective, life was akin to a zero-sum game: in order for one to win, the other had to lose. It was healing to feel like the winner. But I was still left with the question of *why*. In a universe of infinite possibilities, why did I have that kind of mother? Even assuming for the sake of argument that she *was* all wrong and that I was an innocent victim, *why* was I a victim? Until Cayce, such questions had haunted me: why were some children abused, emotionally or physically, while others were as beloved as the Christ child?

The more I read about reincarnation, about the many lives of a soul, the closer I came to the unavoidable truth. It became self-evident and logical. The woman who was my mother in this life was someone to whom I had been closely related in a past life or lives. Quite possibly, our roles had been reversed and I had treated *her* badly. If not her, then someone else. The details were unknown, but the outlines grew increasingly clear. My soul had chosen my mother to be my principal teacher in this incarnation, the one to help me bring the scales of karmic justice into balance.

For a long time I struggled, mentally, to grasp the inner workings — the mechanics as it were — of karma and reincarnation. It was awesome to even try to contemplate the infinite number of pairings of souls and circumstances that had to be orchestrated over the course of eons of time, in the process of redeeming wrongs of the past. But an even greater struggle ensued when I tried to absorb, emotionally, what at first seemed inconceivable: that my soul had *needed* my mother as a teacher.

The implications were staggering. First, I had to acknowledge some seriously "crooked places" in myself that had needed to be made straight. Life hadn't given me just a mild tap on the wrist, but some searingly painful boots to the rear. Second, the metaphysical principle that the soul chooses its learning ground, the family and circumstances of its birth, spoke directly to the question of responsibility. It meant that I, on the plane of the soul, had consented to that set of circumstances for the growth of my soul.

Ultimately, those insights lifted a great millstone from around my neck. Anger and resentment gave way to the possibility of genuine healing. My mother was not the main cause of my suffering; she was merely the main instrument. From that perspective, it became possible to forgive her. Finally I did so and, in the process, felt purged of a negative force that had been draining my vital energy for much of my life. It was as though I'd been living in a prison without realizing it, until I opened the door and walked out.

I wrote her a letter explaining my new understanding of this life and what must have preceded it, and I expressed my forgiveness. To this day I do not know how much of it she was able to comprehend, or accept. But for me, the benefit was immediate and substantial. My heart, long protected by a bulletproof shield, opened again. I was no longer a helpless victim, but a soul responsible for my destiny. Anger and fear were gradually replaced by acceptance and peace. Transformation was underway.

Visions

During my working years, I developed a daily ritual involving a weekly planner, a pocket-sized calendar with a leather cover that I carried in my purse. I used it ahead of time as intended, to keep track of forthcoming meetings and appointments. Afterward, it became a very small diary. At the end of each day I scribbled notes in the tiny amount of remaining space — observations, feelings, insights, anything I wanted to remember.

At the start of 1977, I was working only part-time at the think tank, preparing to leave, and my schedule was sparse. As a symbol of my impending liberation, a sign of my new resolve to live more spontaneously, I decided not to buy a weekly planner. It wasn't long, however, before I had a nagging sense of incompletion. The habit of jotting down notes at the end of each day had become so ingrained that when I stopped, it felt as if something were missing.

A few days into the new year, my head was full of mental jottings. The collection was becoming more cumbersome with each passing day. One morning I surrendered to the impulse to put them down on paper. In a cabinet where I kept supplies, I found only one unused notebook. It was the college-ruled size. The page proportions felt disturbingly wrong. I had gotten used to writing in the unused corners of what was a very small space to begin with. Suddenly I was faced with oppressively large, blank pages.

At first, the length of my entries made it seem as though I had wasted a perfectly good notebook. Then one day, seated at my kitchen table, I found myself filling page upon page. Soon I was writing for hours at a time, then for days, and for weeks on end. In this newest chapter of my life, a total departure from the old, no one I knew could help me make sense of things. The notebook became my alter ego. It was the "place" I went to sort things out.

The more I wrote, the more I realized how superficially I had been living and perceiving life. I'd been something of a workaholic, always extraordinarily busy, especially in the years when I was working on a book along with my full-time job. Rarely did I reflect on what made the world turn. I'd been sailing on the surface of the lake, so to speak, without giving a thought to the life within it or around it, the ecosystem that sustained it.

The notebook turned into a journal, a mode of deeper exploration and contemplation. Subjects seemed to float into my awareness, taking root there through my pen. Words flowed like a river carrying unexpected insights into the nature of things. They originated in a place well beyond my everyday consciousness. In a way that was utterly mysterious, the process of writing seemed to be forging a pathway to that distant, unknown place.

Topics ranged far and wide, from the seemingly mundane to the spiritual. One day I found myself writing about the TV program *60 Minutes*. It was nearly a decade old by then and I was among its millions of loyal viewers. By the end of each program, I had the soul-satisfying feeling that justice had triumphed, or that it soon would. Every Sunday night featured new culprits, new exposés, new hopes that by shining the light of truth on the underside of life, the world would be a better place.

In my journal, where I came to see the reality behind many illusions, an entirely different picture emerged. Viewers believed that the exposure of criminal or unethical conduct on national TV would make people more honest, or somehow improve the moral climate in America. We assumed it was just a matter of a few rotten apples, and that by catching those few in the act of conning or scamming people, they would be rooted out. And so we cheered this televised muckraking.

But there appeared to be a never-ending stream of muck to be raked. Each broadcast exposed more of the darkness beneath the facade of American life. On a weekly basis, there was a feel-good effect. The program offered a safety valve for collective outrage against those who conned, robbed, or otherwise deceived innocent people. But the longer the show ran, the more it appeared that the barrel was full of rotten apples. Over time, the scale of corruption in America transcended our wildest imaginations, while our capacity for moral outrage simultaneously dimmed.

My journal became a refuge from a world that appeared increasingly out of kilter. I realized how often events were shaped by distortions of truth or false premises accepted at face value. We were made to believe, for example, that our government *had* to spend billions of dollars a year on nuclear weapons which could never be used; any attempt to use them against our Soviet enemy would have instantly triggered our own annihilation. Moreover, a handful of these weapons would have destroyed all major enemy targets, yet we continued stockpiling them by the tens of thousands. All the while America's poor, and the world's, suffered in quiet desperation.

The more I wrote, the more I began to see. Veils were being stripped away. The nuclear superpowers seemed like Roman gladiators facing off in an ever-expanding global arena, pouring their peoples' treasure into insatiable machines of death. They were obsessed with the ability to obliterate each other. Equally frightening was the fact that a similar mind-set was creeping into the fabric of American life. The fight-to-the-death, winner-take-all mentality was surfacing increasingly in the corporate world, but was also making inroads into realms ostensibly concerned with the common good.

On some days, writing in my journal cleared cobwebs from my eyes, affording me a glimpse of the reality lying behind the appearance of things, further altering my worldview. At other times, what came through my pen was quite personal and all the more startling. Out of the blue, or so it seemed, a totally new concept would be implanted in my mind. One day, for example, a series of encounters I had had with black people was rapidly paraded before my mind's eye. And then I *saw* that I had been black, or African, in a past life. A link was made between past and present, as if to explain my lifelong affinity for black people.

On another occasion I had a similar inner jolt with regard to France. It was there, in 1965, that I had first experienced past-life recall, long before I understood what it actually was. In the months prior to Peace Corps training, I was living in Paris as an *au pair*. My older brother, who majored in French before entering medical school and becoming a psychiatrist, was doing his military service at a US Army hospital in France. One weekend, he and his wife invited me to join them on a trip to the Normandy coast.

One of the places we visited was Mont St. Michel, a fantastic medieval structure that rises up from the earth like a mountain. The heart of the place, a monastery, can be reached by foot from a village at the base. Visitors ascend a winding stone stairway to a multilevel labyrinth of halls and chapels of Romanesque and Gothic architecture built over many centuries. From the top, there is a dramatic view of the sea lapping at the edges of the spit of land on which it stands. At night, when the tide goes out, it becomes an island.

Almost as soon as we began climbing the wide stone steps, I felt a strange sense of familiarity. I didn't pay much attention to it until we came to a large hall with Romanesque arches called the scriptorium. This was the place where monks of the Middle Ages copied the scriptures by hand. While standing in the center of the room and looking around, I was gripped by an uncanny sensation of having known the place, of having been there before.

When I shared this with the others, the obvious explanation to all three of us was *déjà vu*, the psychological term for the *illusion* of having been in a place where one couldn't have been before. At the time, I knew no other way to explain it. The notion of having had a prior existence sounded like science fiction. Furthermore, living *there* would have made me a Catholic monk, a preposterous thought given my origins in this life. Yet I also knew that *déjà vu* didn't account for what I had experienced. Only years later, writing in my journal, did I understand my affinity for France, which I revisited many times in this life.

In those journal-writing years, the late 70s, there were days when I wrote virtually nonstop for as long as twelve hours. I wasn't able to put my pen down. I would try to ignore hunger pangs and back aches for as long as I could, for fear of breaking the flow. An invisible force seemed to be writing *through* me, informing my mind, illumining both inner and outer worlds. For the longest time I was afraid to stop when I was in the flow — afraid that "it" would stop.

My pile of used notebooks rapidly grew. The more I wrote, the more I understood that another level of reality existed behind the circumstances and events of our lives. This other reality was deeper, vaster, and "older." It preexisted and preconditioned our emotional makeup, our unconscious mind, our childhood programming, our experiences of the adult world. I gradually came to see it as the reality, or realm, of the soul.

The price of entering this realm was steep. After learning to see with the eyes of the soul, I realized the necessity of mustering the courage to face whatever was revealed there. One couldn't afford to be squeamish, I soon discovered, as the light of the soul does not shine selectively. It illumines all things, whether pleasing to our sight or not. It penetrates darkness in the outer world, in other people, and in ourselves, where it is always hardest to look. With time and practice, however, it grew easier for me to bear.

Journal-writing became the vehicle of my soul's awakening, and the major activity in my life. I couldn't explain it to anyone, not even to myself at times. I often passed by a carpentry shop in my neighborhood and observed, with admiration and envy, that the carpenter had an occupation that he clearly loved, and that supported him, because it had value to others. I, too, had found an "occupation" that I loved, but it didn't have a scintilla of value to anyone else in this world.

Still, nothing but abject poverty could have dragged me away from the kitchen table overlooking the Hudson River where I wrote incessantly. Without fully realizing it, I had embarked upon a spiritual journey. Physically, I was still living in Manhattan, the center of a city whose heartbeat had once been very close to my own. Yet mentally and spiritually, I had crossed the threshold into a new universe. I could have been living anywhere on this earth.

One day as I was writing, an image appeared in my mind's eye, as clear as if it were physically in front of me. It was a picture, like a slow-motion picture, of Ben Franklin. He was sitting in a wooden slat-back rocking chair behind a large desk on which huge piles of paper were spilling into each other. He looked somber and disheveled. His hair and face were greasy, the buttons of his shirt had popped open over his protruding belly. He rocked back and forth a few times and then disappeared.

At that moment my telephone rang. I was totally bewildered, having never experienced anything remotely like a vision. I picked up the phone in need of reassurance of my connectedness with the concrete world. The caller was a friend and neighbor, a literary agent, a canny person. To my everlasting gratitude, she did not miss a beat when I described what had just happened. Her response to my inner seismic event was an offer to lend me her copy of Franklin's autobiography, which reminded me that I had a yellowed copy of my own.

I continued writing, with great intensity, endlessly fascinated by this new dimension of reality. About six months later Ben Franklin suddenly reappeared, but the picture had entirely changed. His desk was tidy. He himself looked neat and clean. His demeanor was calm. There was a pleasant, good-natured smile on his face. Then he disappeared, leaving me bewildered again, but with a more peaceful feeling.

The two visions seemed to be telling me something about myself. During the six-month interval, a greater sense of order had descended over my life. The spiritual realm was still fraught with challenges, but I was more comfortable with the course I was on. I couldn't explain what was happening, and still had no concept of God, but realized that a benevolent, invisible force was guiding my writings. As for Ben Franklin and what he symbolized, I was lost. I saw him as a wise and benevolent historical figure, but had no idea where he stood with regard to things of a spiritual nature.

In the summer of '78, I attended a workshop on dream interpretation in Virginia Beach. It was sponsored by the Association for Research and Enlightenment, the organization established to preserve the legacy of Edgar Cayce. I went there with a writer, a feminist whom I had met through a mutual friend. When we returned to New York, she asked if I'd be interested in joining a women's group related to spirituality. While generally hesitant about joining groups, I said I would be willing to explore the idea.

What happened next was truly stranger than fiction. The writer, a friend by then, invited me to her home to discuss the group idea. Another feminist was there when I arrived, a professor at an Ivy League university who was known for the academic scholarship she had contributed to the movement. During the course of the evening, the professor, who had been widowed at a young age, made a startling revelation: she had been communicating with the spirit of her dead husband by means of a Ouija Board. Until then, I had believed that Ouija Boards and Ivy League universities existed in different galaxies.

Seven women gathered at our first meeting. One happened to have a Ouija Board and brought it along. We passed it around the circle, each person placing her fingertips on the plastic pointer and asking a question, all of us waiting to see if it would move, where it would land. When it was my turn, the pointer spelled out "love mama." From then on, no matter what was asked, the answer was the same. We soon discovered that not a soul among us had a harmonious relationship with her mother. Curious about the sender of these messages, I asked who it was. The pointer spelled out "Benjamin Franklin."

Earthly Matters

Just as I was learning to savor freedom from the tyranny of time, its fellow tyrant began hovering. Money started running out. Absorbed in liberating myself from inauthentic roles and searching for my life's purpose, I had become somewhat oblivious to the exigencies of the material world. Before long, however, a new learning cycle began. It fell under the rubric of "the value of money," a phrase with a familiar ring from childhood.

Prior to that time, I hadn't given much thought to money. Making it, spending it, accumulating it for its own sake, were never goals for me. If I earned enough to pay the rent and to travel occasionally, that was plenty. By age fourteen, I knew that I had no taste for opulent living. Being served cold drinks by men who were sweating in their formal attire, while I tanned myself in a bikini beside the pool of my stepfather's country club, caused me intense discomfort. In Africa, I felt more at ease among villagers than among former French colonialists who still had servants posted at every door.

I also had no illusions that money was a panacea. My mother's second marriage had placed her, and by extension me, in the upper income brackets of Americans. It was, in many ways, a rarified place to be. I saw up close that money, large sums of it, was no guarantor of peace or happiness. At times it seemed like an albatross. Concern about investments, markets, rates of return, appeared to be the constant companion of wealth. There was often a roiling sea of anxiety beneath the veneer of financial security.

It had been expected that I would live that life or one like it — marry someone of a similar background, have several children, live in the suburbs, drive a station-wagon, belong to country clubs, women's clubs. My parents could foresee only one possible deviation from that script: widowhood. In exchange for paying my way through college, they extracted a commitment that I would obtain a teaching certificate as a safety hatch, in case I ever found myself alone with children to support.

As I ventured into the world, going where the spirit led me, I had always found work that was meaningful, and often soul-satisfying. Pay had never been a deciding factor. What mattered was the feeling of contributing in some way to the greater good. That was my life for twelve years until Pluto came along, driving a mysterious wedge between me and my past. Suddenly I found myself spending days and nights writing in a journal, existing entirely outside the money stream.

I had left my last job with the notion that I would return to the working world after six months of freedom. Earnings from my book had been sufficient to carry me through that time. But as months turned into years, my savings were swallowed up. To buy more time for spiritual explorations, I began to sell things: stocks and bonds, a fur coat, African sculptures, whatever I owned that had any monetary value.

There was no possibility of returning to the past, and still no hint of the future. An interim survival strategy was a small business venture which I entered into with a friend. We took out an ad in a popular magazine, offering services that ranged from writing and editing to caring for pets and plants. It paid the rent for awhile, but lacking funds to sustain an ad campaign, our initial stream of clients slowed to a trickle. It was clear that I was not cut out for business, on any scale, yet I was destined to learn the value of money.

Before my savings had dropped below the comfort level, I made a declaration on the subject of money that soon came back to haunt me. It was uttered in response to my mother's chiding, during those years, about my impractical approach to living. She felt it incumbent upon her to remind me periodically that "life is a series of compromises," that "nothing is ever perfect," and that "you have to have money to live in this world."

I never responded well to such aphorisms, especially the one about compromises. But feeling besieged by them at a particularly vulnerable moment caused something inside me to snap. I had just submitted a new book idea to an editor who liked the basic idea, but had wanted me to commercialize it in ways I couldn't live with. Upon hearing this news, my mother's response was the standard barrage of adages. I thundered back, as if to make the point once and for all: "Money will never be the deciding factor in my life." Not long thereafter, money became the *only* deciding factor. I ran out of it completely. The Universe, as I began to call the loving intelligence at work in my life, was having its way with me.

The only way I could imagine earning money at that point was something I had once tossed off as a joke. When I left my think-tank job with no ideas about the future, friends and colleagues had asked how I would survive, what I would do to pay the rent. I never took the question seriously since money had never been an issue for me. Life had always produced the right job at the right time. To allay their anxiety, I said in jest, "If worse comes to worst, I can always become a Kelly Girl."

Those were the years when feminism was breaking down ancient barriers. Women were going up the professional ladder, not down. The idea that I might be headed for the bottom, as temporary office work was generally viewed, had been intended as a touch of humor — to blunt the seriousness of people's concern. It seemed funny because it was almost unthinkable. I had always had a secretary of my own, starting with my first job. I was a published author, a newspaper columnist, a member of many boards, a "successful professional woman."

With my bank account nearly empty, I applied to Kelly Girls.

They rejected me. My typing skills had been deemed inadequate. My past credentials were utterly useless. All that mattered was how well I could type. With practice, I finally managed to pass muster with another temporary agency. They sent me to the far reaches of the corporate world. Crisscrossing the island of Manhattan, I went from accounting firms to law firms, from banks and insurance companies to ad agencies. The bastions of materialism became my stomping grounds. There, in the city I thought I knew intimately, I was a stranger.

At home, in my journal, I found myself again. Veils were continually being lifted. New insights into the nature of reality were steadily emerging. My inner vision was being sharpened and honed. The purpose of this lifetime was becoming increasingly clear. My soul was soaring in its own sphere. Yet clearly, that did not exempt me from remedial lessons concerning the laws of matter. I had not adequately assimilated the meaning of: "Someone had to work hard so that you could have this home," or "this education" or "this trip." Belatedly, I was learning about working for money versus working for ideals.

As if to underscore the lesson, my temp agency gave me a long-term assignment on Wall Street, "the heart of the beast" in the view of certain fundamentalist Christians. It was a place where there was no ambiguity about motives. People were there for money, and money alone. Some needed it just to live, to support families; others wanted to amass large sums of it for ego gratification, or power. But everyone was after one and the same substance, as much of it as possible.

Swarms of commuters converged on Wall Street each morning, racing toward seas of towering buildings. Many literally ran from their subway exits down the narrow lanes, through revolving glass doors, lining up beside large banks of elevators, waiting to squeeze into the mass of bodies headed upward. At first, unaccustomed to this powerful wave of motion, I had the feeling that if I stopped moving, or tried to go against the tide, there was a risk of being trampled by it.

Learning to navigate this new territory took time. The density of the population and the height of the buildings made me claustrophobic. Relief came in the form of a few small, open spaces, concrete plazas with potted trees and plants. But even during lunchtime, people moved through them at a dizzying pace. Clothing stores were packed. The dress code was strict, conservative and dictated by men. Women on the way up, including secretaries with ambition, wore tailored suits. The business of making money was all-consuming.

My agency had assigned me to fill in for the vacationing secretary of an executive vice-president at a major bank. During her vacation, the secretary decided to leave the job and the vice-president asked if I wanted to fill it permanently. After being there for three weeks, I accepted almost without hesitation, surprising even myself. I'd grown weary of the nomadic life of an office temp and saw no alternatives on the horizon. Plus, unexpectedly, I had a nice rapport with this man. He loved the money game and had the requisite hard edge to play it, but he also had a large streak of decency that challenged my stereotypes of corporate bankers.

When I agreed to take the job, he asked to see my résumé. Puzzling over it, he realized the strangeness of my situation, but decided nevertheless to try to teach me the fundamentals of banking related to his department. Within a matter of weeks, we both acknowledged that it was a colossal waste of time. I had to bribe myself to sit down with the spiral notebooks he gave me to take home at night, only to discover that I had retained virtually nothing by morning. Learning Russian, which I soon would do, proved considerably easier.

My sole reason for being at the bank, and my reward, was a regular paycheck. Having been financially on the brink for several years, I was overjoyed by that newfound sense of security. It became evident that I had to have known want, seriously so, in order to appreciate freedom from want. And there was nothing like walking through the marbled lobby of a Wall Street bank to create a feeling of abundance, however temporary or illusory.

By the time I left the corporate world, more than three years later, I had learned a multitude of lessons. The most significant ones, spiritually speaking, involved who I really was. The bank was a testing ground for this. I'd arrived there stripped of all my professional identities. But there came a time when I also experienced being stripped of a basic sense of self-respect. It happened when the person who hired me left the bank. He was young, brilliant, ambitious, and gone within a year. While working as his executive secretary, I was very well treated. After he left, I experienced a different side of corporate life.

It was the underside of the business world, something I'd heard about, read about. Ironically, I had even written about it in articles on the plight of working-class women. It was the dehumanization of the powerless by the powerful — demeaning treatment by those who propped up their egos at the expense of those less valued in the corporate hierarchy. In the interim before my second boss arrived, I learned how it felt to be seen as an extension of a desk, or a computer, to be treated like a nameless servant who was supposed to jump at barked commands.

Such occasions proved fertile opportunities for me to remind myself that I was not an extension of a desk, or even a secretary, any more than I had previously been an aide to the mayor or a writer. I was a soul, temporarily working in a bank to round out a life experience (and surely to balance the scales of karma). To survive this awkward passage between two phases of life, while maintaining my sanity and continuing to pay the rent, I recited a mantram, as needed: *I am not an object, I am a soul.*

Signs of a New Time

I first came across the term "New Age" in my neighborhood bookstore. It appeared in a sign above a potpourri of titles ranging from Edgar Cayce and holistic healing to Eastern religion and yoga. The store was owned by a young Jewish man who was strongly attracted to Sufism, the mystical order of Islam, but also interested in the wider field of religious mysticism. Authors of books on that subject were frequently invited to speak at his store. I found myself gravitating there in the late 70s, especially to the new age section.

One day I noticed a special display of books about a place called Findhorn. The name intrigued me and the books themselves had a magnetic quality. They featured photos of lush gardens, radiantly smiling people, and a story that read like a modern-day myth. On a rocky coast of northern Scotland, where plants had never grown, magical gardens were flourishing. Scientists were baffled since the sand content of the soil was supposed to make it impossible for plant life to survive. Something was defying conventional laws of science. I was fascinated.

The Findhorn story had begun in the early 60s with three unemployed British citizens — Peter and Eileen Caddy and Dorothy Maclean. Fired from the management of a resort hotel for espousing unorthodox beliefs, they had been unable to find other work. Approaching destitution, the three adults and the couple's three children moved to a nearby trailer park on Findhorn Bay. They tried growing vegetables but their efforts failed due to the sandy soil. Turning increasingly to prayer, first one of the women, then the other, began receiving guidance. Some of it was highly practical, with detailed instructions for making compost to enrich the soil.

Their garden grew prolifically, and seemingly miraculously. It produced forty-pound cabbages and other oversized vegetables. Articles were published about the phenomenon. Visitors came to witness it and some remained, forming a community in the trailer park on Findhorn Bay. They worked in the gardens and began constructing communal facilities. They prayed and meditated together, seeking guidance for this unprecedented venture involving the mineral, plant, human, and spiritual kingdoms.

As word spread, people from around the world were attracted to the community, which in time outgrew the trailer park. What started with one overcrowded trailer in the early 60s was on its way to becoming an international village by the late 70s. The guidance revealed that the Findhorn gardens, which had demonstrated the possibilities inherent in working with Spirit, had been intended primarily as a lure. The ultimate purpose was to create a "greenhouse for souls," a place to nurture a new, universal expression of spirituality.

The community's focus continued shifting toward spiritual growth with the arrival of an American, in his early twenties, who began giving channeled readings about the advent of a New Age, and a new consciousness. Because of his youth and the wisdom that flowed through him, David Spangler became another Findhorn phenomenon. Books based on his readings appeared in Europe and America. As people came from ever more distant lands, the community evolved into a global center for spiritual transformation.

For me, Findhorn was living proof that another reality was possible. I was enthralled by the discovery of a place where people were searching for truth, studying spiritual principles, and applying them to their lives. They struggled to move beyond self-interest, beyond competition, toward a shared concern for the general good, the whole, the collective. They learned to see the planet and all its creatures as part of one organism, an intricately woven web of life in which human beings, according to the Grand Design, were *supposed* to play the role of caretaker.

It seemed we were failing miserably in that role. But I soon learned, from some of the same books being read at Findhorn, that we were on the brink of an evolutionary leap in consciousness. Higher Forces were preparing human beings for a new era of spirituality, the Aquarian Age. Many souls scattered around the globe were discovering a new dimension of spirituality through inner experience, as I had, and through the ageless wisdom teachings updated for our times. These teachings described an era of spiritual brotherhood, a time when the Christ consciousness would flower in the human heart. Dependence on outer authorities would give way to the authority of the soul, which knows it is one with all of life.

The Aquarian Age was portrayed as the time when humanity would finally "come of age." Gradually, over the course of the next two thousand years, we were to evolve into the role of guardians of Earth life, maturing to the point of being able to consciously cooperate with the Spiritual Kingdom, the fifth kingdom of life on our planet. From that cooperation, the eternal ideal of bringing "heaven down to earth" would finally materialize.

Findhorn was clearly a forerunner. Yet for me, it remained a mythical place for many years — somewhere out there, beyond the horizon. When I first learned of it, I couldn't afford the airfare to travel there. Plus, the unrepentant idealist in me almost preferred not to encounter the reality, as it was bound to fall short of the ideal. It was enough for me to know that there existed on this earth a community of individuals — not a cult or sect under the thrall of a hypnotic guru — who shared my spiritual orientation.

Then, in the fall of 1981, something totally unexpected happened. The spirit of Findhorn came to New York City, to the grounds of the Cathedral of St. John the Divine, which was virtually in my backyard. Former Findhorn members organized a weekend conference entitled "The Earth Community: A Coming of Age." Its aim was to introduce Americans to Findhorn-like communities that had been springing up in the US. Hundreds of kindred spirits gathered there. I felt at home in the world for the first time in many years.

Actually, there was one other "place" where I had felt a similar ease of belonging. Around that time, a small group of friends and acquaintances pooled our energies to create a cable TV series about the new consciousness. We wrote an outline for a program called *New Age Vision*, dedicated to the emergence of Spirit in health and healing, art and culture, the environment, sports. Though we never found a TV outlet, I welcomed this effort as a creative outlet after years of exploring the new civilization in books, lectures, workshops, and my own journal-writing.

But there was a built-in fatal flaw in that and similar projects I threw myself into at the time. It was particularly evident with hindsight. I was so eager for this new civilization to materialize, that I regularly mistook seeds for blossoms. Ignoring the agonizingly slow, incremental nature of organic growth — especially when it comes to something so fundamental and all-embracing as the expansion of human consciousness — I pressed forward with a variety of quixotic ventures.

My expectations of the cathedral event were fraught with the same pitfalls; still it was a major milestone on my journey. It was uplifting and empowering merely to be among hundreds of souls with a shared anticipation of a collective spiritual awakening. Our sense of timing proved to be way off the mark, in terms of the world's readiness for the change we envisioned, but the gathering itself breathed new life into the idea that we were indeed moving toward a new era.

Moreover, before the weekend ended, the New Yorkers present had decided to continue holding meetings. We weren't ready to abandon urban living for rural new age communities, yet we wanted to keep the spirit of the conference alive. As it happened, so did the dean of the world's largest gothic cathedral. A group of us, calling ourselves the Earth Community, met regularly in the dean's office on Saturday afternoons, for well over a year, to plan the agenda for public gatherings following Sunday services.

For a long time, I puzzled over what seemed like an odd amalgam of worlds. The same man who baptized, married, buried and otherwise ministered to some of the oldest and wealthiest Episcopalian families of New York's social establishment, was also playing a prominent role in our ongoing gatherings of Aquarian seekers, most of whom lived on the fringes of the mainstream. I marveled at his ability to straddle such disparate universes.

The worldview of places like Findhorn, and our Earth Community, was antithetical to the one currently undergirding Western civilization. The core of the new paradigm is that all of life is interconnected. The idea that people exist separately from one another, or from other peoples, or nations, or from nature, is an illusion based on our inability to perceive the invisible energies interpenetrating the outer world of form. Leading-edge physicists and other scientists had begun sounding like mystics — asserting, for example, that the flapping of a butterfly's wings could trigger a tidal wave on the other side of the globe.

According to the new science and metaphysical teachings outlining the new spirituality, the premises of our civilization were due for a radical transformation. This was especially so where market forces ruled unchecked, plundering the earth's resources and exploiting its inhabitants for the benefit of a privileged few. The new paradigm challenged the "survival of the fittest" and "looking out for number one" mentality. It spoke to a different reality, that of interconnectedness, which posed a challenge to the viability of institutions that continued promoting the interests of the few at the expense of many.

The early spokespeople for the new paradigm, some of whom preached from the cathedral's pulpit in the early 80s, were saying what had become painfully obvious by the start of our new millennium. Whether we choose to acknowledge it or not, our own security is tightly bound to the security of other peoples, nations, and species. We are part of an interdependent ecosystem. If we destroy any portion of it, if we threaten its delicate balance, we harm our own capacity to survive. We are, in every conceivable way, our brothers' keepers.

The dean of the cathedral was passionate about certain facets of the emerging worldview, especially the environment. He saw the Earth Community as a voice for ecological awareness in New York City, where people often live and work in concrete towers isolated from the natural world. Our Sunday programs, however, rarely drew more than a few stragglers from the cathedral's congregation. With some exceptions, they failed to bridge the gap between New York's old establishment, living in accord with the old paradigm, and our band of new age pilgrims.

This experience gave me an insight into paradigms, in contrast to theories or ideas. Paradigms are not intellectual constructs, removed from life, but become the very foundation of our sense of reality. If we accept the premise that we are not isolated entities, but nodes in a vast network of life, then our consciousness changes in a way that changes everything else in our lives, in the way we live them. From what I could tell, there was a common denominator among those who had made the shift: a heightened sense of responsibility for what it means to be human now, at this monumental turning point — seen by some as the end of history, by others as the portal to a new age.

Between Worlds

In the years leading up to my Russian journey, cataclysmic changes were taking place within me. I was undergoing a process of transformation that was largely invisible, making it all the more difficult to communicate to others. My journal was the only "source" to which I could reliably turn for answers. These answers increasingly came from a place beyond my own soul. I realized that I was being helped by inner teachers. Their precise identity was difficult to discern, but they shone a penetrating light on exactly what I needed to know.

There were always veils I could not penetrate, but in time I perceived a pattern. My inner guides helped me to see the immediate next step, the direction I needed to take for a particular learning experience, even if it *appeared* to be a blind alley. They also helped me to look at my shadow side, the residue of karmic "homework." They rarely told me what I wanted to hear, but rather what I needed to know in order to transmute, purify, transform my inner essence.

At a certain point, I discovered a set of books that ended my sense of spiritual isolation. Known as "the Alice Bailey books," for the woman who received them telepathically, they presented an evolutionary scheme of breathtaking scope. In this scheme, the consciousness of humanity falls somewhere between that of an atom and that of the cosmos as a whole. Against this backdrop, one's sense of self-importance vanishes like smoke. At the same time, these books provide a detailed description of the soul's journey toward the Light. This was the Way I'd been searching for.

I never came close to absorbing the thousands of pages contained in these books, twenty-four altogether, including several written by Alice Bailey herself, but what I culled from them prepared me for the *reality* of a new age. I understood that our current cycle of human history was coming to a close and that we, as a race, were moving toward a higher plane of consciousness. It became clear that humanity is in transition from a materially-based paradigm, governed by what is visible to and measurable by the naked eye, to a spiritually-based paradigm, in which the invisible connective tissue *within* the world of form — the vital essence which ensouls all things — becomes paramount.

According to this teaching, a segment of humanity is about to embark on a journey toward a higher plane of evolution. The path trod in previous times by a few solitary beings, saints and sages, will be trod in the future by a critical mass of individuals, pioneers of the New Age. During the next two thousand years, many people will develop a conscious connection to the Spiritual Kingdom. The divine spark in the human soul will thus become manifest here on earth, redeeming humanity and "spiritualizing" life on our planet.

It was reassuring to learn through these books that those who tread the Path of Light are by no means alone in this process. Illumined beings on a higher plane called Masters of Wisdom are charged with preparing humanity for this next evolutionary leap. The Masters are beings who were once part of the human kingdom but who mastered the soul lessons offered by the cycle of Earth lives. They "graduated" into the Spiritual Kingdom and became part of the Hierarchy of Light. There, under the guidance of the Christ, the perfected one, they oversee the working out of the evolutionary plan in accordance with the will of God.

For now, the part of the Plan which humanity can apprehend concerns the oneness of life, on all planes and in all kingdoms. Awareness of the One Life behind the world of form was initially grasped by a few sensitive souls in the 60s, such as the founders of

Findhorn and certain leading-edge scientists. In the 70s, this awareness spread rapidly to millions of people sensitive to Aquarian energies. And then, amazingly, the Plan began working out in plain view, for the entire world to see, through phenomena that increasingly became part of our everyday lives: electronic technology, the global economy, the changing global climate.

While pondering such things and trying to find my footing in the world, still another kind of learning was taking place. I was being taught tough object lessons about treading the spiritual path. I felt the evolutionary pull of the Aquarian Age strongly; I recognized that I was one of the souls awakening to this new level of awareness with its altered sense of identity. But that, I discovered, in no way exempted me from a seemingly endless learning process — tests and trials that would prepare me to fulfill my *dharma*, my life's purpose.

The challenge was learning to live between two worlds, to bridge the gap between different dimensions of consciousness. Painfully aware of my own shortcomings, I understood that we, as souls, have incarnated on Earth in order to grow, to perfect ourselves — that if we had already attained the perfection of a saint or master, we would no longer be on this earth. What was more difficult to grasp was that despite all our remaining imperfections, it was nevertheless necessary to act. We are not supposed to wait for perfection before contributing, somehow, to the evolutionary process.

Eventually I found a mate, another soul drawn to the same spiritual teaching, which made the inherent challenges of this life somewhat easier to navigate. We were both forty when we met. Before then, before arriving at a certain stage of consciousness spurred on by the living of life, it would have been inconceivable for our paths to have crossed. The material circumstances of our early lives, different in every conceivable respect, would have made the odds impossible.

Evidently, however, our meeting was in the cards. One of the questions I had asked the astrologer, in my early thirties, was whether I would ever find a soul-mate. She didn't answer directly, but suggested repeatedly that I look into an organization near the UN that held monthly meditation meetings. Years later, I finally attended such a meeting, and then a day-long conference. Among the staid esoteric philosophers behind the conference, students of the Bailey books, one person stood out from the rest for his irreverent sense of humor.

Some time later I attended a screening of a cable TV series whose title contained the words "new age." An audience member asked the host what "new age" meant. "Oh nothing, really," he replied. "It's just a trendy phrase." My hand rose involuntarily and I heard myself say, "The New Age is very, very real." The host shot back, "Why don't you come up and tell us about it?" The prospect terrified me, especially after realizing that longtime Bailey students were present, seated, in fact, in the same row as I was. But having no choice, I went to the front of the hall and spoke about the New Age. I barely recalled a word I said afterward, but was relieved to hear, from the person seated next to me, that I'd done the subject justice. Not long thereafter, our parallel paths intersected permanently, in marriage.

Those were the early 80s, the dawn of the Reagan era, when greed and self-interest were becoming more socially acceptable than ever before. With each passing year, the New Age beckoned to me more powerfully. As I gravitated toward a series of ventures described as "new age," a part of me realized they were products of a transitional time and thus experimental, destined to be ephemeral. Yet another part of me wanted to believe, as I hopefully plunged into each new venture, that it would bear fruit. The intensity of my desire for a new consciousness to become manifest frequently clouded my judgment.

Looking back at the 80s, from the vantage point of the present, is like surveying an empty, windswept beach that was once littered with sandcastles. Of course, a case can be made for the intrinsic value of sandcastles. Generally they gladden the souls of those who build them, as well as passers-by, if only for the briefest moment. Each of these "castles" was unique, containing seeds of the New Age and possibly contributing, in some small way, to anchoring the new paradigm. But when the tide comes in and sweeps away such creations, their disappearance can also sadly disappoint.

New age ventures of the 80s became a living laboratory for everything I was learning. At first there were purely voluntary efforts, like the creative collaboration on *New Age Vision* and the Earth Community. Then there was a paid job, nominally so, at a new age center. Excited to find such a job, I grossly underestimated the inherent contradictions in the thinking of a key person there. While presenting programs on the transformation of consciousness, he held firmly to the belief that human nature was unchangeable. Not surprisingly, old age politics quickly entered in, and quickly drove me out. I preferred working on Wall Street to supporting the illusion that there existed a place demonstrating a new consciousness.

While serving my time at the bank, I fed my soul by facilitating a group that became known as The Network — a gathering of seekers from black and white neighborhoods throughout the city. Brought together by a shared interest in the new spirituality, we met monthly, learning to transcend old barriers, to see through each other's eyes. After two years of meetings that were always interesting and often inspiring, the spark simply died out.

It was my next volunteer "assignment" that led me, eventually, to Russia. A friend named Dominique Mazeaud, a woman from France whom I'd met at the Earth Community, involved me in it. She was an art gallery director who spent many of her evenings designing programs that spotlighted artists of the new consciousness. The sponsor of these programs was an organization devoted to "peace through culture," inspired by the philosophy of Nicholas Roerich (1874-1947), a Russian-born artist and philosopher.

Roerich had defined culture as the cultivation of "ur," the Sanskrit word for light. In his view, the main components of culture were the principal avenues through which Light entered into human civilization: art, science, philosophy and religion. Genuine works of culture, those that were truly inspired, transmitted a supernal Light that had the capacity to touch the *human* spirit. Transcending all external barriers, such works were natural pathways to peace and understanding. Thus the phrase: *pax cultura*.

Inspired by these ideas, I found myself involved in helping the embryonic organization hammer out a statement of goals and purposes. The long-range goal was to bring together artists, scientists and philosophers from around the world to work on global problems. Born of the new spiritual consciousness, our purpose was to foster creative synergy and global awareness. We evolved a vision of an "International City," by which we really meant "center." It inspired many of us to give freely of our time and resources, and attracted accomplished individuals in the fields of art, science and philosophy to contribute in various ways.

At a certain point, we outgrew the capacities of a volunteer organization. I was asked to become "the paid staff," at which point I left Wall Street. One of my primary tasks was to raise money. Naturally, I turned to people I had known in the foundation world during my think-tank years, when I had been involved in writing grant proposals for programs related to working-class communities and ethnicity. In the interim, someone I knew rather well had risen to the top echelons of a major foundation. I sent her the "International City" proposal and she agreed to a meeting.

We hadn't seen each other for years. As she welcomed me into her suite of offices, the atmosphere was cordial. We exchanged pleasantries about the intervening years. But once we were seated, she looked at me from behind her oversized desk with an unpleasant glare. Then she began to lecture me. "Every single day," she said, barely concealing her irritation, "we receive thousands of grant requests. They come from communities facing illiteracy, teen pregnancy, drug addiction, crime, homelessness, and despair. What is this International City? Do you really expect me to take it seriously?" It hit me then, as never before, that I had crossed the threshold into a very different universe.

Part Two

The USSR

First Impressions

My Russian odyssey began with a phone call from a stranger. It was the middle of 1985 and I was still working at the Wall Street bank. The caller was on fire with enthusiasm. He had just returned from the USSR and was anxious to make plans to go back the following year. Having heard about my interest in Russia through a mutual acquaintance, he was calling to ask if I would be willing to help organize a group tour. Immediately, almost without thinking, I said yes.

I felt several pulls and tugs toward Russia at the time, some more conscious than others. As a result of the peace through culture work, I'd become interested in the legacy of Nicholas Roerich and his wife, Helena, the author of an esoteric philosophy for the New Age called Agni Yoga. I had also been involved in the anti-nuclear movement of the 80s, where I discovered that ordinary Americans were traveling to the USSR as "citizen diplomats." Frustrated by the failures of superpower diplomacy to curb the growth of nuclear weapons stockpiles, they were undertaking initiatives of their own.

There was another pull whose origins would long remain mysterious to me. The very idea of *Russia* — *not* the Soviet Union — had become intriguing to me. It wasn't easy to separate this *idea* from what I remembered of Dostoyevsky and Tolstoy, or what I felt from the music of Tchaikovsky and Rachmaninoff. Something inchoate, as if from the far distant past, had begun "knocking at my head," to use a Russian expression.

Within months of that phone call, I was enrolled in a Russian course and involved in the planning of a trip for June of '86. Two months before our departure, the worst nuclear accident in history occurred at Chernobyl. Until then, twenty-five people were signed up to go and the waiting list was long. As the radioactive dust settled thousands of miles away and the Soviet Union persisted in denying this reality, our passenger list declined sharply. In the end, we were a group of ten souls, including my husband, me and my co-planner.

Our trip took place near the start of Gorbachev's reign. Many things had hinted at a different climate, from his friendly, engaging smile — new in the history of Soviet leaders — to optimistic accounts of American citizen diplomats. Shortly after ascending to power, Gorbachev had personally welcomed one such a group to Moscow, expressing his gratitude to them for having traveled so far, at their own expense, to meet his people. They reported that he appeared genuinely moved by the concern of ordinary Americans to end the Cold War.

Notwithstanding such anecdotes, there was no reason to expect a loosening of the reins of the police state. We arrived with the assumption that Intourist, the official visitors' apparatus, had retained a tight grip on the comings and goings of tourists through its army of guides and hotel employees. What we hadn't foreseen was the impact of Chernobyl. The tourist boom anticipated for that year had gone bust. Those who braved the fall-out were rewarded by a noticeable upgrade in the quality of food and lodgings, and by an unprecedented, though exceedingly small, degree of freedom.

Our guide, Tanya, was an immensely likeable young woman who disarmed her charges immediately. Expecting a steady stream of state propaganda, we were instead exposed to the most pressing personal dilemma of her life: whether to marry and move to the oil-rich Siberian north, or remain single and moneyless in Leningrad. The obligatory propaganda came with daily doses of official people and places. But Tanya, knowing we had come to meet "real people," occasionally made discreet allowances. One evening, she permitted my husband and me to stray from the official schedule, indicating with a wink that she would look the other way.

We had been given the name and number of a contact in Leningrad, something rare in those days. That was still a time when Soviet citizens receiving calls from foreigners could be charged with espionage or black marketeering. Yet our contact, Vladimir, had sounded elated to hear from Americans. He asked if we could meet him that very evening at a metro station in an outlying district. With a year of Russian studies under our belts, we managed to navigate the Cyrillic subway signs and find our way there. Vladimir was, as promised, instantly recognizable in a tee shirt emblazoned with an image of the Buddha. His demeanor, however, was thoroughly inscrutable.

In stark contrast with the enthusiasm evident in his voice over the telephone, Vladimir's greeting was aloof and circumspect. Motioning for us to follow him, he marched ahead, moving briskly toward an undisclosed destination. We walked in silence for about fifteen minutes, crossing countless streets and boulevards, ultimately arriving at a bus stop. The bus dropped us off outside a sprawling cement-block apartment complex. Vladimir finally saw fit to tell us that we were on the way to an apartment belonging to friends of his.

During this hour-long trek, I realized how naïve it was to have placed our trust in this stranger. The only thing we knew about him, through the London acquaintance who had given us his number, was that he was a student of the Bailey books. The further we ranged from familiar landmarks, the less possible it became to retrace our steps, and the more I smelled danger. Tanya had not forbidden our excursion, but she had not expressly approved it either. Was that a form of cover for her, I wondered? It was still officially against the law for tourists to be out alone, unchaperoned by an Intourist guide.

As we approached the building entrance, Vladimir stopped walking. He turned on his heels and sternly cautioned us, in a whisper, to remain silent. We entered a darkened vestibule with an ominous aura, following him down a pitch-black corridor toward a tiny elevator cage. It, too, was unlit, and lacked both side and ceiling panels. There were only thin wooden planks beneath our feet as the elevator slowly inched upwards in the darkness, its cables creaking loudly. I couldn't help recalling the many times in my life I'd been warned about being overly trusting.

And then, in a heartbeat, everything changed. As we stepped out of the elevator, a bright shaft of light shone through an open door. Standing in the lighted doorway was a slender, dark-haired woman with beautifully chiseled features. Peering deeply into our eyes, she welcomed us into her home with the kind of warmth and eagerness generally reserved, in the West, for old friends. Her expression seemed to be saying: It means so much to have you here. Please come in and stay as long as you can.

Upon entering this apartment, we were transported to another world. It was full of light and color, pulsating with life, worlds away from the dingy building that housed it. A married couple lived there; both were artists. The walls were covered with artwork. One's eyes fell upon objects of beauty and interest everywhere. This experience — crossing a portal from an unlit corridor into an abode blazing with light — was the first of myriad encounters with the stark polarities of Russian life. It became, in retrospect, emblematic of my Russian journey.

The reason for our being there was never explained by Vladimir, who simply stated that the couple, Zhana and Georgi, were his friends. Equally mystifying was their treatment of us as honored guests. Despite the fact that we had just finished a copious dinner at the hotel, and protested at the mere thought of another one, Zhana plied us with platters of delicacies, the kind which (I later learned) Soviet citizens waited endlessly in line for, keeping them tucked away for special occasions.

After the meal, Vladimir immediately cornered my husband, Martin. It became clear that metaphysical teachings were the core of his life. To meet someone who worked professionally with the Bailey books was for him an event of great magnitude. As if to compensate for his earlier silence, a stream of speech burst forth from him like champagne from a newly uncorked bottle. Thoughts, ideas, ruminations — perhaps many years' worth — spilled out with unnatural rapidity and intensity, despite his broken English.

Zhana and Georgi, happily indulging their friend's passion, came to my rescue, inviting me to sit on the other side of the room. We attempted a conversation, but quickly encountered our limits. Their knowledge of English was as embryonic as my grasp of Russian. To close the gap, Georgi brought out a folder of his artwork to show me — illustrations for children's books and a variety of sketches and drawings. When I especially admired something, he would remove it from its folder and present it to me, until I learned to curb my enthusiasm.

With the few words of Russian I could muster, and Zhana's dramatic flair for gesturing, I learned, while looking through Georgi's art work, that they had a son, and that he was going through an adolescent rebellion, which they found quite exasperating. Materially, however, they led a privileged Soviet life. In addition to a comfortable apartment, they had a small art studio, a country dacha, and their own car, quite rare at the time. Their dream was to travel abroad one day, to the West.

Out of the blue, or so it seemed, Georgi asked me whether I liked Dostoyevsky and whether I had read *Crime and Punishment*. When I answered affirmatively, he made a phone call. Ten minutes later a sympathetic young couple, both actors, showed up. A plan had been hatched. Georgi ushered us all downstairs, except for Zhana. She remained home so that six of us, including a few who were rather hefty, could squeeze into one very small car.

Our destination was the apartment building where the real-life Raskolnikov, the central character of *Crime and Punishment*, had lived in mid-19th century St. Petersburg. From the outside, the building appeared to have changed little since that time. Inside, too, everything had an ancient quality, from the cement staircase to the pale green walls, peeling, pitted and covered with graffiti. Scrawled there were hundreds of messages left by pilgrims, people who had visited the building as if it were a holy shrine, recording their names and sentiments for posterity.

Since the hour was fairly late and the tenants were at home, most of our group remained outside. They cautioned Martin and me to be silent and walk very softly. Not only were we trespassing, but being in the company of our hosts was quite illegal. Georgi followed us from the rear for the first few flights, pointing to the top floor, indicating the apartment where the person who inspired the character, Raskolnikov, once lived. We walked up the rest of the way alone, glimpsed the doorway, then quickly descended and rejoined the others on the nearly deserted cobblestone street below.

Georgi and his friends gazed at us expectantly, their eyes gleaming in the light of June's white nights, eagerly awaiting our reactions. Taking us to this "sacred" place, an adventure enhanced by the element of risk, had filled them with a kind of childlike joy. Afterward they drove us around Leningrad, pointing out varied places of historic interest. But it was clear that for them, nothing in their city equaled the importance of the staircase we had climbed. It was a unique, living link to the great writer, the unsurpassed explorer of the human psyche, and thus the most special place they could imagine to bring their American guests.

Before returning to our hotel and the guardianship of Intourist, Georgi drove us back to his apartment to say good-bye to Zhana. His initial reserve was gone by then and he exuded a magnetic kind of warmth. His deep blue eyes seemed to embrace the souls of his guests, much like Zhana's had when she first opened the door and peered into our eyes. Her gaze appeared to bypass everything superficial and external, looking directly, as it were, into our souls.

These exchanges with Zhana and Georgi, transcending the need for language, cast an ironic light on our "cold war diplomacy" mission. There, in the bosom of our enemy, I had experienced being seen, recognized, on a deeper level than I was accustomed to at home. After only a few hours, it felt as if we had formed a special bond. There was joyfulness in simply being together. And their generosity to us was extraordinary. I had noticed a photograph hanging on the wall as we were leaving, an artistic scene of onion-shaped domes atop a Russian church. Georgi immediately removed it from the wall, placed it in my hands, and insisted that I take it home.

At the door, I took out a piece of paper, preparing to write down their address and give them ours. I thought we had forged the beginning of a genuine Soviet-American friendship, one that might grow through correspondence. Zhana's expression suddenly darkened. She asked me to never write, call, or contact them directly. Doing so, someone later explained to us, would attract the authorities' attention and place them under suspicion. That would jeopardize their chances of traveling abroad, their fondest dream.

I left there feeling a bit dazed, as Vladimir guided us back to the metro station. Martin, still the target of a relentless stream of words, was relieved that the evening was ending, whereas I had the feeling that I'd left a piece of myself with Zhana and Georgi, whom I would never see again. Clutching my keepsakes, I tried to digest my first lesson in Soviet-American differences. They lived for the moment, never knowing what the future held. We lived as though the future belonged to us; all we had to do was plan it.

By comparison with that evening, the rest of our two-week stay in the USSR paled into insignificance. There were a few heart-warming encounters in the town of Novgorod, and later in Moscow. But as they were officially ordained, they were always scripted in the main, with some intended outcome or effect. Since "unofficial" contacts were prohibited, those that were allowed could never be taken at face value.

An exception was a curious young couple we met in Moscow. I had called to let them know I had a letter for them from a member of our Russian class in New York. We planned to meet in our hotel lobby, but they had managed to slip past the KGB guards and come up to our room. Both were wearing leather jackets, looking more like affluent Western tourists than Soviet citizens. The woman was also wearing a leather skirt and high-fashion boots, items picked up on trips they took to Czechoslovakia, which made them appear exceedingly privileged.

Nevertheless, they complained bitterly about the hardships of the system, while searching our room for listening devices, looking at the television set and other places unimagined by naïve Americans. To thank us for bringing the letter, they had brought some "souvenirs" for us, which included booklets on Marxist-Leninist ideology. Their signals were so mixed they seemed to cancel themselves out. Looking back, I saw them as a metaphor for those times: change bubbling beneath the surface, while the gears of the old totalitarian system remained in place, superficially shoring up the status quo.

Spiritual Fire

I had never thought about returning to the USSR. There was no apparent reason to do so. But four years later, friends of ours were planning their own "citizen diplomacy" trip and invited my husband and me to join them. At first I was quite hesitant. The prospect of repeating the official Intourist fare of 1986 held no appeal and the odds of finding Zhana and Georgi again, or even people like them, seemed rather remote. In the end, however, something ineffable called me back.

As it turned out, a sea change had taken place in four years' time. It had been impossible to sense the scale of it from thousands of miles away. The first hard evidence was the fact that Intourist, the monopolistic enterprise of the Soviet state, was facing embryonic competition that year. Our trip was arranged by a private tour company, one of the first entrepreneurial ventures to emerge under *perestroika*. Our friends had happened to meet the founders, two men in their early thirties, and wanted to support their fledgling business.

One of the partners, Dmitry, decided to travel with us to observe firsthand the morés of American tourists. Dressed in a blue leisure suit and running shoes, he spent much of the early part of the tour racing to the telephone to make last-minute changes in our itinerary. He was willing to do somersaults to accommodate the group's every wish, arranging for us to cover a huge amount of territory in two weeks' time. From Tallinn, Estonia's capital on the Baltic Sea, we flew south to Tblisi, the capital of Georgia, then took a train to Sochi, on the Black Sea, before flying north again to Moscow and Leningrad.

Dmitry was the new face of Soviet Russia. It appeared that he had long been primed for capitalism, having spent many years in the merchant marines. Life at sea had allowed him to escape the lash of authoritarianism, to some degree, while visiting foreign ports and learning a few things about business. Money spoke to Dmitry. It produced in him a degree of flexibility unimaginable to anyone who ever dealt with state-run Soviet enterprises. He himself was living proof of the changes taking place.

In May of 1990, the air crackled with surprise. The unexpected had become a feature of daily life. Despite Gorbachev's intention to preserve the empire, reforms of *glasnost* were rapidly undermining the old order. The new freedoms of speech and worship had taken on a life of their own, unleashing a powerful drive to throw off the yoke of repression. This was especially evident in Western Soviet republics long resentful of Russia's forced hegemony. One of them was Estonia, where brutal military crackdowns had recently failed to suppress the burgeoning independence movement, and where our tour began.

The scale of change became obvious only hours after we arrived. Our local guide in Tallinn, a professor of art history, had initially greeted us with a cool, academic reserve. That reserve was instantly shattered by the subject of politics. After touring the central square, the site of recent demonstrations, a member of our group had asked a question about the local independence movement. Our guide's response took the form of a billowy stream of invective directed at the Soviet regime. She didn't whisper or look over her shoulder, but spoke loudly, clearly, and deliberately, over the microphone of our state-owned tour bus.

In Moscow, the political fallout of *glasnost* was harder to discern. A Soviet citizen diplomat whom we saw there, a person well known to his American counterparts, was surprisingly uncertain about the future. He had been personally invited to live in Moscow three years earlier by Gorbachev, who had read a newspaper article he wrote on innovative ideas for democratic reform. His fortunes had once seemed absolutely guaranteed. But by mid-1990, he was prepared to be sent home to Siberia, should the political winds shift again.

That was a time when virtually anything seemed possible. Changes in Soviet life were rapid and kaleidoscopic. An encounter took place one evening, at our last dinner in Moscow, which left my head spinning. Members of our group had invited a few Soviet guests to join us, as had our Moscow guide. One of her friends arrived after the meal was over and people had already begun to leave. He sat down in a vacant seat next to me, introducing himself in nearly perfect English. He was Arkady, a charming, strikingly handsome man, perhaps in his late thirties.

As we spoke, I learned that Arkady had just started his own business — the new breed of hydra-headed trading companies springing up at the time. I noticed that he was somewhat tentative about this new venture, yet he seemed unusually comfortable in his own skin, more so than other Soviet people we'd met. He had a kind of *savior-faire* that made him appear conspicuously different. Curious to know what he had done before the advent of business, or "who he was," as Russians phrase the question, I asked. Without hesitation he replied, "I worked for the KGB. So did my two older brothers and my father."

Struggling to assimilate this information and regain my composure, I interpreted Arkady's openness as permission to pursue the subject. But as soon as I posed the obvious next question, why they had left, his face showed signs of vulnerability. Drawing a deep breath, he explained that they had been forced to leave because his mother had been arrested. Her crime was selling things on the street to provide extra cash for the family, a practice still strictly illegal though increasingly common. When the authorities discovered that the arrested woman was related to four KGB officers, they decided to make an example of the family.

In a moment laced with paradox, which I appreciated far better after the fact, I found myself expressing my sincere sympathies to a man born and raised for a career in the KGB. He was clearly still unhappy about the fact that his family had been dismissed from the agency that epitomized, for most Americans, the enemy. If the Soviet Empire was evil, the KGB was its heart of darkness. Yet Arkady had seemed extremely sympathetic and likeable.

Afterward I wondered who he was, in the American sense. Presumably he had shown up at the hotel to meet Americans, most likely to make business contacts. How disappointing for him, I mused. In our ranks were two physicians, a college professor, and a corps of idealists from the non-profit sector. But then our Moscow guide, the person who had invited him, knew that. It began to dawn on me then, in a way that altered my normal mode of perception, that I was in a country where almost nothing could be taken at face value.

There were exceptions, of course. Some of the young people we met along the way, especially those drawn to spirituality, seemed unusually open, transparent. *Glasnost* had profoundly shaped their lives. Those in their twenties had a different, noticeably freer, style of expression. The ones we came to know best were our local guides in such far-flung places as Sochi in the south, and Leningrad in the north. They and their friends, whom they invited to meet "the Americans," gave us a glimpse of the burgeoning spirituality to which *glasnost* had given rise.

By 1990, the communist stranglehold, with its doctrine of atheism, was all but broken. *Glasnost* had flung open the doors of the ideological prison house that shaped the 20th century. Suddenly there was freedom of religion, along with a climate of uncertainty, which seemed to fuel the search for a higher reality. In those years, with the Russian Orthodox Church still on the periphery, seekers were able to roam freely, tasting of this religion and that spiritual teaching, like visitors at a great fair of divine revelation.

One afternoon, on a drive through the mountains of southern Russia near Sochi, there was a sudden commotion in the back of the bus. When I turned around to look, our two young guides were rushing forward. They stopped next to my seat and stood hovering over me, their eyes wide with wonder. They were both students of Agni Yoga, the teaching heralding (in the Russian language) a new era of spirituality. Our friends had mentioned to them that I was familiar with it. They could barely contain their excitement.

Like the incident with our tour guide in Tallinn, this one mirrored another aspect of the change wrought in four years' time. People who had dared to speak of Agni Yoga in '86 did so with considerable trepidation. I first heard it mentioned in the back office of a museum exhibiting paintings of Nikolai Roerich. With the door closed and blinds drawn, museum employees told us how they had secretly studied the Agni Yoga books, copying them over by hand, sometimes photographing or furtively xeroxing the pages. As with all *samizdat* materials, they shared them only with the most trusted friends, always at great personal risk.

One of our Sochi guides had blue eyes of an exceptional shade, a nearly translucent aquamarine. Light streamed from them as she spoke of what she was learning about the inner realms. In a flood of words, she described her spiritual history. It was fairly brief, as she was still in her early twenties, but it covered a breathtaking amount of territory — from the Baptist faith, which she had joined at a Billy Graham crusade in Moscow, to the Ba'Hai religion, introduced to her by American missionaries. Both had captured her interest for awhile. But by the time we met her, she was voraciously consuming the books of Agni Yoga, the yoga of spiritual fire.

Our two young guides had an intensity that transcended mere enthusiasm. They seemed on fire with the search for Truth. While working as guides to earn a living, and to meet foreigners and learn about the wider world, the spiritual quest was paramount for them. What gave meaning to their lives appeared to be the new dimensions of reality opening up as they learned about the inner workings of the universe, the higher worlds, the path of spiritual ascent.

In Leningrad, our guide was about the same age and had a similar fervor in her eyes when she spoke of spiritual things, though her path had led her to more traditional forms of religion. In two years' time, she had been baptized in the Russian Orthodox Church and initiated into Buddhism, and ardently embraced both. For her there was no contradiction or conflict. The same was true for other young people we met. They seemed comfortable picking and choosing, mixing and blending their religions and spiritual practices.

At first there was something slightly disconcerting about all this. It appeared as if the forbidden fruit of the communist era were being superficially, even promiscuously, sampled rather than deeply assimilated. One had the sense of watching people, who had long been starving, overindulge themselves at an extravagant banquet table. But there was also something refreshing, even invigorating, about this avid quest for God. These seekers manifested a spiritual zeal that I had rarely seen among Americans.

Suddenly it dawned on me that I might have been observing, without realizing it, signs of Russia's prophesied future. Prior to that trip, I had done some esoteric research that turned up a startling notion. It seemed that Russia, despite its official adherence to atheism for much of the last century, had a unique spiritual destiny. Prophets and seers of different centuries and different continents had been in remarkable agreement about this. The gist of their prophecies was that Russia, once its soul had awakened — at some unforeseeable time in the future — would play a significant role in spawning a new universal religion.

In this light, I began to see the young people we met as harbingers of this new religion. It was as though they were collecting bits and pieces of it, from East and West, as predicted. Labels meant nothing to them. Dogma of any kind was distasteful. They seemed drawn to the flame of Spirit in whatever form they could find it. Outwardly, their approach resembled a tapestry of contrast and contradiction. But inwardly, from what I could discern, there was a sense of universality that transcended old religious barriers.

During this trip, the idea of writing a book on the soul of Russia began to germinate. I was fascinated by what I had observed, but only dimly understood. For me, writing a book was a way to plumb the depths of questions that seemed, at the time, unanswerable. One of them was personal and paradoxical. I couldn't help wondering why I had found such resonance with the emergent spirituality of people whose country had been, for as long as I could remember, the enemy of my own.

I also wondered why a people raised on atheism, for generations, would be destined to foster a new form of religion. A Russian émigrée living in New York had put forth an interesting theory about this. She hypothesized that Russia's advantage in this regard was having become, in essence, a blank slate in the realm of religion. If a new religious impulse were to take root in the world, it seemed logical to begin with a *tabula rasa*, a place where people were relatively free of religious dogma.

But of course it wasn't that simple. The questions beginning to percolate in my mind contained many layers and dimensions. I had yet to discover the religious origins of Russia, dating back a millennium, or the great legacy of Russian saints, or the powerful role of Orthodoxy in shaping the Russian psyche. On the flight home, as the book idea began to gel, I was mostly aware of the surprising affinity I felt with spiritual seekers I had met there. I, too, had been an atheist before finding myself on the Path. I, too, eschewed doctrine in favor of the ageless wisdom. I, too, felt more nourished by things of the Spirit than things of this world.

Forewarnings

Shortly after returning home, I stuck my toe in the water to test the viability of writing a book. I looked for people to talk with — Soviet émigrés and Americans with extensive Russian experience. In the beginning, my idea was not so much a formulated concept as it was an urge to explore the Russian soul. Still, the more I spoke with people, the more compelling it became and the more I felt drawn to pursue it.

The surge of interest that I felt underscored, by contrast, the staleness of my current work. After the *pax cultura* effort ended, for lack of funding, I joined the staff of another small non-profit organization with a lofty vision. Its aim was to form a worldwide coalition of groups promoting awareness of the impact of global forces on humanity as a whole. The idea was that we were living in a new time, a time when human problems increasingly bypassed national borders. From the spread of terrorism and infectious disease, to climate change and wealth inequality, all nations were affected. Handling these crises required a new mode of perception and a new level of global cooperation.

By the late 80s, the need for a worldview transcending national interests had become self-evident to some. According to the ageless wisdom teachings, it was also an evolutionary imperative. I believed in it whole-heartedly. But my work had lost its luster. I was engaged in editing endless drafts of documents whose impact was minimal at best. In the climate of those times, this organization's goals seemed increasingly unrealistic, and the lack of funds was a constant albatross. It was a case of *déjà vu* all over again.

When the Russian book idea came along, I had reached a cul-de-sac in my work life. My options had dwindled to a precious few. I'd grown weary of working in non-profit organizations with high ideals and relentless struggles to obtain funding. Yet the corporate world, where money flowed, was not an alternative for me except in the direst circumstances. My soul wasn't happy unless I was somehow contributing to the greater good, or at least believed that I was.

Ever since the Peace Corps, I had been hooked on one vision or another for improving the lot of humanity. Invariably, however, each vision had turned into a mirage. In politics, the noblest ideals were corrupted by ignoble means of acquiring power. In softer, gentler spheres where the vision was everything, people like myself abhorred the kind of compromises demanded by people who held the purse strings. In new age groups, where I felt most at home in many ways, there was yet another set of problems and pitfalls.

In part these problems stemmed from a core element of the new spirituality: turning within and attuning to the voice of one's soul for guidance. Some groups experimented with making decisions on the basis of collective inner guidance. But in the 80s, the pre-dawn of the new era, most of us had only a rudimentary grasp of the requirements for Aquarian group work. And few had developed authentic, and reliable, access to inner guidance.

Exacerbating this problem was the fact that within any given group, the capacity of individuals to tap the wisdom of the soul differed greatly. There were times, moreover, when those with the most reliable inner contact received guidance that was dissonant, creating a Tower of Babel effect. That in turn triggered a reversion to the realm of personality, where spiritual insights were defended as ego "positions." In the end, the value of the original guidance became colored, and the sense of group harmony diminished.

And then there was "magical thinking," another common pitfall. It resembled the miscalculation of an infant at the crawling stage who suddenly thinks he or she can walk without any help, and is startled to fall flat on his or her face. In groups working toward visionary goals, often basing their actions on inner guidance, stumbling was inevitable. Learning to navigate new dimensions of consciousness, while living in the world, was sufficiently challenging for an individual. When multiplied by the members in a group, the results could be disastrous. There were times when reason was largely abandoned in favor of the expectation of a miracle. Finally, I saw the futility.

That was when the Russian book idea surfaced. It appealed to me for many reasons, not the least of which was that it could be done independently. I could follow the urge of my own soul, and my own spiritual guidance. Working on this book would allow me, I thought, to disentangle myself from the snares of new age group endeavors. Imagine my surprise, then, when I realized, well into the project, that I had jumped from the frying pan into the fire. The Russia I encountered was riddled with magical thinking, the expectation of miracles, even superstition. Being there, at times, created the sensation of viewing the weaknesses of "new agers" through the distortions of a fun-house mirror.

While peeling away the outer layers of this once dreaded super-power, I began to understand why Russia defied the comprehension of Westerners, why Winston Churchill's inimitable description of it — "a riddle wrapped in a mystery cloaked in an enigma" — had stood the test of time. Behind the walls of the communist empire, which declared strict adherence to atheism, were people whose orientation to life was conspicuously mystical. In this respect, I found myself in surprisingly familiar territory.

But I am jumping ahead. In the summer of 1990, when I set out to talk with New Yorkers familiar with Russia, I was contemplating an adventure into the great unknown. No place on earth seemed more foreign, more inscrutable, than the Soviet Union. After two visits, I had come away with the impression that nothing was what it appeared to be, which amplified the aura of mystery. I had also realized there was something to be discovered that lay beneath the radar screen of many Westerners, something related to spirituality.

My quest began a few blocks away from where I was working at the time, for the project on global cooperation. I began spending evenings and weekends conducting interviews. The few Russians I knew were fellow students of the wisdom teachings, émigrés who had fled their native land and wanted never to look back. Only a few were willing to talk to me. For largely pragmatic reasons, I made my first incursions into the Russian psyche via Americans.

Two of my first interviewees were women in their late twenties with extended experience in Russia. Both had worked for years as tour guides, leading groups of Americans to the USSR in cultural exchanges organized by non-governmental agencies. Both were enrolled in Ph.D. programs in Russian studies at New York universities. Most important, both had lived in the Soviet Union, studying at Moscow State University, for several years during the early 80s.

Curiously, despite the many parallels in their lives, they did not know one another. They had studied in Moscow at different times and had never met. They had been referred to me by different organizations and I interviewed them separately. Because of that, the similarities in their responses were all the more striking, and all the more difficult to ignore or dismiss as the observations of a lone individual.

Both sensed my enthusiasm for the quest I was about to undertake and tried to warn me of what to expect, as an American. Though twenty years my junior, they spoke as elders, like veterans of foreign wars offering advice to a fresh-faced recruit. They, too, had once been misty-eyed about the Russian soul. They, too, had been magnetized by the soulfulness of the people. But both had been badly burned. They had come home feeling used, abused, exploited. BEWARE, they said, in different ways. Don't be fooled by appearances. Russians who befriend Americans *always* want something from them.

That was hardly what I had expected to hear from people who returned to the Soviet Union voluntarily and frequently. Even more confusing was the fact that both admitted that the main reason they kept going back was not the money they earned as tour guides.

They spoke wistfully of the friends they visited while there. The qualities they appreciated in these friends, which they didn't find among Americans, brought to mind my own first impressions of Russians. In the end, I was left with a bundle of contradictions. The warnings, strong as they were, had been undercut by the even stronger ambivalence of these two women.

Far more sobering were the words and forebodings of people in the Soviet émigré community, those who finally agreed to talk with me. Despite their familiarity with the prophecies about Russia's future, mainly in the Agni Yoga books, and despite an acknowledgment, sometimes begrudging, of the creative genius of the Russian soul, they could find nothing positive to say about their native land. The cruelty of Soviet life had left them scarred, unable to imagine any good emerging from that country for generations to come.

In spite of all this, I persevered. Something in my own soul propelled me onward in a search for whatever "evidence" I could find to link the Russian soul with the new era. In its Soviet incarnation, Russia had seemed one of the least likely places on earth for Aquarian energies to take root. Yet despite outer appearances, despite terrifying cruelties, past and present, I had come to believe there was something else, an inner essence, still to be revealed.

I started out with two kinds of clues. One was embodied by the wide-eyed young people searching everywhere for the living Spirit. The other was the collection of prophetic voices. They ranged from Edgar Cayce, Alice Bailey, and Rudolf Steiner to Native American seers, and Russian seers, like Dostoyevsky, who had passionately believed that Russia would some day become a force for universal brotherhood. The question was whether I could link these clues to each other, and to Russia's religious history, in any meaningful way.

Leap of Faith

My decision to follow the call of my soul had immediate financial repercussions. Putting both feet in the water meant leaving my job. To explore Russia in depth would require considerable time and resources. In addition to having to travel nearly halfway around the world any number of times, there would be interpreters' fees and other substantial costs. My first challenge was to find a way to meet these expenses and try, if possible, to compensate for my lost salary.

That presented a conundrum. Unlike many authors who finance their work through book advances, I was not in a sound position to approach the publishing world. There were several strikes against me: I was exploring new territory, I had no relevant professional credentials, and no name recognition. Another possible avenue was a foundation grant, but approaching foundations would have meant that I would have had to disguise the ultimate nature of my search. A proposal to study the Russian soul was likely to raise eyebrows, only.

I decided to try a two-tiered approach, involving two separate books. The first, which seemed highly fundable, would lay the groundwork for the second. It was to be a book of oral histories with a format similar to my book on American working-class women. I would interview Soviet citizens about *glasnost*, exploring the inner changes they were experiencing with the death of communist ideology and the advent of new freedoms.

That was the fall of 1990. No one dreamed that the Soviet Union would implode the following year. But the galloping change already underway seemed poorly understood in the West. Despite a flood of new books, there was a lack of in-depth exploration of the *inner* struggles facing a people emerging from authoritarian rule. My idea was to interview a range of individuals — from diverse professions, regions and generations — to create a picture of the evolving interior landscape. I wrote my grant proposal and sent it off, with optimism, to several foundations.

Weeks passed, in silence. There was no response. I eventually learned that in one case my proposal had worked its way up to the desk of a foundation president, but there it sat. The reason was never expressly stated, but implied was a classic Catch-22 dilemma. I had no professional credentials to write a book about Russia, and could obtain no such credentials until I published something on the subject, for which I was seeking research support, which I could not obtain without credentials.

And there was something else, which hadn't fully sunk in until that time. I had long since passed through a one-way portal on my spiritual journey. It had happened when my working life stopped resembling a career. What was once a normal-looking résumé had metamorphosed into a saw-toothed odyssey. With that deafening silence, the material consequences of my life choices hit home. People within "the establishment" who had once supported my work no longer did. The narrow sluices and fortified gates of the foundation world were permanently closed.

But the soul, I was learning, had its own imperatives. One was a willingness to take a leap of faith. While the doors known to me in the outer world were closed, subtle signs and impulses kept propelling me onward. A growing faith in things unseen became the main fault line separating my past from my present. I had not arrived there easily, nor did I find it a comfortable place to be. Having long held the conviction that religion truly *was* the opiate of the masses, switching gears was a slow and labored process.

This was so despite the many "signs and wonders" I had experienced, starting with "Ben Franklin" surfacing in all manner of places. The guidance I received, in different forms, seemed unimpeachable. Often it was opposite to what I would have done, left to my own devices. I trusted it especially when it went so counter to my natural thought patterns that I could never have imagined it. More than anything else, it was the wisdom and compassion of these inner teachers that was moving me in the direction of faith in things unseen.

And yet this guidance did not necessarily point me toward situations with "happy endings." In fact, following my guidance sometimes landed me in painfully difficult circumstances. It took years to fully assimilate the principle that spiritual guidance was not intended to help a seeker win the lottery or catch the golden ring. Quite the contrary. It was often designed to lead directly into the fires of purification. There were karmic debts to pay and lessons to learn on the road to enlightenment.

I knew for certain that there was a rainbow at the end of that road. Sages had documented that fact over the course of many millennia. But I was still learning, needing reminders, that the path of transformation was — by its nature — unpleasant to the personality. Any desire to shine, to gain worldly recognition, ultimately had to be sacrificed in favor of the soul, which knows we are one with all, and thus seeks the greater good of all. The personality, on the way to becoming a worthy instrument of the soul, had to "die" of the illusion of separation. The finality of that death, it seemed, would have to undergo repeated tests.

Hindsight, of course, brings wondrous clarity. At the time, "the world's" rejection of my request for financial support came as an ego blow and a jolt to my sense of reality. The ground beneath my feet no longer felt solid. I hadn't yet come to grips with the risks of living on the material plane, while following the dictates of my soul. Choosing God over Caesar, as it were, seemed to mean that nothing in Caesar's world could be taken for granted again. As happened when I first left "the world," there was no going back now, but neither was there a clear way forward.

This state of unknowingness was heightened by the character of my spiritual guidance. It was least reliable when it came to questions of a material nature. And yet, paradoxically, as familiar doors closed behind me, I found myself turning to it more than ever, while realizing I couldn't rely on it in a literal sense. In the end, I placed my trust in an ancient spiritual axiom: if one acts in accord with the will of God, as clearly as one can discern what it is, the resources needed to accomplish a given task will be provided. Otherwise, if the motive is self-interest, we're on our own.

By then, the task that presented itself to me had come to feel like a mandate from the depths of my soul. The only means available to pursue it, without help from "the world," were savings belonging to my husband and me. To travel to Russia, I'd have to dip into those savings. Moreover my husband's salary, modest by some standards, would be our sole support. For the first time since I'd begun following my guidance in practical matters, I was being urged to take a financial risk. If it didn't pan out, two lives would be affected.

In the beginning, the risk seemed manageable. I thought of our savings as a kind of down payment on the first book, an initial investment in research to get things started. I would make one trip to the USSR, perhaps two, for interviews that would serve as the basis of a book proposal. I felt confident that the material would be interesting enough to find a publisher, and thus a book advance. My husband agreed. The wheels were thus set in motion.

In March of '91, my education began in earnest. Traveling with a university group during spring break, for convenience, I had less than two weeks to spend in Leningrad and Moscow. Through an extensive network of citizen diplomats, I had come armed with a long roster of potential interviewees. Because it was logistically impossible to make contacts in advance, I expected relatively few to be available when I happened to show up in their city, and fewer still to agree to speak to a stranger.

My expectations proved utterly wrong. Almost everyone I contacted was willing to be interviewed, often on the very day that I called. This surprising turn of events served to underscore my earlier observation that nothing was what it appeared to be. Inside the Soviet "planned economy," there existed a world of unpredictability. People seemed to live existentially, as if floating in time and space. Since economic plans never met their goals, in reality, workers had to be given time off to find the means of survival. They stood in lines to purchase basic commodities, often for many hours each day. Since waiting times were unpredictable, everything else followed suit. In that shadowy zone of freedom, interviews were easily arranged.

My expectations were also largely wrong on the subject of change during *glasnost*. The optimism I had sensed the year before seemed to have evaporated, despite strong turnouts in recent democratic elections. The illusions I was harboring about Gorbachev's reforms were shattered at a meeting I had with a group of psychologists. None could point to any discernable advantages resulting from *glasnost* or *perestroika*. Instead, they cited a marked rise in the suicide rate. They stated that fear had not diminished with the easing of police terror, its locus had simply shifted from the state to criminal gangs. For the first time ever, women feared for their personal safety. There was a growing criminal mentality. Life had changed, yes, but not for the better.

Prior to that visit, I had relied largely on press coverage to gauge the changes taking place in the USSR, beyond my own brief glimpses. It was stunning to realize how biased the reports of American journalists were, how baseless my own expectations were, and how difficult it was to dislodge such biases and expectations. We had all wanted to think that Gorbachev was setting things right, taking steps toward Western-style democratic reform. We wanted to see Russians freed of state tyranny, blessed by the same liberties we had, becoming, in essence, more like us.

By the end of the first week of this trip, my third to the USSR but the first dedicated to interviews, I realized that the truth was far more complex than I could begin to grasp. An elderly gentleman with a long memory and considerable wisdom reinforced this awareness. He was Dmitry Tolstoy, a composer and distant relative of the great writer. Still teaching at the Leningrad Conservatory well into his seventies, he was also a lifelong student of literature, philosophy and history. On a cold March day when city sidewalks were covered with ice, we spoke over hot tea in his simple apartment.

He made two statements that rang in my ears long afterward. One was a poignant observation: "For a thousand years," he said, "the Russian people have known nothing but suffering. This has not changed." The other was his reaction to the purpose of my interviews — my ultimate hope of writing a book about the Russian soul. After staring at me with an expression both patronizing and curious, he warned, "It is folly to even try. The Russian soul is an impenetrable mass of contradictions." He called it "a swamp into which writers invariably venture in vain." Thus, I encountered yet another test of faith.

Rules and Exceptions

As with previous cautionary notes, I duly noted the latest one and promptly set it aside. On the opposite side of the ledger, along with my inner promptings, were all the prophecies about Russia's destiny. They became my secret arsenal, a kind of talisman. The multiplicity of expressions of the same idea, and the uncanny diversity of their origins, convinced me that there had to be at least a grain of truth to them.

Another fact turned up that reinforced this notion. I found an intriguing clue to the nature of Russia's soul in *The Destiny of the Nations* by Alice Bailey. It was a small bit of esoteric information related to cosmic rays — powerful invisible forces that condition life on earth for periods of time. Everything that lives, large and small, material and non-material, is said to be subtly imbued with the qualities of one or more of these rays. This includes the souls of individuals, of nations, and even historical ages.

In a listing of nations and their rays, I noticed that the same ray that governs the Aquarian Age governs the soul of Russia — alone among the world's major nations. The evolutionary purpose of this ray is to "bring spirit into matter." It is said that over time, its radiatory force will increasingly stimulate human awareness of the spiritual dimension of life. Gradually, attention will shift from the outer, material plane to the inner plane of the soul, and the divine spark within all life forms. This shift will eventually give birth to physical plane manifestations of the new spiritual consciousness.

For me, this seemingly small bit of information gave solidity to the prophecies. Amazingly, it also meant that certain writers, luminaries of Russia's golden age of literature, had correctly intuited the future. While living through the violent upheavals of the 19th century, they held onto a vision of their nation's ultimate potential. Dostoyevsky had used the phrase "Russia's unspoken word" to convey what he sensed lying dormant in the depths of his people's soul. He fervently believed that Russia would, one day, "speak her word," that she would become a force for universal, spiritual brotherhood.

During *glasnost,* that sense of hidden spiritual potential had surfaced again. With the emergence of a "spiritual intelligentsia" in the wake of communism, an old ideal of the 19th century reemerged as well. Religious philosophers of that earlier time had encapsulated "Russia's word" in the term *sobornost.* Often translated into English as "brotherhood," *sobornost* literally means "cathedral-ness." It implies oneness in the presence of God. Strikingly, esoteric teachings suggest that this state of consciousness will mark the zenith of the Aquarian Age.

In 1991, when I needed shoring up in the face of forewarnings about the project I was undertaking, my discovery of a link between incoming cosmic energies and Russia's soul seemed quite auspicious. It affirmed, for me, the nature of Russia's spiritual potential, and the promise that this potential would eventually be fulfilled. The big question, of course, was *when.* It could be decades, centuries, or a millennium from now, as one seer had predicted.

By the spring of that year, I had little to go by. There was the light in the eyes of young seekers, the fact that enormous printings of spiritual books sold out instantly, and other similar signs that the soul of Russia, long deemed intrinsically mystical, had remained so despite a century of communist indoctrination. Beyond that, almost nothing seemed knowable for certain. The question of timing remained entirely in the realm of mystery.

Setting aside the unanswerable, I immersed myself in familiar, concrete tasks required for putting together a book of oral histories. I had returned home with a set of interviews to transcribe, and I had arrangements to make for my next trip. In addition, there were new challenges awaiting me. Prime among them was the language. Six years earlier, before my first citizen diplomacy visit, I had studied Russian as a lark. Now it became a necessity if I ever wanted to travel on my own, free of interpreters.

Learning the language was my first in-depth exposure to the Russian persona, or personality, the aspect of a person or a people that veils the soul, until it is redeemed. The Russian persona gave me pause, even more than all the warnings. The more I learned about the language, the more daunted I was by the task I had undertaken. The cultural divide separating the US and the USSR appeared far greater than I had imagined. Learning Russian was not simply a matter of mastering a new vocabulary and a new set of grammatical rules, as with French, or Italian, or even an ancient language like Latin. It was a matter of adapting to a completely different state of mind.

Every language has exceptions to the rules. With Russian, however, the rules were so commonly broken that they seemed to be mere formalities. The exceptions were so numerous that I wondered, at moments of extreme frustration, whether it even made sense to bother learning the rules. For example, verbs of the same category, which theoretically should have been conjugated the same way, often had forms that bore little, if any, resemblance to one another. It struck me that memorizing the conjugated verb forms, one by one, might have been just as efficient, had it been feasible.

It was oddly reassuring to learn that the vast majority of Russians frequently made grammatical errors themselves, including Mikhail Gorbachev, the first Soviet leader with a higher education. I marveled that even a few did not, that any had mastered their Byzantine tongue. Imagine a language in which nouns and adjectives have six different *cases*, plus one form for the singular and a different form for the plural. That means they have twelve possible forms (leaving out exceptions). Choosing the right case for a noun or adjective depends on its placement in the sentence.

To say "wide river" correctly becomes a complex affair, not to mention "wide rivers."

Struggling to find logic in places where none existed, I repeatedly heard myself asking my Russian teacher *why*, in regard to various categories of exceptions. Her undeviating reply was: "I can't explain it. You just have to learn it." That recalled the enigmatic refrain of my grandmother who had come from the same part of the world, *Vy ees ah krookit litter*. I yearned for rationality, efficiency, modernity, but the price of learning Russian was surrendering to ancient, Byzantine modes of thought.

While wrestling with the language, I began to encounter other arenas where rules seemed made to be broken. The first involved my attempt to obtain a visa. I had decided to travel to the Soviet Union on my own, for the first time, in the summer of '91. To apply for a visa as a "non-business" American visitor, I was required to have an invitation from an official, sponsoring Soviet organization. To be official, the organization had to be registered in a manner approved by the state. As it turned out, the specific form of registration required was largely unknown to Soviet citizens.

On previous trips to the USSR, I had become acquainted with a few organizations from which I felt comfortable requesting such a letter. The ones I knew best, however, had come into being during *glasnost*, when many rules were changing. They themselves were not sure whether they were registered in the requisite manner to officially sponsor foreign visitors. Some believed they were, but did not know for certain. The only way to find out was to issue an invitation letter to me, which I would submit to the Soviet Embassy in Washington, and see whether it was approved.

To wade through this red tape, I enlisted the help of a woman in Moscow named Galina, a professional interpreter. I had met her that spring, when she accompanied a group of Soviet psychologists to New York, and invited her to join me that summer as my interpreter and guide. We began the visa process two months before departure time. Galina agreed to call an organization I knew in Leningrad and ask them to write a letter of invitation on my behalf and send it to her. She would then forward it to me by fax.

In 1991, the only fax machines available to the public were at the main post office in Moscow. The waiting time was often four to five hours, assuming the clerk in charge did not disappear on a break. Galina was good enough to endure this trial. She faxed me the invitation, which I submitted with my visa application to an American visa agency in Washington that had mastered the inscrutable ways of the Soviet Embassy. For a reasonable fee, this agency served as intercessor for travelers like me.

Within several days, word came back that the sponsoring organization was not on the "officially registered" list. Galina and I started the process all over again with a second organization. The response was the same. By then, six weeks had passed. With two weeks to go before my date of departure, I discovered another option. For a fee only slightly larger than the sum I had paid the visa agency in Washington, a New York travel agency run by Soviet émigrés offered to provide a fake letter of invitation. They offered this service routinely, for travelers like me. My letter and visa arrived in a matter of days.

Russians are fond of saying, "In the end, everything will work out." When said to foreigners, especially first-time visitors, the intention is to calm the frazzled nerves of those facing an initiation into a system where order, of the kind associated with Western civilization, is largely missing. Russians live with the expectancy that things will go wrong. It is the norm for stores to be out of essential items, for elevators to break down, hot water to be shut off, official papers to be lost. That aphorism really means: eventually, if you live long enough, solutions are often found. And in the end, I did get my visa, just in time.

Galina also helped to arrange my itinerary for that summer. I wanted to travel beyond the Moscow-Leningrad axis, to get a wider cross-section of views and a better sense of the changes taking place across the vast Russian territory. One area of special interest, for its legendary beauty and the literature it inspired, was Altai — the Altai Mountains of southern Siberia, a northern gateway to the Himalayas. It happened that Galina, in the process of calling people whose names I had given to her for the purpose of setting up interviews, had discovered that an interesting conference was to take place there that July.

· The subject of the conference was the culture and spirituality of Altai. To Galina, the word "spirituality" in the title signaled something unusual, since the Communist Party still officially controlled public gatherings. Beyond that, our information was sketchy. A contact who lived in the town where the conference was to be held had just seen a flyer the very day Galina called. He mentioned it when she told him the subject of my interviews. On the basis of that call, Galina suggested that we reverse the itinerary and begin our interviews in Altai instead of Moscow. I agreed.

At the time, that had seemed like a small, inconsequential decision. I made it in a split second on the phone with Galina. We were dealing with the visa nightmare and the itinerary seemed of minor importance. There was still a question as to whether I would make it to the USSR at all. But as things turned out, the decision to attend the conference was fateful. It shaped the course of my life for many years to come. The major force behind the event became a key figure in my quest to penetrate the Russian soul.

She was a writer named Natalya Stepanovna Borodina — Natasha, as she was familiarly called. A woman of sixty with a grandmotherly presence, Natasha was the conference emcee. Between presenters, she offered her own thoughts about the figures being highlighted: Vasily Shukshin, the native writer whose stories illumined the soul of Siberia, and whom Natasha had known as a student; Dostoyevsky, who had spent time in Siberia as a political prisoner and then as a soldier, and whom Natasha considered a spiritual teacher; and Nikolai Roerich, whose Altai journeys had left a great artistic and spiritual legacy.

Flanked by a coterie of lackluster speakers, mostly academic scholars who lifelessly read from prepared texts, Natasha appeared incandescent. One had the sense that their spirits had been extinguished by the totalitarian system, but not hers. She spoke without notes, from the heart, in a voice both powerful and immensely soothing. I needed Galina's help to understand her words, but I could sense from her presence that she was, in many ways, a living exception to the rule.

During the conference breaks, Galina shared with me her own thoughts about what was going on. She felt convinced that Natasha was saying things for those who had ears to hear, making thinly veiled references to the new era of spirituality. Galina, who recognized many of the references from Agni Yoga and other books circulating at the time, was amazed to hear such words spoken in public. She conjectured that it was probably the very first time.

After sitting in the audience for portions of three days, observing Natasha at the podium, I sensed that she held some keys to the mysteries I was trying to unravel. She seemed to embody the old and the new — that which persisted over time, and that which was yet to come. The resoluteness of Mother Russia, the strong, ample-bodied Woman who endured centuries of suffering while keeping body and soul together, appeared to co-exist with the inner, secret, hidden "word" yet to be revealed.

I wanted to interview Natasha. Galina approached her on my behalf, explaining why we were there. We discovered that Natasha lived in Moscow, not Siberia, and had organized the conference at the request of a local cultural official. In the capital, several thousand miles away, most things spiritual, including her own writings that touched on spirituality, were still strictly banned. She had jumped at the chance to present another face of Russia to an audience largely comprised of university students in southern Siberia. As for my interview request, things were too hectic for her there, but she invited me to call her when I returned to Moscow.

Surrealism

It was mid-August when I returned to Moscow and called Natasha. We arranged to meet for an interview the following Monday, at her apartment. That Monday was August 19th. The infamous coup had taken place in the early morning hours. My hostess, Yulia, came in to wake me, apologizing for having to bring me bad news. She stood over my bed with a tear-streaked face and a look of anguish in her eyes. No one knew where Gorbachev was. No one knew whether he was alive or dead. No one knew anything.

TV channels were jammed with ballet and opera. Popular music from Europe and America filled the radio waves. Yulia and I stood at the window looking for signs. An eerie silence blanketed the plaza below, though there was the appearance of normalcy. People stood in line to buy bread, walked their dogs, queued up at the bus stop. They acted much as they would on any other morning, though Yulia noted their numbers were sparser than usual. Suddenly, a loud, ominous roar shattered the calm. A column of tanks appeared, crawling along the wide boulevard down below.

Yulia, torn about whether or not to go to work, vacillated for an hour or so before deciding to venture out. She worked in a hotel complex that had its own TV satellite dish and received CNN, the only possible source of news. Everyone feared that the *putschists* would try to block all communications with the outside world. An acquaintance from Leningrad had called me that morning, one of the few Soviet citizens who had e-mail at the time. Worried that it, too, would be cut off, he asked if I would bring messages to his American friends when I returned home at the end of the week.

Though Yulia was unafraid for her own safety, she felt responsible for mine. Pleading with me not to go out, on the grounds that I might not recognize danger signals, she left me in the care of her neighbor, Olga, whom I had met the night before. Olga arrived within minutes of Yulia's departure. Clutching her ten-year old son, Stepan, with one hand, she grabbed mine with the other and ushered us out to a small balcony overlooking the scene below. As the three of us watched the tanks roll by, Olga shouted to me over the deafening roar, "If this is his future, I will not survive."

Olga's eyes were red from sobbing, as well as drinking too much and sleeping too little. A pretty woman, who loved to laugh and dance, she had gone to bed only a few hours earlier, having thrown a lavish party the night before. All of Moscow had crackled with fireworks throughout the evening in celebration of Aviation Day, an annual Soviet holiday. At Olga's, the merrymaking had been especially intense. Her husband and many of their guests were airplane pilots. It was their special day.

The morning's news had transformed Olga from an intoxicated femme fatale into a terror-stricken mother, watching her dreams for her son vanish with the oncoming tanks. Stepan had the look of a confused and frightened child, unable to decipher the swirl of events around him. Only the night before he had been carefree, happy to meet an American, to practice his English. He had brought out his prized coin collection to show me. When I expressed interest, he had offered me the entire collection as a gift, appearing genuinely saddened that I would accept one coin only. Now, in the blink of an eye, their world had changed.

For me, personally, the implications of this earthshaking event were far less consequential. It was largely a matter of losing my temporary moorings. Everywhere I looked there were contradictory signals. Olga, petrified, had begged me not to go outside, citing orders from Yulia. Yet Yulia had ventured out and many people in the street below appeared quite unfazed. Some had stopped dead in their tracks to watch the sinister parade of military force. Others went about their business, as if refusing to look. Reality seemed to lie in the eye of the beholder.

A stranger in a strange land, totally unaware that the US Embassy in Moscow was advising Americans to leave the country, I was at a loss to interpret the maze of conflicting signs. My main concern was gauging the danger of getting from where I was staying to Natasha's apartment. Our interview was scheduled for that afternoon. I called to see if she was still expecting me, and sensed from her voice that she was in the camp of the unfazed. Sounding oddly upbeat, even buoyant, she never mentioned the morning's happenings. When she confirmed our appointment, my inner voice said to go. The hardest part was convincing Olga that I'd be all right.

Just as I was leaving, a pilot whom I'd met the night before knocked on the door. Olga had commissioned him to walk me to the metro station. Outside in the streets, the tension was greater than it had seemed from nine stories above, which at first made his presence comforting. But it quickly became disconcerting. Gesturing at the tanks rolling by a few yards from the sidewalk we were on, he kept saying, *Normalno, normalno*, while peppering me with questions about life in America, such as the kind of car I drove. I thought he was saying *It's normal, It's normal*, and took it to be a cynical Soviet-style joke, whereas he was actually repeating, to reassure me, *It's all right, It's all right*.

At the metro, the pilot handed me over to my interpreter for the final week of my stay, whose name was Viktor. Galina and I had parted company a few days earlier. After traveling together for five weeks, I had come to feel imprisoned by a totalitarian streak in her. She had no tolerance for divergent views. If I made an observation about something that didn't coincide with hers, she became offended, sometimes even angry. When our judgements about an interviewee were not the same, she sulked. I took refuge, increasingly, in silence. Back in Moscow, I managed to escape.

Now I had a new interpreter. Viktor was a karate instructor in his mid-twenties. He seemed to have arrived from central casting for that day. A few months earlier, he had quit his job as an Intourist guide. He hated having to write reports on Western tourists for the KGB about "suspicious behavior." If there were none, guides were heavily pressured to fabricate something. Viktor began leaving blank spaces in his reports, and finally he left the agency. When we met, through an acquaintance, he was saving money to start a school of martial arts.

Viktor bore a remarkable resemblance to Huck Finn, an older version, with freckles, red hair, blue eyes, and a tall, lanky frame. But he could be as tough as nails. The softer part of him loved sculpture, poetry, and foreign languages, but the other part seemed girded with steel. His overriding mission in life was to conquer fear. In his view, fear was the main enemy of the Soviet people. His method of combating it was to master the arts of self-defense and teach them to others.

I had last seen Viktor the day before, the afternoon of Aviation Day. He had walked me back to Yulia's after two interviews we had conducted. Yulia, who was preparing food for Olga's party, had invited him to attend but he declined. By the time we met again, less than 24 hours later, the world had changed. Viktor chose to ignore this fact. Greeting me with a smile, he asked, "How was the party last night?" Then he fell silent, like everyone else in the metro. After a twenty-minute ride, we exited the station about fifty yards from the Kremlin. Tanks were surrounding the main entrance. Viktor turned away, as if refusing to legitimize the sight with his eyes.

Taking my arm, he ushered me firmly in the direction of Natasha's. I had had barely a moment to absorb the scene, just long enough to notice something that seemed askew. Walking between the rows of armored vehicles stationed outside the Kremlin gates were a dozen or so middle-aged women. Some looked old enough to be grandmothers of the soldiers perched on top of the tanks. The women were speaking to the young soldiers animatedly; some were shaking their fingers at them. They appeared to be warning the soldiers, pleading with them, not to fire on their own people.

A few blocks away, Natasha was entering the vestibule of her building when we arrived. She and a woman companion were carrying bags of groceries. Her expression was difficult to read. She didn't appear as sanguine as she had sounded on the phone that morning, but still made no reference to the day's events. She simply apologized for being late, explaining that the tram and bus drivers had gone on strike while she was out, which meant she had to return home on foot.

Her apartment was huge by Soviet standards. It was immediately evident that she led a privileged life. The main room alone, containing a long, oval-shaped dining table, appeared larger than many apartments I had visited. She invited me to wash my hands, leading the way down a long hall, past several closed doors, to a spacious bathroom where an elderly woman handed me a clean towel, smiled, and promptly left. The woman was clearly a household servant, the kind of soul I had never expected to find in the capital of communism.

That was a day when it was hard to be certain of anything. My senses were assaulted by things that didn't add up. In the metro station, impassioned young men were giving fiery speeches, imploring passersby to demonstrate against the coup. Their body language suggested it was a matter of life and death. Yet only a few people stopped to listen. The vast majority walked right on by, averting their eyes, like Viktor had. Hurrying me past one of these speakers, he tried to change the subject entirely, mentioning that he had seen a long line outside the new McDonald's in Moscow earlier that day.

Things became increasingly surreal at Natasha's. Viktor and I had come there to conduct an interview with her. Natasha, without explanation, invited us to sit down at the large dining table, along with a young man already seated there. The table was covered with a white linen tablecloth, a dozen place settings, and numerous wineglasses. She introduced us to the young man, named Mikhail, and left us there, mentioning that she would be in the kitchen helping to prepare the meal.

Mikhail appeared lost in reverie. Languidly draped over his chair, he had a blank stare. His face, framed by long blond hair and a blond beard, was angelic. It was an unforgettable face, one that I knew I had seen before, recently in fact. Yet we had never met. I stared at him furtively, frantically searching my memory, afraid my mind was playing tricks on me. Separating reality from illusion, the challenge that had greeted me from the moment I awoke that morning, had reached a new height.

It finally dawned on me that I'd seen that face in a movie, the month before. It belonged to an actor who had starred in a film shown at the conference in Altai. Natasha had written the filmscript. It was an adaptation of Dostoyevsky's *The Brothers Karamazov*. The man sitting across the table had played the part of the beautiful, pure-hearted monk, Alyosha Karamazov.

On that day, he appeared pensive and somber. I assumed that he, Mikhail, was upset by the morning's ominous events, but evidently I was wrong. With a dismissive wave of the hand, he told Viktor and me that the coup was of little concern to him. He had recently entered Moscow's theological seminary and had been contemplating the day's religious significance, when we arrived.

August 19th was Transfiguration Day, one of the twelve holiest feast days of the Russian Orthodox calendar. He and Natasha had attended morning services at the Ascension Cathedral, inside the Kremlin. The Moscow Patriarch had presided over the largest public celebration of this feast day since the Revolution. That explained the groceries, the fancy tablecloth, and the women's voices in the kitchen.

The entire day resounded with paradox. The coup plotters had unintentionally chosen one of the holiest days in Russian Orthodoxy, which had marked its first millennium three years earlier, to attempt to resurrect the atheistic Soviet regime. The capital was filled with sights and sounds of totalitarian terror alongside quiet celebrations of Christ's revelation of his divinity. As I sat listening to Mikhail sanguinely explain the holiday's significance, I waited with baited breath to see what would happen next.

Battling Fear

Food platters covered the dining table when the women finally reemerged from the kitchen and took their seats. The male guests, already seated, eagerly eyed the delicacies arrayed before them. Natasha entered last, standing at the head of the table and nudging everyone to rise. Facing the east corner of the room, the "icon corner" in Russian Orthodox tradition, she made the sign of the cross and recited a prayer. Mikhail joined her; many of the other guests appeared unfamiliar, perhaps uncomfortable, with this ritual.

Wineglasses were filled and refilled many times during the meal, yet the atmosphere remained solemn. Whether it was partly due to the day's religious significance, or entirely due to the tanks outside, was hard to tell. Brief utterances, long silences, and somber faces suggested that the news hung heavily in the air. Yet from what I could tell with my limited Russian comprehension, it was never discussed. Viktor confirmed that the sole comment, made in passing, had been from Natasha. She mentioned that she had walked by the Russian "White House" just when Yeltsin climbed on top of the tank and spoke to the gathering crowd.

Curiously, it fell to me, the only foreigner, to raise the subject. Sitting there, taking part in a meal consecrating an Orthodox holiday, I was thoroughly baffled as to why Natasha had confirmed our meeting that very morning. With my tape recorder in my purse and my interpreter ready to conduct an interview, I needed to touch solid ground. When the meal was drawing to a close, I asked Natasha if she had picked up a copy of Yeltsin's statement, which we'd seen circulating in the metro.

She indicated that she had, and had given it to a man seated opposite her, at the other end of the long table. The man, named Slava, had barely lifted his head from his plate. I noted that only peripherally, as everyone looked preoccupied on this day, but I was also vaguely aware that he had kept his distance from me. It would be four years before I learned the extent to which Slava resented my being there. He was certain that "the American" was gloating over Russia's misfortunes. My presence, for him, was like rubbing salt in a wound.

Slava, a professor of literature whom Natasha referred to as "the professor," was the only one who had seen Yeltsin's statement. Even after the subject had been raised, no one else at the table appeared interested to know what it said. Nevertheless, in response to my request, Natasha asked Slava to read it out loud. Casting a dubious glance my way, he slowly put on his glasses, reluctantly pulled the wrinkled sheet of paper out of his jacket pocket, and began to read.

Yeltsin's appeal was powerful. It was a call to freedom that sent a chill down my spine. He implored the Russian people to oppose the coup organizers' naked attempt to grab power, to forcefully restore a dying dictatorship. This was a crossroads unlike any other. Yeltsin urged resistance. In a moment of extreme uncertainty, his words seemed to fill an existential void. Gorbachev's fortunes were still a mystery. The *putschists* had not yet shown their faces. Almost nothing was known, yet the nation's fate hung in the balance.

When Slava finished reading, he asked for more wine. The room was still. I was completely baffled. The muteness seemed like unaccountable obliviousness. Understanding the currents and crosscurrents, fallout from the communist century, would take me years. The sordidness of life, the sense of powerlessness, had led people like Slava and Mikhail to take refuge in personal pursuits. Others present were casualties of the regime. Natasha's husband, a theater director, was an alcoholic, his spirit crushed by the censors.

Her mother, once a member of the Central Committee, had become senile during *glasnost* upon learning that the hands of Lenin, her lifelong hero, were "drenched in blood."

These discoveries would come much later. On Monday, August 19, 1991, I was completely in the dark. The lack of responsiveness to Yeltsin's words set me further adrift in that sea of surrealism. No one at the table appeared even mildly stirred. Was it really possible that no one cared about the coup's outcome? Was I was the only one cheering on the forces of freedom? The deafening silence made the gulf between our worlds seem all the more unbridgeable. I wondered, again, whether I had gotten in over my head.

Sitting there in a state of confusion, fragments of that summer's interviews floated to the surface of my mind, piercing the impenetrable fog. The drama unfolding that day had temporarily blotted out all that preceded it. For weeks I had been hearing a chorus of unhappy voices, some wishing unabashedly for a return to pre-Gorbachev days. *Perestroika* was a bust. People were already cynical about democracy, Soviet-style, dismissing it as "a joke." *Glasnost* had brought new freedoms — of religion and speech — but even they appeared to be a mixed blessing.

Freedom of the press had resulted in numerous unintended consequences. People raised on a diet of propaganda were suddenly awash in the terrible truth. Newspapers had published an unending flood of documents revealing the brutal atrocities committed by Soviet people against Soviet people, in the name of building a communist utopia. This produced a widespread crisis of conscience, and pitted the younger generation against their elders for failing to resist the evils of Stalinism.

That crisis, however, had been short-lived. It was superseded by a more urgent one: a growing fear for survival. While Gorbachev shilly-shallied about "the market," the "jungle of capitalism" as portrayed under communism, market forces were already unleashed and had taken a heavy toll. By the summer of '91, there was massive insecurity. Many people would have gladly traded *glasnost* and *perestroika* for a return to a system of guaranteed food and shelter, even if it meant a return to totalitarianism.

I began to understand, that summer, the degree to which fear had shaped the Russian psyche. It was raw, ancient, and hard for Westerners to grasp. Fear had been a constant fact of life since the incessant wars of marauding Slavic clans, before the first chronicles of Russian history. Gorbachev's reforms had spawned *new* fears. People longed for the days when the state provided everything, when children had culture palaces and summer camps, when streets and parks were safe. The tanks in Moscow that Monday heralded a return to those days. For many, the prospect was not entirely unwelcome.

Such thoughts would come into focus later. On the first day of the coup, I was confronted with question marks at every turn. At my disposal, during those tense and anxious hours, were only crumbs of information and superficial impressions. As the afternoon wore on, many bottles of wine were emptied and the possibility of conducting an interview became increasingly remote. I had all but given up the idea when suddenly, out of the blue, a window of opportunity appeared.

Natasha's guests were slow to respond to Yeltsin's words, but when they did, the reaction was loud, boisterous, and intensely emotional. Some began shouting, interrupting each other. Natasha sat back and listened, staying out of the fray. Over the din, I screwed up my courage to ask whether I could speak with her briefly. She nodded her assent, rose from her seat, and led Viktor and me into an adjoining room, a library lined with glass cases full of leather-bound books.

She appeared relieved to be away from the fracas. It seemed she had been quietly mulling things over from a deeper, wider perspective and was glad for the opportunity to offer a different view. Her answers to my questions took us light years away from that moment in time. With a sweep of the hand, she dismissed the day's events as a political battle between forces that were flip sides of the same coin. In her view, they were fighting over spoils of the Stalinist system, whereas the system itself had to go.

In Natasha's mind, Russia's future depended on a spiritual awakening. She said she saw signs of it already, especially among young people. Her hopes were tied to the coming of age of this new generation. She believed that a "breakthrough to Spirit" was inevitable, citing examples of the rending of the veil between material and spiritual realms. Such a breakthrough, in her view, was the only thing that could save Russia. And she believed that Gorbachev and Yeltsin both knew this to be true — "deep in their souls."

Much of what Natasha said had an uncanny ring of familiarity. It turned out that she was, in fact, a student of the wisdom teachings. She, too, perceived the current times as transitional, preparing the way for a new stage in the evolution of consciousness. Her sense of Russia's destiny reflected what I'd come across in my research. She drew an analogy between the nations of the world and a symphony orchestra, making the point that each nation had its own note to play, in its own time. Russia's note, to be sounded in the coming era, was to make manifest "the living connections between heaven and earth."

Realizing that the time was short, I asked her more about the day's events. She returned to the spiritual realm, speaking of Transfiguration Day. Her eyes sparkled as she explained that this was the day when Christ brought his closest disciples to the mountaintop *not only* to reveal the light of God in Him, but to demonstrate, more importantly, the divine potential in human beings. That was what mattered most to her. As for the political events, she was praying for calm to prevail. Stating that she firmly believed in the power of prayer to move mountains, she said her own prayers were focused on avoiding bloodshed.

The telephone rang throughout our interview. After about forty-five minutes, Natasha excused herself, returning to her callers and guests. I felt like a miner striking gold when the whistle blew, signaling the end of the shift. We had strayed far from the subject of my oral history book, but in Natasha's case, especially on that day, the impact of Gorbachev's reforms seemed irrelevant. Her soul, and what it reflected about Russia's soul, were what interested me. I was left with a stream of unasked questions, such as how she had found her way to spirituality during "the godless years," but it was time for me to go.

Before leaving, a younger woman who appeared to be part of the household approached me. She spoke English and seemed eager to make a connection. I asked her how she was coping with the day's events. She replied, calmly, that whatever happened was God's will, so she was not afraid, adding that others there shared her belief. I had no way of knowing for certain what was responsible for that peaceful sanctuary — whether it was faith, denial, or something else. But as I walked outside, I had the sensation of stepping out of a timeless realm, separate and apart from the swirl of events, and into a world filled with fear.

It was early evening, a time when Moscow's streets were normally full of activity, but there were few souls around. Empty streetcars, abandoned by drivers protesting the coup, lay strewn diagonally across wide boulevards. In the metro station, people eyed one another with suspicion, something I had never experienced before. I was aware that my Americanness was conspicuous to Russians, who were careful observers of clothing, shoes, and demeanor. But the harsh glare of many pairs of eyes suddenly made me feel vulnerable.

I was on my own for the first time all day. Viktor had been obliged to leave Natasha's before I did. Coup or no coup, it was Monday, the night he taught his weekly karate class. The day before, he had invited me to observe the class and I promised that I would. Now I had to decide whether to keep that promise, which meant venturing into unfamiliar territory in a city that felt more alien with every passing hour, or return to the safety of Yulia's.

It was dusk when I found myself walking down a wide boulevard in the direction of a large school, which Viktor had told me I couldn't possibly miss. The main thoroughfare of this outlying residential neighborhood had few streetlights and was virtually deserted. The occasional shops I passed along the way were dark. On the side streets, there wasn't a soul in sight. I held my breath each time I heard footsteps approaching from behind.

During my walk from the metro to the school, which seemed to take forever, I drew courage from many of the day's images: Yulia caring more about news than safety, Viktor's one-man crusade against fear, grandmothers boldly counseling soldiers not to fire on fellow citizens, Natasha's determination to dwell on the coming age of spirituality. Still, when I reached the school and saw Viktor, I breathed a huge sigh of relief. And I received a lovely reward — a broad smile, an expression rare for him.

In the hall outside the school gymnasium, twenty young men with lean, muscular bodies were lining up when I arrived. They were grinning, clearly happy to see each other. While waiting for latecomers, Viktor asked me if I had any questions for his students. I asked them if they felt as self-confidant and nonchalant as they *appeared* to be. They replied collectively with a laugh and a resounding "Yes!" When the last student showed up, he excused his lateness by quipping that too many tanks had gotten in his way. Peals of laughter filled the hallway.

Inside the gym, Viktor led the young men through a sequence of karate drills with military-like commands. He was tough, pushing them beyond what seemed humanly possible. At one point he turned to me and whispered, "The purpose is to build their minds as much as their bodies." Many were in training to become personal bodyguards, a new career in Soviet life. The first businessmen, emerging from the shadows of the black market, needed protection and were willing to pay for it handsomely. These future protectors of capitalism, appearing completely unfazed by the *putschists*, defiantly honed their skills.

Mood Swings

The following evening, one of the *putschists*, a military man, made an appearance on TV. Wearing a uniform plastered with decorations, he declared the imposition of martial law. Presumably, one of the purposes of his appearance was to restore calm. But as he announced a curfew, to begin that night, his hands shook quite noticeably. While promulgating a long list of prohibitions, the shaking worsened. The incredible irony of this scene caused an outburst of laughter at Yulia's, where friends were gathered around the TV. From that moment on, the coup seemed destined for infamy, though of course no one knew.

A journalist whom I'd interviewed was there that evening. A single mother in her thirties, Tanya worked for the USSR's most popular progressive newsmagazine. She was planning to travel around Moscow to gather stories the next day, and invited me to join her. Wednesday at noon, when I arrived at her office, things were spiraling downward. The *putschists* had begun their reign of terror by shutting down progressive media outlets. That morning they had padlocked several newspaper offices and shut down their bank accounts. Tanya's magazine received warning that it was next.

Collecting back pay was first priority for her and her colleagues. If the *putschists* won, their survival would be at stake. We sat in the lobby talking for hours, as she periodically checked her place in line. It started at the bursar's office and snaked around the magazine's winding corridors. Editors were huddled behind closed doors listening for news about Moscow from foreign radio broadcasts, planning stories for the next edition, if there ever was one. Reporters ran around chasing down rumors. They were expecting soldiers to burst through the doors at any moment and arrest the entire staff. Yet they weren't cowed. Here was a place where the freedoms of *glasnost* really mattered.

Simple habits of daily life took on tremendous significance that day. It might have been the last day, the last time, for many things. Dozens of journalists converged on the cafeteria just before the 3 PM closing time, uncertain they would ever return. For Tanya, and surely others, the cafeteria was their main source of sustenance. Working long hours, she rarely cooked. For years, she had eaten her main meal there and brought home her daughter's dinner from there. At stake that day was even more than freedom of the press, and work that she loved, there was also a life support system. Given all that, the level of calm seemed remarkable.

It was also remarkable to hear laughter during those incredibly tense hours. Some of the rumors flying around the cafeteria were imbued with a special brand of Russian irony that can defuse the most dreadful situations. Between rumors, there were long, somber, quiet spells. After one such period, a rumor surfaced that turned out to be false but signaled the dénouement. The *putschists* had reportedly been spotted at the airport, ready to flee the country. Before that rumor could be verified, it set off a wave of quiet jubilation. Then came the real news, over the radio. It sounded like a miracle. Yeltsin, on the balcony of the White House, was announcing that the forces of freedom and democracy had won.

An explosion of joy reverberated throughout Moscow. Throngs of people converged on the White House, including Tanya and me. The sun appeared for the first time in days. People looked dazed, as if they didn't quite believe what they saw and heard. Tanya began interviewing people, several of whom had been there for three days, defending the White House, the new symbol of Russian freedom. One man, in his sixties, clearly hadn't washed, shaved, or slept. But he had an almost beatific smile on his face when he spoke about how he felt at that moment, what it meant for his children, his grandchildren.

As dusk fell and the air grew cold, small fires were lit and people huddled around them. The previous two nights, such fires were the only source of warmth for those who stood guard, ready to fight the *putschists*, prepared, quite possibly, to die. That night their expressions were radiant. The triumphant words of Yeltsin, sympathetic military leaders, celebrities, the congratulations pouring in from world leaders, lingered in the air. In the warm glow of the small fires, friends held each other in long embraces, strangers caught each others' eyes and smiled. As we walked around, observing the scene, Tanya turned to me and said, "For the first time in my life I feel proud to be Russian."

Once the dust settled, a seamier view of things emerged. There were rumors that the victory had been engineered by the new capitalists, those who were getting rich fast and had the most to lose if the *putschists* won. It was said that *they* were largely responsible for rallying the troops, building the barricades, feeding the protesters. Some journalists reported that contrary to appearances, it was businessmen, not ordinary citizens spontaneously sharing their wares, who had arranged for the free sandwiches, pastries, cigarettes, and hot tea available in the rain-soaked, muddy plaza where the three-day demonstration took place.

Like so much of what happens in Russia, the whole truth may never be known. But certain things were observably, undeniably true. People had risked their lives in the name of freedom. Several had been killed. Thousands had kept vigil over the site to secure, with their bodies if necessary, the jerry-rigged barricades intended to keep army tanks away from the White House. A relative handful of nameless Muscovites, along with kindred spirits in Leningrad and elsewhere, had managed to turn the tide of Russian history.

Two days after the victory, on my last day in Moscow, Viktor accompanied me on a tour of the site. I wanted to see what remained of the historic battlefield for Russian freedom. To my surprise, it was nearly deserted, apart from clusters of exuberant young people savoring the victory. Some were perched on top of one of the army tanks "liberated" by the pro-Yeltsin forces; others draped themselves over the piles of metal tubes and pipes that had formed the barricades. A few strolled around carrying flowers and signs saying "No to Fascism!"

In some ways, things appeared to be returning to normal. Outside the doors of the White House, a small group of elderly people stood arguing heatedly, as Russians are wont to do. Not far away, another feature of Russian life came into view, though far more dramatically than usual. Parallel realities, seemingly unrelated, flanked both sides of a wide boulevard. On one side, a mob unleashing decades of pent-up rage was engaged in toppling the statue of Felix Derzhinsky, founder of Stalin's secret police, the personification of Soviet-era cruelty. On the other side, a huge line formed outside Moscow's main department store for children, just reopened for business.

One came away from scenes like this with the impression that everything, and nothing, had changed. It was like being in Alice's wonderland, passing through the looking glass time and again, never knowing for certain where one was, or how the wind was blowing there. I was, therefore, extremely thankful, the following day, when Yulia, Olga, and Olga's husband, the pilot, accompanied me to the airport. It was impossible to know what to expect from the airport authorities, a quasi-military corps in Soviet times. If they had been sympathetic to the *putschists*, they might well be in a foul frame of mind. And if so, they would likely be more aggressive than unusual toward American travelers.

On a normal day during the Soviet era, getting out of the country was like running a gauntlet. Several groups of airport personnel could make one's life miserable. First came the customs agents who rifled through your personal belongings, laying claim to anything from a water color painting to a jar of honey as "state property." Whether it was a bribe they wanted, or the object itself, a war of nerves ensued. The passenger could try staring them down, standing firm, insisting the item was legally acquired, or call upon a Soviet friend, more adept at playing the game, to intervene.

Next came the airline clerks. They could also prey upon "rich foreigners," charging extra for every kilo of overweight baggage. Or they could haphazardly, even mischievously, send your baggage to the wrong destination. Finally, there were the airport police, whose job it was to see that visas were properly stamped and dated. If something was incorrect, if a date had expired, for example, they could haul you into custody as your baggage flew homeward.

That Saturday, the mood at the airport was hard to gauge, even for my Soviet friends. I was anxious, as my bags contained the fruits of six weeks' work: dozens of taped interviews, notebooks full of reflections. Adding to my anxiety was the fact that I had neglected to obtain a special stamp in my visa upon arriving in Moscow, a new rule for visitors traveling alone. It required a long trek across the city on my only day in Moscow before leaving for Siberia, and given my earlier visa experience, I hadn't taken the rule all that seriously. Yulia and her friends were also worried about that. They had a lively argument about the penalty I could incur.

As it turned out, the mood of victory seemed to have swept Sheremetyev Airport. The customs agent was a lovely young woman who smiled and let my suitcase pass along the conveyor belt without even opening it, though boxes of cassettes were clearly visible on her x-ray screen. The airline clerk, a Russian employed by an American carrier, could have almost passed for American. He spoke English flawlessly, helped me with my luggage, and tried to make things easier rather than more difficult.

After waving good-bye to my friends, who stood watching over me from the non-passenger side of the railing, the most difficult hurdle awaited me: the airport police. A hostile officer could have detained me for not having the proper Moscow stamp in my visa. From a distance I could see two green lights, indicating two booths were open. I paused, took a deep breath, asked inwardly which way to go, and veered right. The officer took my visa and placed it on a pile. He never even looked inside. With a genuine smile, as though we were allies now, one happy family, he wished me a pleasant journey home.

Whether I was truly in danger I'll never know, but I felt jubilant to be leaving with everything in tact. And equally jubilant to be reentering a world of order, where the flow of life was governed by accepted practice, rather than mood or temperament, or the threat of force. It was also a world in which things generally functioned as intended. In the world I was leaving behind, the ladies' room in the departure lounge was unusable that day. Someone, perhaps a kind soul, had allowed a group of gypsy women to do their laundry there, turning the doors of the stalls into drying racks, which caused an unfordable stream to flow out of the restroom.

On the airplane, fortune smiled on me again. Tourist-class seats had been overbooked and I was among those bumped up to business class. Not much of a drinker in normal times, I couldn't have been happier about the beverage service. I wanted to forget the anxieties of the day, and the week, even more than I wanted a clear head to make notes. The sun was shining brilliantly, the meal service was gracious, everything was clean and functioning as it was supposed to. I had already entered a different zone of reality.

The Irrelevance of Facts

At home, I received several requests to write about my experiences in Moscow during the coup. Not being a seasoned observer as yet, I found the challenge of distilling the essence of what I had encountered to be formidable. Russia remained extremely foreign, defying my comprehension more often than not. Without a solid understanding, I lacked the capacity for meaningful analysis. In the end, I was limited to writing about what I saw, heard, and felt.

Years passed before I could even identify the underlying reason for this pervasive sense of incomprehension. Clouding my perception were fundamental differences in the nature of our societies, so fundamental they were easily overlooked. The heart of the matter was the role that information played. Democratic societies flow from consensual realities that are based on shared information. Facts are not always available, or reliable; they may even be intentionally distorted to manipulate public opinion. But in healthy democracies, people generally believe they're making choices based on dependable information. This makes it possible to trace how they got from A to B in everything from elections to wars.

In Russia, consensual realities had never existed. Information had always been censored and pre-packaged, first by czars, later by communist dictators. People were conditioned *not* to believe so-called facts. It was understood, for example, that history had been completely rewritten after the Revolution of 1917. A new set of "facts" was promulgated for children to learn at school and at home. Knowledge of real history, including family history, was exceedingly dangerous, particularly if one's relatives were such "enemies of the people" as capitalists, clergy, aristocracy, or intelligentsia. A fact casually revealed by a child's slip of the tongue could have jeopardized many lives.

In the 1990s, facts were freely available for the first time. Their cumulative effect had been powerful enough to undermine remaining myths of the communist century. Yet they remained oddly irrelevant to many Russians, including the most highly educated. People found it laughable, or extremely naïve, to believe that objective, indisputable facts existed anywhere, about anything, so accustomed were they to Soviet-era encyclopedias known to contain large doses of fiction. During *glasnost*, when journalists began quoting sources, the sources were immediately dismissed as unreliable. All information was presumed tainted, or distorted, to suit someone's political purposes.

That mindset had multiple consequences, some more benign than others. On the lighter side, I noticed that Russians often felt free to play with "facts." Some even took a certain delight in embroidering things just to make life more interesting. Once in a conversation about politics I mentioned to an acquaintance that I had worked for the mayor of New York when I was young, many years ago. Not long thereafter, she publicly introduced me to a large gathering as the "vice-mayor" of New York. Later, when I told her how mortified I was, she seemed genuinely bewildered.

Dismissing the relevance of facts had far more nefarious consequences. Perhaps the most corrosive was a culture of distrust, an environment where nothing was taken at face value. There was an underlying assumption that people were not speaking the truth, or that their motives were other than what they appeared to be. Even the so-called "best people," those who were highly cultured and intelligent, suspected each other of being less than truthful. It was as if they had grown up in Plato's cave never seeing the sun, only its shadows. They'd been conditioned to assume it was not possible to see the light directly.

By the fall of '91, I still hadn't quite grasped this phenomenon. But as I searched for a framework for writing about the August coup, I was uncomfortably aware of seeing only the tips of icebergs. Moreover, two years later, when I started compiling my interviews for the oral history book, I found myself up against a similar challenge. I had crisscrossed the Russian Republic three years in a row, from '91 to '93, focusing on twelve individuals. My plan was to explore the changes they had experienced during those years, in the hope of being able to paint a picture of collective change.

Instead, what I ended up with were sketches of twelve lives, during one of the most turbulent periods of Russian history. Shortly after Yeltsin replaced Gorbachev and the USSR was effectively dismantled, the turbulence had intensified. In early '92, under pressure from American economic advisors, Yeltsin instituted "shock therapy." Suddenly, without warning or preparation, state subsidies, the backbone of Soviet life, had been terminated. Price supports for food and other essentials had disappeared. The floor fell out from under science, culture, health, and education. Factories, entire industries, were abandoned. Everyone was left to fend for themselves.

Almost overnight, much of the population was reduced to a state of grinding poverty and humiliation. Many pensioners lived on a diet of bread and tea. *Babushkas* formed lines outside metro stations to sell anything they could — used clothing and shoes, cigarettes, newspapers, even pornography, which began proliferating wildly. Scientists, the élite of the Soviet era, faced the choice of remaining at work they loved and being destitute, or turning to trade — buying and selling goods — which many saw as tantamount to selling their souls.

One of the twelve people I interviewed in depth for my book was a woman named Sveta. She lived near Novosibirsk, the largest city in Siberia, in a place called *Akademgorodok*, "little academic city." Since the early 60s, when the first buildings were constructed, many of the best scientific minds in the USSR had been concentrated there. Sveta was the daughter of an internationally renowned mathematician, and became a mathematician of high standing in her own right. After her father's death, she also turned to writing, starting with his biography.

When I first met Sveta in '91, a month before the coup, she was a youthful, high-spirited grandmother of forty-six. She was also a journalist by then, having left mathematics to write about the truth of those times. The facts revealed during *glasnost* had assaulted the ideals of her youth, but hadn't completely annihilated them. Sveta remained idealistic, believing that the truth she unearthed as a journalist could help right past wrongs. As a mother and grandmother, she felt deeply committed to her country's future.

A year later, she seemed completely changed. When we sat down at her kitchen table in the summer of '92, with my tape recorder still off, she turned to me and said, with deep sadness in her eyes, "Thank you for being interested in us. We have lost interest in each other." In the intervening year, the awful truth about the past had been compounded by an ugly set of facts emerging in the present, many of which were by-products of Yeltsin's program of shock therapy.

Nightmares about capitalism, drummed into the head of every communist schoolchild, were coming true. "Jungle capitalism" was taking root on Russian soil. People were thrust into a sink-or-swim world where it was "up to each man for himself." In such an environment, the crooked finger of dishonesty beckoned everywhere. At the upper levels of the hierarchy, Communist Party bosses swiftly "privatized" the wealth of the socialist state, the supposed communal property of the people. At the bottom levels, where many verged on starvation, stealing took more banal forms.

Sveta's eyes filled with tears as she spoke of what it was like to live in such times. Financially, things were so bad that she couldn't afford to buy her granddaughter an apple once a week, though she had taken a second job to supplement her journalist's salary. Even more painful to her was the moral decline of her newspaper. The brief life of press freedom had effectively ended. Capitalist censors had already replaced communist ones. Advertisers wanted to see good news about market reforms, not terrible facts about rising rates of child abandonment, hunger, prostitution, alcoholism, and suicide.

Of all the changes that offended her sense of dignity, the most egregious one had to do with money. Sveta genuinely believed in the communist ideals, like most people I had met of the post-war generation. They grew up seeing themselves as pioneers of a new world order based on justice — social and economic. A model Soviet citizen was someone who considered the good of the whole before thinking of himself. The accumulation of individual wealth, seen as the selfish obsession of the capitalist enemy, was viewed as a form of evil.

By '92, Russia's "new democrats" had a new face. Many, including prominent officials who had once embodied the hopes of millions, declared publicly, on TV and elsewhere, that acquiring money was all that mattered. "They don't care how you get it," Sveta said, throwing up her hands in disgust. "The authorities are actually encouraging people to lie and cheat and steal if they have to, to do anything necessary to get money. This is now the measure of a man."

Many people with whom I spoke echoed Sveta's sentiments. After a few short years of optimism inspired by the hope of fair elections and decent elected officials, cynicism and despair had become widespread. The old Communist Party bosses had simply "changed hats," as the saying went, retaining power under a different name. At first, some politicians uttered lofty words about democracy while lavishly lining their pockets with cash, shipping the excess to Swiss bank accounts. Then they stopped uttering the words. "Getting money" superseded all else, and was now supposed to become the collective pursuit.

Russians were used to hardship. Throughout their history, the masses had remained mired in poverty while those at the top of the pyramid enjoyed enormous wealth and privilege. The Bolshevik Revolution had succeeded in redistributing wealth by means of violence and brutality on a numbing scale: a civil war, the liquidation of privileged classes, the forced collectivization of the peasantry. Finally, after recovering from the staggering human loss and suffering of World War II, the masses had experienced some material progress. It was small by Western standards, but no one starved.

People had widely accepted the low standard of living as a necessary sacrifice. They believed they were involved in a great human experiment to create a better life for all, for people everywhere. What helped make the sacrifice palatable was the state's guarantee of jobs, housing, food subsidies, health care, education, pensions, even summer camp for children. But what gave their lives meaning was *The Ideal*. And then, in the blink of an eye, everything was gone: no more safety net, no more ideals.

In the early 90s, a plaint I commonly heard was: "We have nothing left to believe in anymore." None of the Russians I came to know could conceive of "getting money" as a reason for living. In those years, some were adjusting to the need to earn money as a necessity, in order to do what the soul yearned for: to read, write poetry, listen to music, be out in nature, travel. Money, in and of itself, seemed to hold little interest. The kind of people who lived for money had always been associated with criminality: the black market during the Soviet era, the mafia thereafter.

Eventually I realized that Russian idealism, paradoxically, had a role in undermining the salience of facts. The *need* to live for higher ideals, for something beyond money, or matter, was at odds with the ugly facts of life that people were powerless to change. I met many staunch defenders of communist ideals who were loath to acknowledge the violence used in the quest for those ideals — even in the 90s, after everything had come to light. It was as if their minds, or emotions, could not contain both. The Russian soul yearned for higher things. Facts were not convenient. They interfered with the only reason to get out of bed in the morning.

Nourishment

Studying the Russian language was excellent preparation for understanding the Russian character. As was the case with rules governing the language, there were few social conventions that were not frequently broken. In fact, people seemed to take conspicuous pleasure in breaking all kinds of rules. But in my experience, one social "rule" was consistently upheld: Russians were exceedingly generous and hospitable to foreigners.

By all accounts, this was especially so in the case of Americans. Despite Cold War propaganda, which induced morbid fears in the Soviet people about US government plans to annihilate them all, there remained a reservoir of good will toward Americans. Some said it was the legacy of World War II, when we were allied in the battle against Hitler's Germany. Others traced it back to an earlier episode in the 20th century, when American supporters of the communist revolution were elevated to almost mythic status.

Whatever the origins of this good will, it had forged a mysterious bond with Americans that completely bypassed the Iron Curtain. I heard an especially poignant illustration of it from a scientist, the sole Communist Party chief among my interviewees. He was thirteen years old during the Cuban Missile Crisis, when our nations were a hair's breadth from nuclear war. The following year, when he heard the news of President Kennedy's assassination, he wrote in his diary, which he brought out to show me: "I cried for myself, and for all Soviet and American citizens. We have all suffered a great loss."

In the 70s and 80s, some Soviet citizens became attracted to Americans for more materialistic reasons. As travel behind the Iron Curtain increased, Americans left behind a growing trail of artifacts. People with money, mostly black marketeers, grabbed at the chance to buy used American clothing — everything from blue jeans, always in demand, to the shirts on travelers' backs. American magazines that leaked through Soviet borders were even more corrosive to Soviet propaganda, which denounced capitalism for the widespread poverty it generated. Glossy, full-color ads portrayed an America awash in luxury, the envy of all.

For a whole gamut of reasons, some more identifiable than others, most ordinary Russians liked and admired Americans. The admiration, at times accompanied by a toxic form of envy, resulted in large part from our ability to create material abundance, to live on this earth surrounded by comfort and beauty. The affection seemed to stem from something more elusive, something about themselves that Russians saw mirrored in us.

Despite myriad differences of history, culture, and standard of living, Russians often commented on how much alike we were, as people. They pointed to the openness and friendliness of Americans, saying they felt a greater affinity with Americans than with most Europeans. Likewise, Americans travelling to the USSR during *glasnost* were often surprised by the sense of familiarity they experienced. In place of anticipated tensions, many cited an uncanny sense of ease. At times, Russians almost seemed like long-lost cousins. And they lived in a way that evoked a certain kind of nostalgia for some of us.

Being in the USSR in the early 90s was like travelling back in time. For me, it brought back visceral memories of childhood, in the late 40s and 50s, a simpler, more innocent time. Visits with extended families had been much-anticipated events. They usually coincided with birthdays or holidays, but the real cause of celebration was being together, with aunts and uncles and cousins one didn't ordinarily see, and sharing a festive meal. That was how it often felt to be among Russians.

By '93, nearly every family I knew had been badly hurt by

Yeltsin's economic policies, including Natasha's, which had once seemed so privileged. Although they were better off than most, I noticed that meat was served in increasingly smaller portions. Still, no matter how simple the fare, the guest from afar was always honored. The centuries-old tradition was never broken. There was always a special meal and a special bottle of something to drink. There was always toast-making, story-telling, and the simple pleasure of being together.

There was, of course, another side to this picture. American visitors to the USSR, even first-time tourists, were forewarned to arrive with "souvenirs" to present to people one met along the way. Later, as friendships developed, my bags were laden with gifts for every member of a family with whom I stayed, and for the families of those whom I interviewed. It was expected. Americans were seen, monolithically, as the rich cousins living in the fantasy world portrayed in magazines.

Such rituals aside, however, visiting with Russians in the early 90s had intrinsic satisfactions. The old order remained sufficiently intact to sustain a favorite Russian pastime: spending time around the kitchen table in the company of people one liked. It was a form of recreation whose descriptive name can't be properly translated into English. The literal translation is "to sit well." To sit well was to be among friends, to eat, drink, laugh, sing, to take pleasure in each other's company, and to feel no pain, for as long a time as possible.

It was worlds apart, in every way, from the Manhattan lifestyle of that era. By the early 90s, home hospitality was sharply on the decline. No one had time to prepare dinner for friends anymore; it was easier to meet in a restaurant. It seemed that all of life had moved into the fast lane. More than ever, time was money. People had agendas and needed contacts for careers, investments, advancements. Résumés were tailored to fit on one page. Having long since departed from my own résumé, I was largely a spectator. But the lifestyle all around me seemed rather chilling.

In Russia, paradoxically, I found myself becoming engaged with people on a different, purely human, level. Professional labels were irrelevant, for all intents and purposes, though simply being an American, and one who was exploring the Russian soul, gave me ample "credentials." People like Sveta from Novosibirsk genuinely appreciated my continued interest in them, especially at that time. But for reasons unrelated to who I was, or the work I was doing, the experience of being there was nourishing to me.

First, on the most primal level, the aroma of food wafting out of the kitchen always greeted visitors. Cooking was done in pots and pans, not microwavable pouches. And it was done by women who were overextended in every way, oppressively burdened by life's unequal demands, which made the recipient of their efforts feel all the more grateful. As they cooked, served, and inquired into the comfort of their guests, the women smiled. There was almost a self-sacrificial quality to all they did to make American guests feel welcome.

Being in a Russian kitchen also evoked memories from childhood. They were visceral memories, like sitting in the lap of my Grandma Pearl, enfolded by her unconditional love. In part, what conjured up such images was the setting — the warmth of the hearth, the aromas of food not unlike what my grandmother used to prepare. In part, it was the feeling of acceptance, without expectation of achievement, performance, or worldly success.

In the early years of my Russian journey, I didn't spend much time or energy analyzing that feeling. I knew, intellectually, that Russia was a land of polar extremes. And I knew the other side of Russians — from history, from literature, from Americans who had felt violated, and from Russians themselves, quick to point out the impure motives of their countrymen. Still, I allowed myself to be seduced by the experience, a recurring one, of feeling recognized as a soul, a fellow human being.

Russians had a way of looking deeply into another's eyes, especially when they first met, as though they were exploring who was *really* there, behind the outer facade. They seemed to function on the premise that eyes really were the windows of the soul. Before the advent of capitalism, everyone had more or less the same, meager standard of living. The inner self mattered more and the eyes were the first measure of that.

At home in America, on the other hand, souls seemed increasingly buried under layers of material affluence, outer signs and symbols of success. I was still living in the world's financial capital, while having abandoned worldly pursuits for the spiritual path, which made for a heightened sense of isolation. I understood that that isolation was part and parcel of the Path, the natural result of withdrawing from collective perceptions of reality, but a part of me missed the sense of connectedness I'd always felt with people —with friends, groups, organizations. The companionship of fellow seekers was a special balm.

In Russia, I had the impression of encountering many fellow seekers. Kindred spirits seemed to appear everywhere. It was hard to be certain, as I realized that things were rarely as they appeared. But in the course of my interviews, and widening travels, there were moments when eyes met eyes and I experienced a genuine communion of souls. Those moments were as nourishing to me as the aromas wafting out of warm kitchens. I was like a sponge soaking up nutrients that I needed, but hadn't really known I was lacking, before finding myself in the lap of Mother Russia.

Cruelty and Kindness

Being a writer was especially useful for penetrating the outer veneer of Russian life. My interviews, many of which continued for days, allowed me to dig well below the surface. The climate of those times was also favorable. There were no censors, no fears of KGB eavesdroppers, no prohibitions whatsoever. It was a field day for a person with natural curiosity. My only limitations were the patience and fortitude of the people I was interviewing.

When it came to finding satisfying answers to certain questions, however, I often came up empty-handed. The reasons varied. At times interpreters made honest mistakes in conveying either the intent of my question or the response. At times, I learned after the fact, interpreters had changed the wording of a particular question "for my benefit," presumably to save me from embarrassment, but without informing me, thus the answers made no sense. At still other times, both question and answer were straightforward, but I was unable to grasp the response. The cultural gap was simply too great.

One such question had to do with the myth of Lenin, Father of Russian Communism. Unlike Stalin, whom Khrushchev had deposed from the status of demigod, Lenin had maintained that status until the revelations of *glasnost*. But how? I wondered. He was almost universally viewed as an unblemished hero, for seven decades, despite the fact that he fomented violence, mass murder, on an unprecedented scale. His proclamations of the need to annihilate whole classes of people, in order to usher in the rule of the proletariat, were learned by every schoolchild.

By '91, with the flood of published documents, no one could reasonably deny that the means utilized in the movement to bring about a communist utopia had included massive crimes against humanity. But there still appeared to be a disconnect when it came to means and ends. People were reluctant to acknowledge that eliminating entire social and economic groups, for the purpose of creating "a happy life" for the majority, amounted to genocide. Illusions about the ends also remained. The USSR was a socialist state, claiming to be on the road to true communism, something indefinable even by Party leaders. By the end, everyone claimed to have known the dream was unattainable. Still, that dream would not easily die.

The system of indoctrination had been powerfully effective. Like all Soviet citizens, my interviewees had gone through it. They were professors, scientists, psychologists, engineers, artists, linguists, actors, writers, and journalists who as children automatically became Octobrists, then Young Pioneers, participants in the monolithic movements that molded them from ages five to fourteen. At fourteen, everyone was inducted into Komsomol, the Communist Union of Youth, with the exception of avowed rebels. The best and brightest were appointed Komsomol leaders. Those so inclined were groomed for Communist Party membership, the system's ultimate prize, the guarantor of career advancement and privilege.

As it happened, a majority of the people I interviewed, mostly in their thirties and forties when I met them, had been Komsomol leaders. They were different, however, from their parents' generation, which had fallen under Stalin's "hypnotic spell." Their eyes had been fully open to the system's dark side. They realized rather early that Party officials were corrupt, that the system rewarded dishonesty and punished those who dared speak the truth. While only two interviewees had ever been Party members, all, without exception, defended what the Party stood for — a society where resources were shared on the basis of needs and means.

Communist ideals retained such a powerful hold that they continued blurring the atrocities committed in their name. A professor of English eloquently suggested why this was so. At fourteen, she and her classmates had eagerly anticipated their induction into Komsomol as a kind of sacred rite of passage to becoming builders of communism. Instead, she had encountered gross hypocrisy among Party officials, which shattered her faith in the system. Yet thirty years later, she clung tenaciously to the ideals it had stood for. "Russians need ideals in order to live," she said. "They are like stars in the sky. We have only the illusion of getting closer to them, but if they disappear, something in us will die."

Throughout my travels, there were questions that hounded me. I posed them time and again, directly and indirectly, because the answers always seemed elusive. For one, I was always surprised by the goodness of many people I met. How, I wondered, had such people survived a police state of such brutality that virtually no family escaped unthinkable horrors in the generation or two after the Revolution. Thereafter, at the very least, everyone suffered horrendous human rights abuses, massive corruption, official hypocrisy. How had they managed to survive with their humanity in tact?

Behind this question were many of the stereotypes that had fueled the Cold War. They were primitive, yet contained grains of truth, large or small, as stereotypes do. America had been widely perceived by our enemy as a paradise for the pleasure-seeking rich and a place of destitution for almost everyone else. We often saw the Soviet Union as a massive prison system that kept rebellious inmates in check by ruthless force, and muted the groans of everyone else through cradle-to-grave economic protections.

Prisons are widely known as breeding grounds for brutality. In the USSR, one didn't have to look far to see the face of brutality. "The authorities" were trained to assume a mask of severity for purposes of intimidation. Among ordinary people in public places, there were many gnarled faces, frozen expressions of pain and bitterness, eyes that appeared to have never known human kindness. One might expect that in a police state. The question was: what accounted for the smiling faces and the open hearts? What explained the kindness and generosity?

Some people postulated God as an explanation, belief in a just God with a higher, if unknowable, purpose. More commonly, however, they spoke of friendship, the kind of friendship forged in dire circumstances. A biochemist, a bearish man with a warm smile, had described a friend as someone he would be willing to die for, to protect with his own life. He said he was a very rich man, having several friends who felt that way about him and about one another. Such friendships, he said, more than marriage, served as fortresses of trust, islands of goodness, in a world of brutality and betrayal.

Friendship seemed to be of equal importance to women and men, but it had a different quality for women. While men commonly sought to deaden their feelings with vodka, women more often sought solace by sharing their woes. In the Soviet Union, as in previous Russian centuries, suffering was universal. It was part of life, even seen by some as redemptive, beneficial to the soul. Redemptive or not, it was never far away. What made it bearable for women was sharing it with a friend over tea in a warm kitchen. The heart of a friend often took the place of a psychiatrist's couch in the West.

The threshold for pain and suffering in Russia seemed unimaginably high. It was often physical as well as emotional, beginning at the most primitive level of daily existence. There were, for example, no public toilets to speak of. This remained true through the late 90s, except for élite establishments in Moscow and St. Petersburg catering to foreigners and Russia's nouveau riche. Being unable to relieve oneself for extended periods of time takes a heavy toll on the body, as I learned. It was amazing to discover what the human mechanism is capable of, out of absolute necessity, but the price of prolonged distress is high.

There were times when I found myself in urgent need and asked to be taken to the nearest toilet, if there was one. Having arrived, I often found myself unable to use it. In rural areas, the "facility" was usually a place of raw sewage, a wooden shed containing mounds of human waste. In cities and towns, the lavatories in schools and offices usually had no seats, never any toilet paper. As they were rarely, if ever, cleaned, the stench was putrid. Not uncommonly, toilet stalls had no doors, even in concert halls. I witnessed women having to squat, in their finest clothes, in full public view.

At times I worked up the courage to ask Russians, who endured such conditions, how and why it could be. Some explained that until the 20th century Russia was a largely agrarian society. Toilets were holes in the earth. During the communist era, cleaning products were largely unavailable. As for the present, like many things in Russian life, it simply was the way it was. A few staunch defenders of Russia's soul retorted, in reply to that question, that Western standards of cleanliness reflected an obsession with material comfort. People who lived for higher things, they said, were used to making material sacrifices.

Try as I did to view it that way, I couldn't help seeing Russian facilities as a form of social debasement. Toilets in apartments were constructed in a way that actually forced people to confront their own wastes. Why, I wondered? What did it reflect? How far back did it go? I thought of the Mongol Yoke, Russia's two-hundred-year-long humiliation, when princes had been forced to prostrate themselves before vengeful khans. In the 90s, five centuries later, there was a common expression: "Scratch a Russian and you'll find a Mongol," a person with his boot on another's neck, one who controlled others, in part, through humiliation.

It was years before I discovered satisfying answers to such questions. In the meantime, I found myself caught up in the astonishing play of polarities that seemed to pervade Russian life — stark opposites like the pure- and evil-hearted characters of Russian folk tales that profoundly shaped the culture for centuries. By contrast with the United States and other Western nations, where people's values and behaviors tend to cluster around the middle of the spectrum, what was striking about Russia were the dramatic contrasts in human nature: kindness and cruelty, good and evil, beauty and ugliness.

Cruelty, evil and ugliness were to be expected in a totalitarian dictatorship. As for kindness, goodness and beauty, at a certain point I stopped asking how they survived, realizing the futility of hoping for a logical explanation. It was like asking how flowers managed to grow through narrow sidewalk cracks, pressing mightily upward between thick slabs of concrete. The answer clearly had to do with resilience, spiritual resilience in the case of Russian "flowers." It was so powerful that it couldn't be crushed by objective reality. Such people, undoubtedly old souls, eventually became the focus of my quest.

But first, there were many miles to travel and lessons to learn. The problem of perception faced by travelers to foreign lands, the challenge of seeing the true nature of people beneath layers of cultural conditioning, was multiplied tenfold in Russia. Even in the final years of the Soviet Empire, the scent of terror hung in the air. People were raised with the awareness that the KGB had tentacles everywhere; that penalties for speaking against the authorities were severe; that trials had preordained outcomes; that imprisonment meant torture. They became accustomed to having two "faces" — one presented in public, the other reserved for intimate friends.

Initially, like most American travelers to the USSR, I assumed that the system's enforcers were cut from a different cloth than ordinary citizens. To my mind, "the authorities," as they were called, represented a different species. They had no kinship with "keepers of the peace," as policemen once were seen across much of America, at least by white folk. I viewed them collectively — the KGB, the high Party officials, the armies of guards and police — as people cut off from their own humanity. And I saw the ordinary people under their control as their victims.

Then I was offered a different view. A brilliant woman named Nadia, someone who enjoyed clearing the cobwebs from people's eyes, decided to set me straight. She was a professor of psychology at Moscow State University who had received training in the West, and had become one of the first psychotherapists in Moscow with a private practice. Her clientele was not, as one might have expected, comprised solely of the more progressive elements of society. It represented a cross-section of the population, including Party officials and various other "authorities."

Noting my surprise at hearing this, Nadia, the professor, gave me a lecture. "You are wrong," she said, "if you think they are different from us. They are part of us. They *are* us. They all have spouses, children, parents, friends, lovers. It is not a question of them against us. We are not separate from them. You must understand this if you want to understand us." It was difficult to assimilate her words initially. Once I did, the old souls, the flowers squeezing through the sidewalk cracks, became all the more central to my search.

A Turn in the Road

My path across Russia was fairly regular during the first few years. I usually started in Moscow, flying several thousand miles southeast to southern Siberia. From the town of Barnaul, near the Altai Mountains, I took the bus a few hours north to Akademgorodok, the scientific community near Novosibirsk. From there I flew westward to Leningrad — St. Petersburg again by 1992 — and then took the train back to Moscow.

Of the scores of people I met along the way, the twelve I chose for my oral history book were the most interesting to me, and among the most articulate. They were especially adept at expressing what it was like to live through the implosion of the communist state, the collapse of the Soviet Empire, and the subsequent chaos that was euphemistically called, by Westerners, the transition to democracy and capitalism. My hope was that their stories would be as riveting to readers as they were to me.

The first literary agent I contacted responded instantly, sharing my enthusiasm. Bubbling over with excitement, she referred to my book proposal as a "hot property." Large dollar signs flashed in her eyes in anticipation of the advance she thought it would bring. Given her reputation and the list of authors she represented, I began to breathe a sigh of relief. Finally, I thought, the spell of financial barrenness would be over. But things turned out otherwise.

As it happened, the fall of '93 was not a propitious time for a book like mine. The velocity of change in the former Soviet Union had created a situation in which numerous books were out-of-date before they came out of the publishing pipeline. My book was less time-sensitive than many others, but publishers had been burned and were skittish about anything connected with the USSR. Adding to the general environment of risk was another red flag, in my case: the fact that I had no certified credentials related to my subject.

In spite of all this, several publishers expressed interest in the proposal. For them, the final nail in the coffin was, in the words of one, "The author lacks a clear point of view." These publishers were looking for a strong narrative to bind the oral histories together and make sense of those times. But I was still peeling away the outer skins of the onion, scratching the surface of the story of an enigmatic people undergoing tumultuous change. I had hoped the voices in the book would be strong enough to speak for themselves. What these publishers were asking for was something beyond my reach at the time.

Facing that truth came hard. Among other things, it meant no income. I hadn't earned a dime since the start of my Russian explorations, and living in New York in the 90s was becoming exceedingly expensive. My husband worked for a non-profit agency. His salary was quite adequate for one person, barely so for two, especially if that second person was engaged in long-distance travel. My preoccupation with Russia was consuming our savings and moving us perilously close to the financial edge.

I was at another crossroads. With no revenue in sight, my venture began to seem like an expensive vocation, a luxury we could no longer afford. From a purely practical standpoint, it made sense for me to put it aside and find some gainful employment. But the voice of my soul refused to be silent. It kept urging me to keep on going, to dig deeper, to uncover more of the essence of the Russian soul. To my amazement, my husband's support remained unwavering. Though I came up empty-handed time and again, though our resources were fast evaporating, he never really flinched.

With money removed from the equation, at least temporarily, the way ahead looked clear. Several objective factors supported my inner guidance, persuading me to pursue the quest. First, though the oral history book appeared doomed, my research had produced a foundation of knowledge; the lay of the land was at least familiar. Second, it seemed likely that I was the only writer exploring Russia through the prism of the new spirituality, looking for seeds of Aquarian culture. And finally, I was being led directly into the heart of Mother Russia. It was as though I'd been given a compass, a map, and a personal guide.

My guide was a young woman I'd met in Moscow on the day of the August coup in '91. She was among the guests at Natasha's for the celebration of Transfiguration Day. Though I had barely spoken with her that day, I was impressed by her poise, her statement of faith in the will of God. I became acquainted with her the following year, when I returned to interview Natasha at length. Her name was Lida. She became an essential part of my journey, leading me toward the back roads and remote outposts of the Russian interior.

Lida was born outside the USSR, though she lived there for most of her life. She had attended elementary school in a town near Moscow where her father, a nuclear physicist, was conducting research. Later she returned on her own for university and graduate studies. Despite the harsh conditions of Soviet life, she preferred it to life in western Yugoslavia, which she viewed as philistine. In Russia, there was an intelligentsia steeped in philosophy, literature, spirituality; people who lived for things beyond small material comforts.

In her twenties when I first met her, chronologically young enough to be my daughter, Lida was an old soul. And it happened that we were, in certain ways, on a parallel quest. For years she'd been searching for Old Russia, a country that existed in her mind's eye, the pre-Bolshevik Russia widely portrayed in the great 19th century literature and art. Before meeting Natasha, in 1990, she had traversed much of that huge expanse of land searching in vain. Finally, a year before I met them both, Lida encountered a rare preserve of that earlier time.

It was a small city, two hundred miles south of Moscow. The old quarter had fatefully escaped the Bolsheviks' wrecking ball, remaining almost exactly as it had been a century ago. Lida described a place of colorful wooden houses, a well-preserved cathedral, wide streets lined with old trees that formed leafy canopies overhead. Even the modern section of town had lacked the oppressive feel of most Soviet cities, dominated by huge, monolithic apartment compounds. She fell in love with it.

The town was called Belaya. I had first heard about it in '92, from Natasha. During portions of three days, while learning many interesting things about her life, I also had my first encounter with the force of her will. Though I'd traveled nearly halfway around the world to pose questions related to my oral history book, Natasha had her own agenda. After humoring me for awhile, staying within range of my questions, she completely abandoned the interview etiquette and took over. There was a story she wanted to tell. By the end of the first day, I decided to sit back and listen.

At first, the significance of her story, and of Belaya, largely escaped me. Natasha had a unique style of speaking, especially when she was excited. It was staccato, episodic, a little like abstract art with a line here, a splash of color there. One had to struggle to decipher cause and effect, chronology, the connective tissue that holds a story together. But it turned out to be an extraordinary tale of another Russia that existed beneath the facade of the Soviet state, carefully hidden from view.

With some help from Lida, who was then living in Natasha's apartment, a fuller picture emerged. Natasha had discovered Belaya thirty years earlier, when she was thirty, during a painful personal crisis. It was 1962, the time of Khrushchev's "thaw," a sort of fleeting preview of Gorbachev's *glasnost*. The reins of censorship had been loosened enough to allow the publication of *One Day in the Life of Ivan Denisovich* by Alexander Solzhenitsyn, the first exposé of atrocities inside of Stalin's prison labor camp system. Everyone read it. Teachers discussed it with high school students.

For Natasha, it was excruciating. The book cast a horrifying light on the system in which her mother figured prominently. From an early age, she had inculcated Natasha with the highest ideals, prepared her to sacrifice everything, if need be, for her country's noble human experiment. At the same time, Natasha had been showered with privileges. As a teenager, when her mother headed the Party apparatus in central Moscow, she had met the best and brightest in Soviet culture. When her mother became part of the Central Committee, the world was her oyster. She traveled abroad, visited the US, even dined with John F. Kennedy months before he became president.

Then along came Khrushchev's campaign to expose Stalin's "cult of personality." Solzhenitsyn's book appeared. Natasha felt she had to see with her own eyes whether it was true. Along with several friends, she set out on a trek through northern Siberia looking for the labor camps. What she found was devastating. It forced her to confront some terrible facts. Everything that had once seemed rock-solid was suddenly subject to questioning: the parades and pageants to Soviet glory, the lofty ideals, the unbounded pride in country.

She was left with an overpowering urge to discover her roots, the truth about her forbears. Stalin had ruthlessly expunged family histories. People suffered terrible fates for having the "wrong" ancestors. The higher one rose in the Party, the more one's family history was sterilized. Any ties to religion had to be totally purged. In a rare moment of candor, during an intense emotional ordeal, Natasha's mother had confessed to her that her own mother had been devoutly religious. Before then, all that Natasha knew of her grandmother was that she kept beautiful gardens in Belaya, in the heart of Russia's rich "black earth."

Shortly after returning from Siberia, Natasha set out for Belaya, where she had never been before, in the hope of finding the gravesite of her grandmother. Along the way, life took a completely unexpected turn. Upon arriving in Belaya, she went to the address given her by an uncle, a place for her to stay. He had told her that a middle-aged couple lived there; both were physicians. The man who opened the door, however, wore the robes of a Russian Orthodox priest.

Natasha recounted what happened next, thirty years after the fact, with much self-deprecating irony. She greeted the couple as

Daughter of the Communist Party, member of the Soviet élite, a self-described "boss" filled with arrogance. The priest's wife immediately set about preparing a hot meal for the hungry, weary traveler. Natasha consumed every morsel placed before her, unabashedly asking for more, while aggressively lambasting her host, the priest, for having abandoned his post as a surgeon at a time when the nation faced a shortage of doctors. Moreover, she defied him to explain how an adult could possibly believe in God in an era when men were already traveling into outer space.

During the next few years, a seismic change took place within Natasha. The abrasive young woman, sophisticated member of Moscow's literary intelligentsia, set forth on a journey that would transform her into a humble disciple of the priest, Father Alexei. "It started with his eyes," Natasha said. "Months later, I couldn't stop thinking about them. I saw God for the first time in his eyes. It is something you know when you see it. There was a kind of love and compassion there that I had never seen in another human being."

Something else she had never seen, and at first adamantly refused to look at, was a Bible. Eventually, however, Natasha agreed to bring a copy of the Gospels with her to Moscow. Despite her lifelong convictions, she found herself reading it, thinking about the eyes of the priest. A year later she returned to Belaya, to the horror of her mother who believed she'd fallen into a cult. After several more yearly visits, she went there to stay. Leaving a husband and young child in Moscow with her mother, distraught but resigned by then, Natasha placed herself under the tutelage of Father Alexei, for nearly seven years.

After being there for some time, she began inviting trusted Moscow friends to Belaya to meet Father Alexei. At first they traveled there one by one, with extreme caution. Under Brezhnev, the reins of totalitarianism had been tightened again. To be caught in possession of a Bible was a crime that could land one in the gulag. Contact with a priest could destroy a career. Belaya became a secret shrine for a handful of Moscow's intelligentsia. It remained that way until Father Alexei's death in 1985, when Gorbachev came to power.

During my visit in 1992, Natasha spoke of Belaya incessantly. No matter where our conversations began, they ended up there. There was a reason, though it emerged in small bits and pieces requiring time and patience to assemble. Belaya, as it happened, had been the site of a miraculous religious event. The event took place in 1395. The six hundredth anniversary was coming up. Natasha wanted to create a gala celebration. To help launch the planning for it, she was inviting friends from Moscow to travel there the following year. For reasons that were obscure, she wanted me to join them.

I couldn't fathom what meaning this central Russian town might have for me, not to mention a religious event that happened six centuries ago. But Natasha kept insisting, lacing her arguments with references, religious and historic, that were absolutely foreign to me. When I remained hesitant she declared, with barely disguised annoyance, that if I ever wanted to understand the soul of Russia, I had better make the journey to Belaya. In the end, it was Lida who filled in some of the missing blanks and persuaded me to go. Through her eyes, I caught a glimpse of what I might find there.

Part Three

Mother Russia

Midnight Trains

T he way into Russia's heartland was carefully paved. I arrived at Natasha's in May of '93 only to discover that her friends had metamorphosed into "the Moscow delegation." Our delegation of twenty included two Americans. With me was my husband, Martin, who had decided to join me on this trip. Since train tickets for Russians cost a fraction of the price for foreigners, the Americans' tickets had been bought under assumed Russian names. We were instructed to pretend to be Russian when the train conductor came around.

Eight of us, nearly half the delegation, congregated at the train station on an unusually warm and balmy spring evening. The others were to leave the following day. Standing on the dimly lit platform, waiting to board the train, the atmosphere was electric. Voices were hushed in keeping with the canons of public behavior from Soviet times, but excitement flashed in the eyes of our fellow passengers. Natasha's vision and boundless enthusiasm seemed to have infected everyone.

The train ride was to last twelve hours. In the US, it would have taken perhaps one-third as long to cover the distance of some two hundred miles. But rather than feeling inconvenienced by the length of the trip, our fellow travelers seemed delighted by the prospect. There was a great romance about train travel from Soviet times. The longer the journey, the greater the sense of adventure.

To anyone who grew up with freedom of travel as a birthright, the limits of Soviet life throttled the imagination. Before *glasnost*, all movement had been tightly monitored and restricted. To go almost anywhere, permission was needed from authorities, often several tiers of them. Most people were locked into one city, town, or village, often one dwelling, for their entire lives. Exceptions were those with specialized education or training to fulfil work quotas in a more desirable place, or with a marriage offer from such a place. When it came to foreign travel, only a small elite could cross a border, even to a neighboring Soviet-bloc nation.

Travel was the stuff of dreams, especially foreign travel. In reality, it was largely confined to circumscribed areas of the USSR, and to trains, for journeys of any distance. Few people owned cars, and poor roads and scarce service stations discouraged long trips. Buses lacked lavatories; planes were expensive. Overnight trains were not only comfortable and affordable, they sparked the sense of romance that comes with waking up in a new, or different, place. On the way, there were simple pleasures, like sharing food with friends, a ritual that generally began before the train pulled out of the station.

And so it was that evening, my first experience on an overnight train in Russia. As soon as the bags and parcels were tucked away, packages of homemade food began appearing on the small pullout table in our compartment, which Martin and I shared with two of Natasha's friends. Settling in for the long ride, snacking on victuals, I sat back and took a deep breath. It was the first chance I'd had to take stock of things since leaving home. I realized, suddenly, that the actual purpose of our voyage still remained obscure to me. While conferring the title "delegate" upon us, Natasha had neglected to offer any further information about our mission.

What little I knew, thanks to Lida, was that people believed a miracle had taken place in Belaya, in 1395, which had saved Russia from annihilation by the Mongol conqueror, Tamerlane. The Russian Orthodox Church had celebrated this miracle until the Revolution. By 1993, it was gone from the collective memory, along with most other religious history. The mission of Natasha's friends, who included theater and film directors, was to help the people of Belaya design the first celebration of this event in nearly a century.

The story of the miracle required piecing together over time, like a giant jigsaw puzzle whose fragments were scattered all about. Part fact and part legend, it hinged on divine intervention in human affairs. The main figures were the Mother of God, Our Lady of Belaya in this instance, and Tamerlane, a descendant of Genghis Khan. With a horde of 400,000 on horseback, Tamerlane was on a rampage to conquer the Kingdom of Muscovy, on his way to subjugating all of Europe. At the southern perimeter of the land of Rus, in September 1395, he entered the fortress town of Belaya. When the local prince refused to surrender, Tamerlane obliterated the town. And then he had a dream.

Asleep in a tent on the outskirts of a ravaged Belaya, the story goes, he awoke in a state of terror. In his dream, he'd seen a beautiful maiden surrounded by bands of saints and angels pointing their swords at him angrily. The maiden warned him, sternly, to leave the Russian land and never return. The ferocious warrior, a Muslim, was shaken to his core by the maiden, whose identity was unknown to him. He called on his seers. They explained that to Christians, she was the Mother of God. They advised him to retreat, as no amount of physical force could defeat her. Tamerlane turned his hordes around, headed southward, and left Russia forever.

Icons depicting Tamerlane's dream kept the story alive in the popular imagination for ages. They featured the Mother of God, and the bands of saints and angels; some contained renderings of Mongol warriors' tents. It was believed that the scene had been recorded by Tamerlane's scribes and had eventually found its way back to Russia, where the original icon was "written." For centuries, a plethora of such icons hung prominently in Belaya's churches. On the 500th anniversary of the miracle, in 1895, the town folk had raised funds to erect a new church honoring the Mother of God of Belaya, for her deliverance of Russia from Tamerlane.

If Tamerlane's dream had been the whole story, it could easily have been dismissed as mythology. But there was more to it, recorded in ancient Russian chronicles. In late summer of 1395, news that Tamerlane's hordes were heading northward reached Moscow. Terror-struck Muscovites began round-the-clock vigils, praying unceasingly to their protector, the Mother of God. Until then, they had believed that the Mongol Yoke, which oppressed and humiliated Russia for over two centuries, had finally been broken. In 1380, at Kulikov Field near the Don River, Grand-Duke Dmitry had won a stunning victory over the Mongols under the spiritual guidance of Sergius of Radonezh, Russia's holiest monk. Fifteen years later, Sergius and Dmitry were both dead. Dmitry's heir sought divine protection for Moscow, the new capital of Rus, from its most sacred icon. He ordered Church authorities to bring the icon to Moscow from Vladimir, the interim capital. A long, prayerful, tearful religious procession accompanied Our Lady of Vladimir to Moscow by foot, a journey of several days. As Our Lady entered Moscow, news arrived that Tamerlane's hordes had suddenly, inexplicably, turned around and headed south.

Six centuries later, Natasha's delegation was heading south from Moscow to Belaya. All of us were largely ignorant of the above details at the time. But whereas Russians seemed inclined toward the miraculous and the supernatural in general, miracles on a scale that changed history remained outside *my* ken. Besides, I had come there for other reasons. It was an opportunity to see a different face of Russia. Lida had argued convincingly that a visit to this relic of Old Russia would expand my education — that I would encounter there, in the provinces, a purer, more timeless embodiment of the Russian soul.

As it happened, my education began shortly after boarding the train. The women in our compartment were two of Natasha's oldest friends. One was a cultural official, a former Party chief, the person behind the conference where I had met Natasha two years earlier, and who had just established a new museum featuring Russian spirituality. The other was an actress known and beloved by generations of Soviet filmgoers. The women train conductors, thrilled at the sight of her, tried to do whatever they could to make her journey more comfortable. They immediately rushed to find plastic hangers so that she could hang up her dresses.

Irina Leonidovna Mikhailkova, still very beautiful in her late sixties, was like a force of nature. She was part earth mother, the one who thoughtfully, generously prepared edibles enough for all four of us. And she was an irrepressible fount of songs, poems, stories and jokes. She regaled us for hours, untiringly and unselfconsciously, like a spring that never ran dry. Lida, who was assigned to another compartment, spent most of her time in ours helping translate Irina's outpourings. But it was almost unnecessary.

In Irina's presence, you could learn by osmosis. As the night wore on, she expressed an extraordinary range of emotions, fluctuating between joy and sadness, laughter and tears. It was hard to know whether she always acted this way, or whether it was the midnight hour and the intimate setting that brought back a flood of memories and the feelings they induced. To the accompaniment of the rhythmic, lulling, clanging of the train's wheels, Irina laughed heartily one moment and wept the next.

Her life had been filled with high honors and awards as well as tragedy and suffering. The episodes she chose to share with us were laced with mystery, beginning in her youth. During World War II, she and her husband had both been drama students, living with his mother in Leningrad. It was the time of the German blockade. People were dying of starvation all around them. The streets were filled with corpses, as the living became too weak to bury the dead.

One day an elderly man with a long gray beard approached Irina on the street. He told her that if she memorized a certain German phrase, and recited it when she encountered German soldiers, she and her family would have enough to eat. She did as she was told and the result was unimaginable quantities of bread and milk. Some time later, she entered a church, which was permitted by Stalin during the war. Her eyes were immediately drawn to a particular icon. Irina was certain that the face in the icon was the face of the old man she had met. A priest told her that the image on the icon was that of St. Nicholas, patron saint of Russia.

Not long thereafter, Irina's husband and mother-in-law both perished. Irina was helped to escape Leningrad on a truck driving across the frozen Lake Ladoga. Bombs fell all around them, narrowly missing the truck, forming craters everywhere, yet they made it safely across. Again, Irina saw signs that St. Nicholas had protected her. At the end of the story, she opened the top button of her blouse and slowly pulled out a chain with a locket. Inside the locket, which she opened reverentially, was a miniature icon of the saint. She'd worn it secretly all those years. The winner of countless Peoples' Awards, the highest Soviet honor, was a devout believer.

Though our train wasn't due to arrive in Belaya until midday, the passengers were jolted awake at 7 AM by a blaring noise. Over a crackling loudspeaker, on that sunny spring morning, came a syrupy rendition of "Autumn Leaves." Struggling to pry open my eyes, I noticed that Irina had long since been up and dressed. She had already dealt with "our nightmare," as she dubbed the lavatories on overnight trains, and was standing at the window in the corridor, exclaiming over the magnificence of the countryside. When she saw that we were awake, she motioned to Martin and me to come take a look.

The train moved so slowly that we could almost inhale the aroma of the velvety green, hilly terrain with lavender and white lilac bushes blossoming everywhere. Irina loved this part of central Russia and was exhilarated. There was no trace of the pain she had felt the night before upon recalling the loss of her second husband, and then of her son — her only child, a poet, who died in his youth of a drug overdose. Bursting with joy she announced, practically shouting, "This is a new day. The sun is shining. We are blessed to be alive."

Irina's faith was as valuable to "the Moscow delegation," I later realized, as her celebrity. The realm of religion was still fraught with uncertainty and paradox in those years. On the one hand, churchgoing had become so commonplace that people often dismissed it as a passing fad. Former Communists, lifelong atheists, turned up in church all of a sudden, lighting candles, even becoming baptized. On the other hand, the official penalties for such behavior had been quite severe until fairly recently. Believers, long accustomed to concealing their faith, were swimming in strange, uncharted waters.

For Natasha, moving out of the shadows, in terms of her own spirituality, presented an unusually delicate dilemma. In bygone times, the public alibi for her attachment to Belaya was that her mother had been born there. When questions arose about the frequency of her visits, and her taking up lodging in Father Alexei's apartment, they were squelched, ironically, by her mother's position in the Central Committee. Now, in this new time, part of her task was to reveal, in bite-size portions, the true reason for her connection to Belaya — to explain why a writer from Moscow was organizing an historic religious event in this provincial town.

There was a lot to reveal. Her story involved not only Father Alexei, but an underground stream of spirituality that had connected him, and thus Belaya, to the heart of Russian spirituality during the Golden Age of the 19th century — the legendary monastery of Optina Pustyn, not far from Belaya. Optina was a place where pilgrims from every corner of Russia traveled to receive spiritual guidance from its illumined monks, the Elders. Those pilgrims included Tolstoy, Dostoyevsky, Gogol and many other well-known figures. They also included a small boy who visited there in the years just before the Revolution. A half-century later, he was the priest in whose eyes Natasha saw God.

As a boy, Father Alexei had been taken on annual pilgrimages to Optina by his mother, starting at age five. Her spiritual father was the last Optina Elder. When the Bolsheviks removed him by threat of force, Elder Nektary sought refuge in a neighboring province. Mother and boy continued to visit him. At age twenty, the young man asked for Elder Nektary's blessings to become a priest. The Elder, who had the gift of clairvoyance, counseled him to become a physician until age fifty, when it would be safe for him to enter the priesthood. And so it happened.

In the mid-1950s, the Church assigned Father Alexei to Belaya, a sleepy, provincial city, where he quietly served the priesthood for twenty years until he was stricken by a paralyzing illness. He, too, was clairvoyant, and remained so despite his illness. During the darkest days of Communist atheism, he held to a vision of the spiritual flowering of Belaya. Just before his death, in 1985, he had shared this vision with Natasha, his closest spiritual child. It became her legacy to nurture the vision — to keep it alive, sharing it only with her most trusted spiritual brothers and sisters, until the ripeness of time.

During *glasnost*, Natasha proceeded cautiously, with the instincts of a skilled politician. After Father Alexei's death, she had journeyed to Belaya far less frequently. Since '91, there was a new head priest, an unknown quantity, and a new mayor, the first democratically-elected city administrator, a former school teacher. He was the first non-Communist to govern the town since before the Revolution and he was also, Natasha discovered, a believer. She quickly turned him into an ally. It was under the auspices of this new mayor, at his official invitation, that the Moscow delegation was traveling to Belaya, to rejoin the interrupted stream of Russian spirituality.

Holy Places

Belaya had a reputation for natural beauty. From the rolling "black earth" of its surroundings, a vast expanse of fertile land, to the people themselves, particularly the women, it was known to be a place of exceptional beauty. True to its billing, the town's Department of Culture sent three strikingly attractive women to meet our delegation. They stood on the platform waving, smiling warmly, as the train pulled into the station.

The van waiting to ferry us to the hotel was, in stark contrast, aged and badly weather-beaten. The Hotel Belaya, the only hotel in town, was just over twelve years old at the time, yet the typically shoddy construction of the era gave it a dilapidated feel. The room assigned to "the Americans" was spacious, its walls covered in an attractive floral wallpaper. Lida had heard it was the hotel's best room. The main problem, predictably, was the toilet. It ran incessantly, giving off a foul odor, and there wasn't a sign of toilet paper.

This last problem was thoughtfully solved for us by Irina. A veteran traveler, having toured the far reaches of the Soviet empire many times during her long career, she was extremely resourceful. And having once visited the States, she evidently empathized with our plight. After the official welcoming luncheon that day, as we were leaving the dining hall, Irina sidled up to me and opened her purse, stealthily withdrawing a large wad of paper napkins she'd collected from nearby tables, generously sharing her cache with Martin and me.

Our first outing took place that afternoon, an excursion into the surrounding countryside. A bevy of women gathered outside the hotel after lunch to board the dilapidated, gray van assigned to our delegation for the length of our stay. The only men in our company were the driver and Martin. The other men had drunk "to the bottom" with each of the many toasts offered at lunch, quietly disappearing afterward. By that point in the day, our delegation almost had the feel of a women's committee.

As we drove through the town, I was at a loss to see what Lida saw, at first glance, apart from the magnificent old trees forming leafy canopies over the wide streets and boulevards. Through my American eyes, everything had a shabby, run-down look. We passed by several piles of rubble where churches once stood. Nearly all the buildings were badly in need of plaster and paint. At closer range, however, beneath the deteriorating facades, there were outlines of great architectural beauty. There was artistry in the wooden houses with their decorative, hand-carved shutters, vestiges of the lifestyle of Belaya's wealthy merchant class before the Revolution.

Heading out of town for our first adventure, the group was exuberant. Despite physical discomforts and a hint of danger, it seemed as if nothing could dampen this spirit. The springs of the old van were not made for the deeply rutted roads we bounced along. Its windows were sealed shut, permanently, trapping the sun's rays like a greenhouse and creating a suffocating heat. An extremely tense moment occurred when the heavily loaded vehicle crept across a teetering wooden bridge. As we held our collective breath, Irina began to lead the women in rounds of song. They all knew all the words, as the same songs had been taught at all Soviet schools and summer camps.

What had inspired the group's exhilaration was our destination. It seemed that several of the women had already been there, and passed the word along to the others. When we arrived, the reason for their excitement was immediately clear. It was a place where white stone cliffs towered, dramatically, over a winding river far below. Leading out to the cliffs was a wide, soft, grassy plateau offering an awesome vista. Fleecy clouds dotting the azure sky seemed almost close enough to touch. In this spot, where pagan rituals had been celebrated long ago, one truly had the illusion of standing at the juncture between heaven and earth.

The beauty of this place evoked a spontaneous celebration from our companions. The women, mostly of middle-age, kicked off their shoes and frolicked in the emerald grass as unselfconsciously as school girls. They whirled and danced until they finally ran out of steam and meandered quietly, one by one, toward the cliffs. Sitting perched on the large boulders in silence, motionless, they looked like human sculptures. A rapturous gaze appeared on many faces, forming an unforgettable picture of Mother Russia in the embrace of Mother Nature.

Those were interesting times. Despite the persistence of old forms, signs of a new era sprouted everywhere. That evening, an "official" ceremony took place that ended in a completely unexpected way. The Moscow Delegation had been scheduled to take part in the formal founding of a *zemlyachestvo*, a kind of confraternity of people spiritually linked with the *zemlya,* the land, of Belaya. We were expecting the deputy chief of the Department of Culture to preside over a quasi-formal induction ceremony.

Present that evening, in addition to several residents of Belaya, was the initial membership, consisting largely of Natasha's out-of-town friends: a group of Muscovites, one person from Siberia, one from Yugoslavia, and two from America. Each of us was to receive an official *Zemlyachestvo* identity card. Similar to widely used Soviet-era "cards," it was a small folder covered in red imitation leather, embossed with gold letters, bearing an official Belaya stamp and place for a photo and signature.

In true Russian fashion, the "presentation ceremony" turned out to have no resemblance whatsoever to what the words implied. It was a purely social event. Each of us was casually handed a bright red folder after which tea and a delicious, ornately decorated cake were served. All of that took place within a half hour's time.

Afterward, the deputy chief of the Department of Culture, one of the beautiful young women who had welcomed us at the train station, suddenly "changed hats."

She turned into a charming, blushing bride, married just the week before. For her, our gathering was an occasion to share a pivotal experience of her life and the life of the town. She had had a formal church wedding, one of the first such weddings to take place in Belaya since the Soviet era, when marriages were perfunctory rituals conducted in state wedding bureaus. The main event of the evening was her wedding video — raw, unedited footage containing every detail of the long, elaborate pageant inside Belaya's large cathedral.

This was, ironically, a genuine cultural event. Few Russians alive at the time had ever seen such a ceremony. From the bridal gown, to the ornate crowns worn by bride and groom, to the richly embroidered robes of the priest who conducted innumerable rituals symbolizing the joining of two lives by God, everything was brand new. The women in the room were transfixed. It was close to midnight by the time we left, yet several wanted to stay on and see what remained of the four-hour tape.

The following day began with the delegation's *raison d'être*: a planning meeting for the 1995 celebrations. The meeting took place in a building where Lenin's image remained visible everywhere. In attendance were Belaya's leaders in higher education and culture, along with the Moscow delegation, which had doubled in size overnight. The first speaker was the head of the pedagogical institute, the local college. He reported that students of history and archeology had already begun researching the events of 1395, laying the groundwork for reconnecting Belaya to its pre-Revolutionary past on the basis of fact.

The new mayor, the former secondary school teacher, spoke next. He reported on a recent meeting he had had with Yeltsin, whose results were discouraging. Having traveled to Moscow in the hope of procuring resources for Belaya's historic celebration, he felt he'd been summarily brushed off. "We'll be lucky if they issue a new stamp for the occasion," he quipped. Furthermore, thanks to rapidly vanishing subsidies from the centralized economy, he revealed that the town's coffers were growing increasingly bare.

As if to counteract that gloomy note, the mayor ended his remarks with an upbeat expression of appreciation to the Muscovites, which was also a statement of faith. What made it all the more stunning was that he uttered the statement while standing beneath a huge oil painting of Lenin reading a copy of *Pravda*. After thanking the Moscow group for coming to Belaya and providing inspiration, he said, with utter sincerity, "With your continued involvement and with the aid of the Mother of God, I know we will succeed."

It was another classic moment of Russian surrealism. Lida's jaw dropped. She whispered that she thought she'd travel to Mars sooner than hearing a Russian politician speak such words. Yet believers were cropping up in all sorts of unexpected places, as the veneer of atheism quietly slipped away. There in the provinces, Lenin was still omnipresent — in names of streets and public squares, in imposing statues and paintings. But there were growing signs that he was going to have to co-exist with the Mother of God.

As the mayor sat down, he invited the Moscow delegates to speak. Among those who had arrived overnight was a producer named Mikhail. After years in classical theater, Mikhail had turned to organizing largescale public events, including religious ones. Just the year before, as the Russian Orthodox Church was emerging from the shadows, he had helped orchestrate a nationwide observance of the 600th anniversary of the death of Sergius of Radonezh — the saint most revered in Russia's history for his role in breaking the Mongol Yoke.

Mikhail arrived in Belaya brimming with ideas. His main idea involved a religious procession winding through the streets of the town. Led by young girls in white dresses, representing purity, it would start at the gates of a ruined convent high on a hill overlooking the town. For the two years leading up to the event, Mikhail proposed a series of projects symbolic of purifying the spirit, the "water of life," such as cleaning up Belaya's badly polluted streams and rivers.

That provoked the morning's first controversy. Whether it was sparked more by Mikhail's rather slick, big-city style of presentation, or by the content of his ideas, was hard to say. A young, dignified-looking man, who turned out to be the grandson of Father Alexei and a physician, rose in protest. He spoke somberly, with a hint of anger. "It is pointless to purify our rivers," he said, "if we don't first purify our souls. That is how we must prepare ourselves. Otherwise this event will merely be a show." A thunderous silence followed. The meeting ended inconclusively, but not without a note of optimism, shortly thereafter.

One of the highlights of our stay in Belaya was a visit to the place where Father Alexei had lived. His widow, in her eighties, received our group for tea one afternoon. The apartment consisted of one comfortable-sized room which served as dining room, living room and sleeping quarters, and one tiny room that contained a desk, a single bed, and a reclining chair. This was Father Alexei's room. From its small window, we could see the graceful, sloping brick wall of the destroyed convent on the hill across the river.

The apartment, which also contained a primitive kitchen and bathroom, represented the heart and soul of Belaya for Natasha. She had lived here for seven years under the tutelage of Father Alexei, and it was to these rooms that she returned constantly, while he was still alive, after resuming her Moscow life. She used to say that he taught, mainly, by the example of his love. Many souls had come to this humble dwelling, one floor of a small house, in search of this priest's healing love.

Upon entering the large room, I noticed something I had only read about previously. It was an icon corner, a feature of nearly all Russian homes, from the humblest to the grandest, before the Bolshevik Revolution. The east corner of the room was blanketed from top to bottom with icons of Christ, the Mother of God, and many saints. Hanging on adjacent walls were tapestries of scenes from the life of Christ and still more icons. From certain angles, one had the impression of being inside a chapel.

The small room remained exactly as it had been when Father Alexei was alive. Nothing had been moved since his death eight years earlier. It, too, had an icon corner. A small table in that corner held several large crucifixes, along with a plethora of icons of different sizes, shapes and materials. The wooden desk was covered by a plate of glass under which were dozens of photographs, mainly of his spiritual family, just as he had left them.

It was a room of invisible presences, most powerfully of all, that of Father Alexei himself. Paralyzed with an undiagnosed illness seven years before he died, he had spent the last years of his life in a reclining chair. Natasha beckoned me to enter the room while the others were having tea, closing the door behind her. After sitting in the well-worn recliner for several minutes with her eyes closed, she stood up and motioned for me to sit there, as if she were inviting me to enter a sacred shrine. That was the "place," I understood later, where Father Alexei had described to her his vision for Belaya. And that was where she most wanted to be, at that moment, to seek guidance on how to implement it.

East and West

A cathedral stands on the crest of a hilly slope overlooking Belaya. The designer of this once-magnificent 19th century temple was the architect of Moscow's original Church of Christ the Holy Saviour, as well as the Great Kremlin Palace. Belaya's cathedral had been spared the fate of its Moscow cousin; it had managed to survive the Communist wrecking ball. But like all such religious structures, it endured punishing indignities at the hands of the atheistic state. Large portions of it had been commandeered to serve as a food warehouse and had taken a terrible beating.

The day after seeing the cathedral in the wedding video, we paid a visit there, though not to the sanctuary. The new head-priest had invited the Moscow delegation to lunch. An acolyte met us at a side entrance, ushering us into a low-ceilinged subterranean passageway. At the end of a dank, narrow hallway, past a warren of small rooms, we entered a large rectangular hall with a small window. After having served as a state granary for many years, this chamber had been turned back into a refectory.

Upon entering this hall, I had the unexpected, inexplicable sensation of feeling at home. It was one of many such moments during my Russian journey when I stopped dead in my tracks, aware of how implausible everything seemed. I hadn't known a soul in our group apart from Natasha and Lida until a few days earlier, yet it had already become "our" group. And while Russians had an uncanny way of absorbing you into their midst and making you feel you'd always belonged there, there was something else.

It struck me like a flash of lightening when we entered the refectory. I was flooded by a sense of familiarity reminiscent of my first visit to Mont St. Michel in France, nearly thirty years earlier, when I *knew* that I had been there before — especially in the scriptorium where the monks had copied over the Gospels. In Belaya, the sensation was less acute, more diffuse, but was vivid enough that I couldn't ignore it.

When I was young, this kind of sensation would have ended up in the dustbin of *déjà vu* and life would have gone on. Even after the Mont St. Michel experience, which occurred years before I discovered the theory of reincarnation, I had lived comfortably with a degree of unknowingness. But now I knew about the Law of Rebirth, and I was faced with another past-life recollection as I entered a church structure. The thought of having once lived in such surroundings was nearly inassimilable at first, given my parentage in this lifetime. Yet it occurred to me, that day, that perhaps I *had* been Christian in the past, and Russian (as well as French), and that perhaps I had even known some of my travelling companions before.

As for this particular space, the refectory, there was nothing remarkable about it, unlike the flying buttresses and Romanesque arches of Mont St. Michel. The narrow, rectangular hall was not especially inviting in the usual sense of that word. It was dimly lit and sparsely decorated. There was little to relieve the starkness of the gray walls except a crucifix or two and a simple icon of the Mother of God. Yet it felt strangely, mysteriously, comforting to be there.

The head-priest was a gaunt, fair-skinned, youthful-looking man named Father Dmitry. He sat slightly apart from the group at the head of the long wooden table, almost like a distant observer. He said very little. His demeanor was circumspect, at times a bit severe, yet he was a generous host, repeatedly inviting his guests to help themselves to more food and drink. Despite a lavish amount of the latter, I noticed a certain stiffness among my companions that hadn't been present before.

Only later did I appreciate the groundbreaking nature of this meeting, the reason why it seemed everyone was walking on eggshells. Layers of distrust separated Father Dmitry and Natasha, who were destined to become the main protagonists in an ongoing drama, but were virtual strangers in '93. It was still an "in-between" time. People were feeling each other out and trying to read the tea leaves. Communism was officially dead but not yet buried and no one was certain that it, or another form of totalitarianism, would not be resurrected.

A vast and ancient reservoir of suspicion continued to keep strangers at arm's length. Only a few years before, the Church itself was anathema, and its place in the new order was not yet clear. Moreover, there was habitual distrust between people from different spheres of life, in this case the Orthodox Church and Moscow's world of culture. And then, residents of the provinces historically resented the privileged residents of the capital. Plus, Father Dmitry, who now resided in the provinces, had recently arrived there from Siberia, whose natives were suspect to Muscovites for their unpredictability.

The fact that this gathering took place at all was significant. Different worlds had come together, either to collide or to learn accommodation. A troupe of talented Muscovites, by no means all Christians, was there to present the new head-priest of Belaya with a plan to resurrect an ancient religious holiday in *his* city. Father Dmitry, preoccupied with restoring the cathedral and forty other churches, was not particularly responsive. He seemed to be observing, withholding judgement, until Mikhail trotted out some of his theatrical motifs. Visibly put off, our host swiftly brought the luncheon to a close.

This was an unusually fluid period with regard to religion. There were no signs, as yet, that the Russian Orthodox Church would soon become a behemoth issuing its own anathemas. People still felt free to explore the many faces of God. A student of Agni Yoga, which criticizes orthodox religion for its dogmatic deadness and sterility, could still freely walk into an Orthodox church, light a candle, draw inspiration from the sacred music, and even take part in liturgical rites, without fear of censure.

Though this era of openness was destined to be ephemeral, it offered myriad foretastes of a new, inclusive kind of spirituality. To my astonishment, of all the examples pointing in that direction, I discovered none more arresting than the spiritual identity hidden in the depths of Natalya Stepanovna Borodina. It was said that the new religion would be born of a recognition of the common sacred truths at the core of all religions. As it turned out, Natasha's soul had long been incubating common truths of both East and West.

Before making this discovery, I had thought I understood Natasha's worldview, more or less (apart from her unorthodox relationship with the Orthodox Church). I knew she had read the Agni Yoga books, often described as a synthesis of religious truths. She had also read Theosophy, a teaching devoted in part to proving the common origins of the world's major religions as a foundation for universal brotherhood. These two teachings, brought into the world by Russian-born women, Helena Roerich and Helena Blavatsky, had attracted millions of Russian readers. So in this regard Natasha was hardly unique.

The most interesting thing about her was a private, totally concealed dimension of her spiritual life. Lida had discovered it by happenstance, and shared the secret with me in a moment of weakened resolve to never mention it to anyone. It seemed that Natasha consciously recalled a past lifetime which bore directly on this one. In that earlier life, she had been a 19th century British writer and disciple of a great Hindu master. She had helped spread the master's teaching to the West. In this life, she had translated his writings from English into Russian, publishing several pamphlets anonymously before mysteriously abandoning the project.

To me, this was extraordinary. I had never known anyone who recalled a past life with such specificity, or who had carried forward the same work from one lifetime to another, from one part of the world to another. Natasha was consciously living out what I then knew largely in theory, apart from occasional flashes of intuition. I marveled at the identities coexisting inside of her, and at the sheer complexity of living her life. Publicly, she was a writer and daughter of a high Communist Party official; privately, she was the spiritual daughter of a Russian Orthodox priest; in the depths of her soul, she was a former disciple of an enlightened Hindu master.

The implications were staggering. I began to see Natasha as a symbol of Russia's potential future, as well as a clue to understanding the unfolding Aquarian Age. In my mind, she became a kind of living laboratory of the predicted synthesis of religious truth and the revelation of the One Soul of humanity. I began to imagine how quickly barriers would fall away if people consciously realized — as she did, in the very fiber of her being — that all religions are pathways to God, tailored to different cultures and epochs of history.

It was not uncommon for people to experience fleeting glimmers of the past as I had — of having been in a particular place before, of knowing someone who is ostensibly a stranger, of feeling an inexplicable affinity for a language, a culture, a part of the world, or an era of history. Moreover, a large majority of the earth's population is raised with a belief in reincarnation — mostly in the East, with small but growing numbers in the West. Yet Natasha's story suggested what could happen, within the soul of humanity, if those intuitions and beliefs ripened into fuller awareness.

Her life seemed to illustrate what students of the ageless wisdom know in principle: that all souls incarnate in different races, religions, countries, genders, and material circumstances on the journey toward illumination. By the end of that long journey, when the perfected human being is released from the cycle of earth lives, ready to enter the Kingdom of Souls, each individual soul has experienced all aspects of the human condition. The sense of separation that divides civilizations is replaced, over the course of time, by a conscious awareness of oneness and a shared spiritual identity.

I began to realize that Russia had some geographical "advantages" that promoted this process. Lying at the juncture of

East and West, it encompassed aspects of both civilizations. Perhaps, I mused, this was another reason why, in the unforeseeable future, Russia might be fertile soil for a new spiritual dispensation. For the present, however, it often appeared to tilt toward the East, to the constant frustration of Westerners. Many Russians seemed to have a foggy sense of time, a lack of interest in the material order, and relatively little concern for individual human rights, along with a strong affinity for timeless realms, for the cosmic order, and for humanity in general.

Lida and I became engaged in lengthy debates about the relative merits of these characteristics, versus the practical materiality of Westerners, both during our visits to Russia and in-between. We exchanged voluminous letters for several years, including long periods when she was living in India, studying Eastern philosophy. In Lida's eyes, there was no contest: an affinity for the transcendent was vastly superior to total immersion in material-plane pursuits. Paradoxically, despite my alienation from the prevailing wave of materialism at home, and my understanding that both "sides" of the human experience were necessary to the coming Aquarian civilization, I often found myself defending the West.

We both subscribed to the concept of "a new heaven and a new earth," as found both in the Bible and in the ageless wisdom teachings. According to the latter, the coming era will manifest a new fusion of spirit and matter. Up to now, human experience has been largely marked by a separation of the two. That separation will come to an end when humankind, the mediator between the higher and lower kingdoms, awakens spiritually. As segments of humanity become increasingly responsive to the spiritual kingdom, to divine purpose, life on Earth will be uplifted, redeemed, and transformed.

My side of the argument with Lida was that before this transformation could happen, people of an Eastern orientation needed to take a different view of the material plane. After all, the material world will form the "receptacle" of Spirit in the coming age. Unlike the past, when holy people sought refuge from the world in caves and monasteries, in the future such people will lead lives that may appear worldly, on the surface, but they will be infused with a consciousness that is holy, thereby "bringing spirit into matter." Among other things, I contended, this meant that toilets mattered.

Interestingly, I met an Orthodox priest in Moscow, named Father Nikolai, who shared my view. Given the story of his life, his priorities were all the more striking. As a young scientist, he had become a follower of Father Alexander Men, the scientist-turned-priest who was assassinated, many believed, for "bringing the word of God to the Soviet people." On his way to the priesthood, Father Nikolai had suffered his own harsh fate for refusing to cooperate with the KGB, in an era when the Russian Orthodox Church survived by offering up names of church-goers (who were then severely penalized). His punishment was spending twenty years as a deacon before being allowed to be ordained as a priest.

In 1990, Father Nikolai was assigned to a crumbling church in Moscow that had functioned for decades as a Soviet printing facility. Despite the overall decay of the structure, his first priority was to construct an attractive restroom that would always be kept clean. I couldn't help asking him why. He replied, "Because Christ was born in a human body. He came to earth in a human body simply to show us that our true nature is divine."

For most Russians, however, it was a challenge to live in the world of form, within the constraints of time and space. The present moment always felt too small and constricting, too confined by mundane demands. It was the Russian proclivity to brood over eternal questions. Contemplating abstract, philosophical ideas was more compelling than repairing leaky faucets. Pondering the vast reaches of the cosmos was inspiring; dealing with the here and now was fraught with unpleasantness. A part of me understood, and empathized.

Black Magic

After leaving Belaya that May, of '93, Martin and I traveled to southern Siberia with Lida, who accompanied us as our interpreter and guide. The three of us had planned to do some traveling in the region, once I completed the last round of interviews for my oral history book. In previous years, my schedule had always been too tight to venture far. That year I looked forward to exploring the mythical land of Altai, the vast mountainous region to the east, stretching all the way to the border with Mongolia.

I also looked forward to meeting a boy who lived in Altai. Almost a year earlier, I had accepted an "assignment" on his behalf, at the request of an interviewee, a computer engineer named Andrei. When I last saw Andrei, in the summer of '92, he was living in Barnaul with his wife and daughter. The family had moved from Leningrad to that city, to be close to Altai. By that fall, Andrei had moved to Altai on his own, I later learned, leaving his family behind.

In late fall of '92, back in New York, I received an e-mail from Andrei containing an urgent appeal for help. He had met an eight-year-old boy in Altai, named Stepan, who needed reconstructive surgery. Stepan's face and body had been badly scarred from a fire that had taken the lives of both his parents and consumed their home. He had gone to live with his aunt in Altai, whom Andrei described as a wonderful woman. At her request, Andrei asked if I could possibly find a way to bring Stepan to the US for surgery.

It was understood that everything would have to be donated.

Not only the surgeons' fees and hospital care, but transportation, food and lodgings. When I said that I would try to help, e-mails began pouring in from a small hamlet in Altai, the place where the "wonderful woman" named Valentina was living. Each message from Andrei bore added information, such as the need for Valentina to accompany Stepan to the US. And each message ended with an impassioned plea for help and an exclamation like: "Wouldn't it be the most wonderful thing if we could help this poor boy!"

Despite the enormity of the task, I decided to give it a try. To my surprise, things began to fall into place much more easily than anticipated. A friend with whom I had once traveled to the USSR, a physician at a New York hospital, was willing to help. She sounded rather optimistic about enlisting a sympathetic colleague to do the surgery. My Russian language teacher had a friend who worked at a travel agency and offered to try to obtain free airline tickets. Through a Russian Orthodox church, I found a woman with an extra bedroom who was ready to provide lodgings for Stepan and Valentina.

When I boarded the plane for Russia in May '93, I had in my hands two round-trip airplane tickets and a promise of lodgings. The plastic surgery was uncertain. Once the doctors saw photos of Stepan's disfigurement, they thought he would need a series of operations and hospital stays. The costs had been estimated in the hundreds of thousands of dollars. The optimism of my physician friend evaporated. Still, I thought to myself, these things *do* happen; perhaps I'd find another hospital. There was still a high level of American goodwill toward Russians.

As our small plane approached Altai, I was eagerly anticipating my first encounter with Valentina and Stepan. Though I couldn't make any promises regarding the surgery, I thought the airline tickets would be a tangible sign of Americans' concern for Stepan and cause for hope. A number of people already knew of his plight and were anxious to help. I was planning to look elsewhere for volunteer medical assistance. Stepan's story had become part of my life. I was finally going to meet him and his "wonderful" aunt.

From the moment we landed in the small hamlet where they

lived, nothing happened as expected. Andrei met the three of us at the local airstrip and drove us to the main street, a dirt road frequented by cows, goats, and chickens. This was a place where strangers did not go unnoticed. As we stood in the middle of the road discussing our lodgings, a woman in business clothes passed by. Andrei excused himself to speak with her. He informed us, on his return, that she was Valentina, and she had the key to our lodgings. We *might* meet her the following day.

The fact that our lodgings were still a question, though the time of our arrival had been confirmed weeks before, seemed as bizarre as the behavior of Valentina. Andrei himself, who had been a most willing interview subject for several years, and who had pleaded with me to help Stepan, was a changed man. He seemed to be a total stranger. There wasn't a hint of the boyish charm he had exhibited in the past.

Andrei finally obtained the key to the official guest house, a cottage of several rooms, and left us there to fend for ourselves. Without Lida, we might not have survived. I was suffering from the flu and feeling weak. The toilet did not flush. Cooking implements and dishes were lying around caked with food, leftovers of the previous guests' meals. The store on the main street sold sausage and canned meats, and two of us were vegetarians. Lida managed to find some cheese and fix the toilet. We lived mainly on bread, cheese and tea.

Our first evening in the village, a priest named Father Vladimir came to visit. He was another spiritual "child" of Father Alexei, a spiritual brother of Natasha. For most of his life, he had lived in Moscow and worked as a psychiatrist. After meeting Father Alexei and spending time in Belaya, he had felt called to become a priest. Father Alexei blessed him to enter the priesthood at age fifty, and to fulfill his dream of building a church in Altai, where none existed at the time. They had all been destroyed.

However, the spiritual potency of the enormous territory of Altai was legendary, and made manifest in a multitude of ways. The region was home to indigenous peoples with their own religions and shamans, as well as small communities of "Old Believers" —

descendants of Russians who had sought refuge there after a bloody Church schism in 1666. Those groups had been joined, in more recent times, by an array of new age spiritual seekers looking for a natural life in a pure environment. Governing all of them were officials of the Communist Party, *presumably* atheists.

Father Vladimir showed up looking as if he had been through a war. He was worn and weary, dressed in a dirty, ragged cassock, his face full of pain. After a brief greeting and a polite attempt at pleasantries, he began to unburden himself. He already knew Lida, and evidently decided he could trust Martin and me — more recent friends of Natasha. For hours, he recounted the nightmares he had encountered in Altai while struggling to build a church.

In that sprawling enclave, like a large village, there were factions and sub-factions with constantly shifting loyalties. The first group to rally around Father Vladimir on his arrival in late '91 was led by none other than Valentina — Stepan's caretaker. A year later they turned against him, accusing him of all kinds of evil-doing. Their protest turned ugly and violent. The church-building effort, in which they had participated enthusiastically, completely ceased.

This was only the beginning of his miseries. The greatest albatross, Father Vladimir claimed, was black magic. Altai was a place where it was believed that the veil between spirit and matter was unusually thin. People came there for its unspoiled natural beauty and its powerful spiritual energy. This energy was said to affect everyone somehow, consciously or unconsciously, for good or for ill. The problem was that certain individuals, in Father Vladimir's view, were directing it toward dark purposes.

He cited many cases of mysterious disappearances, inexplicable behavioral changes, psychotic breakdowns, violent attacks, even murders. The local people tended to be highly unstable and easily influenced by those in power. Valentina, as it happened, wielded power of two kinds. She had been head of the Community Party, chief executive of the local area under the old regime, and still held a high administrative post. She was also believed capable of wielding occult power.

After talking for quite awhile, Father Vladimir's demeanor

changed. It was as if an enormous weight had been lifted from his shoulders. A smile appeared on his face. He thanked us for coming, saying that this was the first time in months he had been able to relax in friendly company. Noticing my worsening flu symptoms, he took pity on me and offered to help. He was a natural healer. Sitting in a chair behind me, he placed his hands on my neck, shoulders, and temples. My head cleared. I felt better than I had in days.

The next morning was magnificent. The sun's rays sparkled like diamonds on the rushing river, swollen by spring rains, just outside our cottage. Snow-capped mountains were visible in the distance. We had arranged to take a day's drive into the pristine wilderness, following the course of the river in the direction of Mongolia. Feeling healthy and energetic, I was eagerly anticipating this outing, planned many months in advance.

As we prepared to leave, an attractive, intelligent-looking woman in her thirties appeared at the cottage door. Lida recognized her from a conference they had once attended together. She was an attorney living in a nearby village. She and her neighbors were spiritual seekers, students of Agni Yoga and other esoteric teachings. They had moved to Altai, often cited as "the last ecologically pure area of Russia," to live in harmony with nature. She had heard, somehow, that we were in the area and had walked a long distance to meet us.

Moments after she showed up, Andrei arrived to pick us up in a small van we had paid him to rent for our forays into the countryside and for the long drive back to Barnaul, where we would fly back to Moscow. Since we were locked into this arrangement, I held out hope that his behavior the day before had been an aberration. But things got worse. When Andrei saw the woman at our door he flew into a rage and *ordered* us to stop speaking with her. The woman, oddly, did not object. Nor did she seem very surprised. Gracefully, she backed away.

But I was livid. I had never in my life been told whom I was allowed to speak with. Lida, realizing how upset I was, begged me not to confront Andrei. It was never clear to me why she did so: whether she understood the cause of the enmity between him and the woman, or whether she didn't care. What concerned her most was the fact that we were totally dependent on Andrei for transportation. He claimed to have rustled up the only available van and driver in that remote region, on the promise of US dollars.

The day proved to be a very mixed blessing. We drove through some of the most beautiful country I'd ever seen — gently rolling hills adorned by a profusion of spring wildflowers, majestic mountains as far as the eye could see, rarely a sign of human civilization. The main inhabitants were flocks of sheep and herds of wild horses suckling their newborns, frolicking in the lush green valleys. On a human level, however, with Andrei and the friends he brought along, the day was a trial by fire. As a final gesture of good will when we returned, I handed him the airline tickets. He took them in silence. There was still no mention of Stepan.

That evening, we had an invitation to dinner at the home of a local resident, a former Muscovite, yet another friend of Natasha. We had barely changed our clothes and washed the mud off our faces, coagulated dust from the unpaved roads, when Father Vladimir arrived to take us to the house. The central room had an icon corner, which we stood and faced as he blessed the meal. Ten minutes after we sat down to eat, our hostess, Marina, wearing a lovely dress, excused herself to go outside and milk the cow. She returned perhaps fifteen minutes later, placing a glass of warm milk for each of us next to our vodka glasses.

During Marina's brief absence, I had become seriously ill. I experienced a shooting pain in my jaw that seemed to come from nowhere. It was so searing and throbbing that I had to leave the table. Marina's sister, a retired dentist who happened to be there, offered to locate the source of the pain. She took me into a darkened room and tapped gently on each tooth with a metal tool, but there was no sign of the cause. I became so faint that I had to be held up during the short walk back to our cottage. Father Vladimir tried his healing hands again, but this time to no avail.

Pondering the sudden, mysterious onset of the pain and its

severity, Father Vladimir mentioned the possibility of black magic. Lida, too, began to consider it. Given all that had transpired since we arrived, and the stories we had heard, I found myself contemplating what had previously seemed unfathomable to me. But Altai was a place where many things were unfathomable. Writhing in agony, I began to wonder, in spite of myself, whether Valentina, whom I had not yet met, had possibly, for reasons beyond my imagining, "cast the evil eye on me" . . . .

The next morning Valentina showed up at the guest house. It was as though she'd walked on stage in the wrong act, and didn't even seem to notice. She was there to tell us, with a friendly smile, that a picnic was being held that day in our honor. A group of men were already at the site in the nearby hills barbecuing the meat; the women had been preparing delicacies for days. She said she would have us picked up within an hour. When Lida explained that I was ill and unable to attend a picnic, she looked visibly annoyed, inconvenienced. Eventually, however, she offered to take me to the local clinic.

The clinic's dentist, like Marina's sister, was unable to locate the source of the pain. Looking perplexed, he took Valentina aside for a consultation. Shortly thereafter a nurse came scurrying out with an unopened box. Lida explained that it contained vials of a pain-killer, special medicine kept in reserve for VIP's. The nurse unceremoniously pulled down my pants, jabbed the needle into my thigh, and handed me the box and the syringe.

As we walked out into the sunny splendor of Altai, Valentina tried to console me, saying that I could inject myself whenever the pain returned. But the pain never left. At the picnic site, a sublime setting with breathtaking panoramas, I finally met Stepan. He was playing with the other boys, but was obviously sad. The picnickers reveled in the food and drink, singing and dancing to the accompaniment Andrei's guitar. Noticing that I hadn't eaten, Valentina asked me how I felt. I replied that it seemed the medicine hadn't taken effect yet. At that point she informed me that the medicine was five years old, but it was all they had.

The following day we left Altai for Barnaul. It was a fourteen-hour journey in a small, crowded, over-heated van. The windows worked, but had to remain tightly closed to keep out the dirt. There were cavernous ruts in the unpaved roads and the van had no springs. Every bounce was agonizing. Lida tried to help by massaging my jaw with an herbal cream. I laid back with my eyes closed, opening them occasionally, just long enough to glimpse some of the most glorious landscapes on earth passing by.

The next day was my 50th birthday. Our hosts in Barnaul, old friends by then, had prepared a special meal. My appetite was restored just in time by a friend of Father Vladimir, a local physician trained in Eastern and Western medicine, a beautiful, gentle young man who came over immediately upon hearing of my plight. To my surprise, when Lida explained what had transpired in Altai and the suspicion of black magic, the good doctor didn't laugh. He seriously took it into consideration. Deciding to treat my ailment with acupuncture, he placed needles in my hand at a meridian associated with the jaw. The pain of the needles was initially worse than what it was attempting to cure. Eventually, however, the acupuncture plus homeopathic tablets that he gave me, all free of charge, made the pain go away.

Several weeks later I saw my dentist in New York. He discovered that I had a root canal problem. But neither the sudden onset of the pain nor its unremitting intensity sounded normal to him. In fact, he said it was highly unusual. Yet in Altai, everything was that way. I never heard from Andrei again. The airline tickets expired six months later. Though Stepan's eyes had glowed with hope when we spoke, briefly, of the possibility of his coming to the US for treatment, it was not to be. And no Russian whom I knew could ever explain why.

Into the Breach

T he following year, 1994, was the first year that I hadn't been to Russia since 1990. It began as an uncomfortable hiatus, since I was in a blind about how to proceed. Having promised to be in Belaya for the historic celebration in the fall of '95, I had a large gap to fill. But it was more than just a gap in time. After coming to terms with the fact that the oral history book was not to be, at the end of '93, it had slowly dawned on me that the failure to find a publisher was a form of salvation. I had homework to do.

One of my hopes for the book of oral histories had been to convey an aspect of the Russian people largely unknown in the West — the spiritual dimension re-emerging with *glasnost*. To illustrate this phenomenon, I had chosen twelve individuals from scores of people I had met. One of them was Andrei, of Altai. Initially, he'd seemed like a perfect fit. He had abandoned an unhappy life, working under the boot of a tyrannical director at a dysfunctional scientific institute in Leningrad, and had set out to forge a life of freedom. His goal was to disseminate spiritual knowledge through a center that he was helping to establish in Barnaul.

The problem, which erupted with blinding clarity in '93, was that I hadn't really known Andrei. The persona I initially encountered and the one that later emerged were sorely at odds with one another. This turned out to be the case, though less dramatically so, with a few other interviewees. Had the book been published as originally conceived, readers would have learned interesting things about the lives of twelve individuals in those times. But I would have known they were reading *partial* truths, especially in certain cases. That realization would have put me in the awkward position of wanting to sabotage my own work.

In analyzing this near-miss, I came face to face with a disconcerting truth about myself. The lack of balance in my initial perceptions of Russians pointed to something unbalanced in me. It dawned on me then that Russia was going to be more than the subject of a book; it was also going to be a learning ground for my soul. Whatever else was destined to transpire there, I was being given an opportunity to deal with some longstanding personal issues. One of them had to do with dualities. I had a tendency, common among idealists, to want to focus only on the light and to ignore the shadows. Yet the same light that drives us onward toward the goal, I realized, can also blind us to perils along the way.

What drew me to Russia was the light I saw in many people I had met. Granted, the individuals I had come to know were among those whom Russians called "the best people." Still, through them, what was lacking for me in America during the 90s appeared abundantly present there. Despite their suffering, or perhaps because of it, people seemed propelled toward things of the spirit. Among those oriented toward the new era, there was a deeper sense of expectancy than in the US. The dawning of a new age seemed to take on greater livingness there.

At the same time, my interviews had starkly revealed the dangers of focusing on the light and overlooking the darkness. In a sense, that had been the story of Russian communism: a fanatical attachment to the ideals of justice and equality, and a blurring of the savagely brutal methods used to achieve those ideals. In the end, however, when the dark side exploded into full view, it had been devastating, most of all to the fanatical idealists.

Lida, who played a growing part in my quest to unravel the mysteries of the Russian soul, exhibited the classical symptoms of an idealist. Her imbalance was not unfamiliar to me — that is, the nature of it — but the scale of it was. She had idealized Mother

Russia to the point that criticism of any kind upset her, even my revulsion at "the facilities." She struggled mightily to keep the negative side from her field of perception, and also from mine. Lida had fallen in love with the *idea* of Russia — the idea, linked to the flowering of Christianity there, that Russian soil was sacred. That idea had been sustained by the great souls whom she had met.

She loved to regale me with tales of her heroes, several of whom were teachers who had influenced her at formative times in her life. One was a primary school teacher, imprisoned by his own country during the Great Patriotic War for "the crime" of having been taken prisoner by the Germans, thus deemed a Western spy. Though he'd endured years of unspeakable torture, he was a gentle soul, always speaking to the children about love, brotherhood and the preciousness of life. Another of Lida's heroes was a professor of philosophy. He repeatedly put himself at risk by speaking to her, after class, about his belief in God.

By '94, Lida had become my sounding board. We exchanged voluminous letters about once a month, often as long as fifteen or twenty pages. Hers were written in a tiny script, mine typed and single-spaced. Our lives afforded us this possibility. She had returned to India to be near her spiritual teacher and to work on translating spiritual texts. I was living in New York City and writing occasional articles, spending much of my time studying early Russian history, reading Russian religious philosophers, trying my hand at a different style of book, and waiting for inner direction.

Our correspondence covered a wide array of topics — spiritual and philosophical ideas; growing up under communism, capitalism; the changing lives of women, changing weather patterns, changing human consciousness. But the core of it was always Russia. Still a citizen of Yugoslavia, she wanted desperately to obtain Russian citizenship. To do so, she was willing to endure untold trials and tribulations, including leaving the country periodically to avoid prosecution for breaking laws pertaining to temporary residents.

Her efforts to obtain citizenship once included marrying someone she didn't love, while at university. The marriage ended in two years and her battles resumed, continuing unabated. To obtain a temporary permit to live in a major city entailed endless lines, humiliating grillings, long periods of waiting for a reply, having to offer "gifts" to clerks, living in fear of being charged with bribery, and finally, at best, obtaining another *temporary* stamp. It was the same in "democratic" Russia as it had been under Soviet rule. Yet this was the only country in which Lida could imagine spending her life.

For my part, Russia had become more like another dimension than another country. I came to see it as a different state of consciousness with a different mode of existence. It was a place where I felt stretched and pulled, turned inside out. There was much that attracted, much that repelled, and much that I still failed to comprehend. After the episode in Altai, and my encounter with a different Andrei, I felt even more like a stranger in a strange land, unsure of my own perceptions.

Into the breach stepped Lida. She seemed to have appeared, magically, as a kind of guiding spirit. During two years' of correspondence, I shared with her countless reflections, observations, questions. She responded generously with her own thoughts, corroborating mine sometimes, offering divergent views at other times. Our letters turned into a kind of basic training, essential to my venturing further into Russia. In the process of formulating my own thoughts and questions, and assimilating her responses, I eventually acquired the sense that I was standing on solid ground.

Prior to that time, I had felt like a lone explorer, navigating foreign territory on my own. The accuracy of my observations depended on my ability to see beyond masks and veils into the true nature of people and events. Lida was immensely helpful in this regard, if not always objective. She was wise beyond her years, extremely intelligent, knowledgeable about many things, plus she had grown up and been educated among Russians. Our correspondence was rounding out my limited firsthand experience.

There came a time, however, when I feared our relationship might be in jeopardy. I had always assumed that our exchange was rooted in a shared fascination with Russia's mysteries. Then suddenly Lida began to write of her "devotion" to me. Alarms went off in my head, for many reasons. Chief among them was the Russian tendency to idealize and idolize, which inevitably led to disaster. There was a deep-seated cultural pattern of creating heroes, placing them on pedestals, and then systematically, ruthlessly, knocking them off.

I had been clued in to this phenomenon by a Russian psychologist, whom I had asked about the intense public mourning that accompanied the deaths of many actors, poets, musicians, film directors. She conjectured, with irony, that the outpouring of love and adoration for the deceased was directly proportional to the severity of criticism he or she suffered while still alive. "Something in the Russian nature," she observed, "makes it easier to praise people in death than in life." The reason was envy, in her view. An unconscious battle raged between admiration and envy, with the latter often destroying that which was most admired.

Lida had first used the word devotion while living in India, where devotion is part of the spiritual culture. Still I recoiled from it, trying subtly to quash any such notion. Then it took another bent. As our letters continued over time, she began turning me into a mother figure. In a sense, this was not so surprising. I was roughly her mother's age and while her mother had been cruel and repressive, I was very supportive, especially regarding her spiritual journey. But then she revealed her motive for wanting to make me into someone I wasn't. She confessed that it was her nature to be extremely competitive, and hoped to avoid driving me away by turning me into her "good mother."

Naturally, this development put me on my guard. Yet I did my best to minimize it. Our exchange was invaluable. Her letters contained pearls of insight immensely helpful to my search. In addition, during my two-year absence from Russia, she had become my only living link, as I was hers. The adage "out of sight, out of mind" seemed especially true of Russians. Being outside the country was like falling into a black hole. Those who remained there evidently felt betrayed by those who left, even if they did so by necessity, as in Lida's case. Letters, for a host of reasons, were virtually a lost cause.

Lida was a crucial link in what I realized, after the fact, was a carefully orchestrated chain of events propelling my journey onward. She emerged as a central figure at a time when I was feeling adrift, bereft of my original clarity, unsure of my direction as a writer. As my understanding of the Russian soul grew deeper, so did my uncertainty about how to approach it. The Belaya events of '95 were out there, somewhere on the horizon. They had the potential of bringing new clarity and focus. In the meantime, there was Lida, reassuring me, bolstering my confidence, keeping me on course.

Without her, it's hard to imagine how I would have sustained my connection with Russia across that large expanse of time. I began to experience, as never before, one of the toughest challenges of living a spiritually guided life: keeping the faith when things do not manifest in the world of form as envisioned. At such times, doubt creeps insidiously into the recesses of the soul. Like a thief in the night, it can rob you of the will to proceed, unless there is an unshakable conviction that everything happens for a purpose, and that time is a relative phenomenon.

Lida's presence in my life seemed intended to counteract the doubt. During the period of our voluminous correspondence, it wasn't so obvious that it was part of a larger design. It only became so later, looking back. When I first met her at Natasha's, in August '91, it had seemed purely by chance. Likewise, my meeting with Natasha in Siberia, a month earlier, had seemed accidental. And the fact that our interview date coincided with the first day of the coup as well as the first public celebration of Transfiguration Day for most of that century, all seemed strictly coincidental, at the time.

On that unforgettable day in Moscow, I had with me a long list of contacts given to me by Americans. Though I didn't realize it at the time, Lida's name was on the list. The friend who had given me her name had spoken glowingly of her. He mentioned that she was relatively young and not Russian by birth, but said she was one of the most helpful people he had met in Moscow, and one of the most charming. The problem was, he wasn't sure where or how I might find her. She had moved and he didn't know where she was living at the time, or even where to look.

She Who Inspires

The air hummed with excitement at Natasha's in late August '95. It was a way-station for people en route to the historic celebration in Belaya. They were friends, acquaintances, members of her spiritual family, all part of a far-flung network of kindred souls invited there from remote corners of the former Soviet Union, as well as India and America. Sitting around the kitchen table, people shared news from places as distant as the Baltic States in the west, and Altai in the Siberian southeast.

Being there amidst the continuing flow of new arrivals, with the doorbell ringing constantly, was like being in the middle of a large extended family whose members hadn't seen each other for a long time. But in this case, they weren't blood relatives. What drew these people together was a link to Natasha and a shared attraction to the new wave of spirituality. They were part of what was being called the "spiritual intelligentsia."

By then, Russia appeared to be teeming with such people. In the US, there was a parallel surge of interest in the new spirituality, but it was camouflaged by the trappings of consumerism. Our standard of living had a way of masking, no doubt dulling, the hunger for spiritual truth that was spreading around the globe. That hunger was especially acute in Russia. And it had a history. Russian minds were being prepared for the New Age, in part, by inspired writings of pre-Revolutionary religious philosophers and metaphysicians whose works were again freely available.

At the same time, in this land of unparalleled contrasts, daily life was increasingly apocalyptic. The kind of criminal and deviant behavior that had formerly been suppressed by force was now rampant. The girl-next-door had turned into the local prostitute, seducing neighborhood boys to support her family. Mafia gangs extorted protection money from budding entrepreneurs, including sidewalk vendors. Murders were committed for an apartment, a car, a computer. People spoke anxiously about the death of conscience in Russia, the result of a collective "forgetting about God."

The people who gathered at Natasha's seemed to exist on a different plane of consciousness, while having to wade through that swampland on a daily basis. All of them, professors, scientists, writers, actors, filmmakers, had suffered ever since Yeltsin's "price liberalization" of '92. Their state salaries either shrank drastically or disappeared entirely. Some survived by living on increasingly less; others had help from family members. Yet they appeared somehow immune to the prevailing mood of panic and the calls from authorities to go out and "get money" however they could.

Natasha seemed to play a vital role in those times. Her apartment was like a sanctuary from the surrounding chaos and bleakness in '95, just as it had been on the day of the coup four years earlier. She herself seemed to embody continuity, stability, and even optimism, as the old order crumbled. She had a vision for the future, extremely rare at the time. And she was determined to rescue from the past, from the chapter of Russian history just ending, a modicum of decency and pride.

It was common at the time, especially among the Western-oriented intelligentsia, to sweepingly condemn the failed socialist state. Many people laughed, with typical self-deprecating humor, at the massive Russian-style bungling of the communist experiment. Instead of leading the way to a glorious future, providing an example for the whole world to follow, so went the jokes, Russia's only success was to demonstrate to the entire world what it must *never* do.

Natasha often stood alone, even within her own circle, in defense of the vision of communism. She couldn't simply write it off as an historic blunder. There were still the values, the high ideals. Her childhood was emblazoned with object lessons in self-sacrifice, sharing, concern for the happiness of all. Later in life when she read the Gospels, it occurred to her that the ideals of communism, often called the "religion without God," had in fact been "borrowed" from Christ's teachings. For her, this was the ultimate proof of communism's superiority over capitalism.

She had an inner light that burned brightly, if not always steadily. When standing before an audience and speaking from the heart, she had an immense capacity to inspire. Many people sought her out, as I did, as Lida had. They wanted to be in her aura, in her circle, at her kitchen table. This seemed increasingly so as the chaos and confusion of Russian life intensified. Bereft of ideals and a sense of direction, people had lost faith in the future. Natasha, who appeared as solid as the rock of Gibraltar, helped shore up that faith. She seemed to see and know more than others did.

Her vision of the future, at least in the near-term, revolved around Belaya. She saw it as a place where the sleeping soul of Russia could be readily reawakened. Not only was it quiet, away from the big-city turmoil, but she sensed the possibility of tapping into the powerful stream of spirituality that had once flowed there. Subtly, she held out the promise that those who went to Belaya would be blessed by the aura of great souls who had lived there. That August, her ability to inspire was reflected in the large gathering of individuals ready to make the pilgrimage.

Since the visit of our "Moscow delegation" two years earlier, Natasha had traveled to Belaya many times to help organize the forthcoming celebrations. Cutting through the initial distrust of Father Dmitry, she had developed a warm relationship with him. He himself became an enthusiastic supporter of the holiday and convinced the regional Church hierarchy to put its growing weight behind it. In the realm of politics, however, there had been a setback. After one term in office, the mayor whom we had met, the Orthodox believer, had been replaced by a communist who eschewed religion and refused, at first, to cooperate.

After each trip to Belaya, Natasha returned home with new tales to tell. With every telling, around the kitchen table, her exploits took on added embellishments. She had a natural gift for feeding the Russian attraction to that which is larger than life. Russia's soul, steeped for centuries in a highly mystical religion and the magic of enchanting folk tales, had always been stirred by wonder, mystery, beauty, and goodness — all that transcends the ordinary and mundane. Despite the bursting of illusions which accompanied the collapse of communism, that longing for the magical, the mythical, remained.

And so it was that Belaya began to acquire the aura of a mythical city. That aura grew powerful enough to attract people from far-distant corners of the land to make the long journey to central Russia. In the end, sixty souls traveled there to take part in the 600th anniversary of "the Deliverance of Russia by the Mother of God." Few, if any, had heard of the holiday before. Few, if any, would ever have visited Belaya. But all had been caught, one way or another, in Natasha's magical web.

About twenty of us journeyed there in a borrowed van. The trip was by far less memorable than our adventure on the overnight train in the company of Irina, but twice as fast. And it afforded me a bird's-eye view of the spiritual intelligentsia of that time. Before the van left the station, everyone held a book in his or her lap; some were already engrossed in reading. The titles, under the rubric of spirituality, broadly speaking, ranged from the Hindu *Bhagavad-Gita*, Greek mythology, Agni Yoga and Theosophy, to the Christian Gospels.

Father Vladimir had traveled all the way from Altai to be there, a journey of several days. He sat in the back of the van surrounded by several new disciples, among them a prominent Moscow economist and two nuclear scientists. Together they quietly recited Orthodox prayers, seemingly oblivious to the other passengers. But when he finally encountered Lida and me, Father Vladimir appeared strangely remote. Given the relationship we had formed in Altai two years earlier, his behavior was extremely puzzling. For Lida, who felt great affection for him, his cool indifference had come as a blow.

We hadn't yet understood the tumultuous change rocking the world of religion in Russia during our two-year absence. In an amazingly short span of time, members of the free-wheeling spiritual intelligentsia had found themselves pitted against the reemerging Russian Orthodox Church. The only institution to remain structurally in tact, the Church had filled the power vacuum left by the implosion of the communist state. And it quickly set about reasserting its authority, resorting at times to issuing anathemas.

Until then, spiritual seekers had been delighting in throwing off the fetters of dogma, reveling in freedom from the fear of being watched, judged, or condemned for veering from a given party line. The breadth of the search for spiritual truth, suggested by the reading matter of my travelling companions, was striking. This posed a problem, however, for the Russian Orthodox hierarchy. Many of the books of interest to the spiritual intelligentsia had an Eastern cast. Principles such as reincarnation were at odds with Church doctrine on the life of the soul. Some books, moreover, were openly hostile to organized religion, especially to Russian Orthodoxy, long accused of obscuring spiritual truth.

The reassertion of Church doctrine had had a direct impact on Natasha's spiritual family. During Lida's absence, she had become *persona non grata* to Father Vladimir. Her long sojourns in India were suddenly cause for suspicion, along with her inclusive approach to spirituality. She had undergone a Hindu initiation ritual, as well as a Russian Orthodox baptism, and was an avid student of Agni Yoga and other metaphysical texts. A few years earlier, that was not unusual. None of the spiritual "children" of Father Alexei, including Father Vladimir, had raised an eyebrow.

But everything was changing. New lines were being drawn. Father Vladimir was in a vulnerable position. Before entering the priesthood, he had spent years reading metaphysical books and shared many of Lida's beliefs, including the notion that souls evolve through a chain of incarnations leading toward the perfection embodied by saints and masters. But just the year before, such beliefs had become dangerous. In 1994, the Moscow Patriarchy officially branded them, and the teachings in which they appeared, "anathema." People who held those beliefs and did not recant them, before a priest, were to be excommunicated.

Thus, Father Vladimir tried hard to avoid us. He had come to Belaya to honor the vision of Father Alexei, at the strong urging of Natasha. She had convinced him to make the four-day journey and to take part, as a priest, in the church ceremonies. But even she, evidently, could not combat the fear creeping into their ranks. Already facing problems with new age groups in Altai, Father Vladimir seemed to view Lida's spiritual path as another threat to his dream of building a church there. Dogma was reasserting itself in Russian life. Among its casualties were the bonds that had once existed between spiritual brothers and sisters.

Ultimate Paradox

Skies were overcast during the day's trip from Moscow to Belaya. The grayness outside accented an odd stillness inside the van. Nearly everyone read or slept the whole time. It occurred to me that if the passengers had been Americans embarking on an adventure together, there would likely have been a steady stream of chatter, bursts of animated conversation, laughter. Then it dawned on me, after hours of nearly unbroken silence, punctuated only by speech barely above a whisper, that I was witnessing the residual effects of a police state.

When we pulled up in front of the Hotel Belaya, almost seven hours after leaving Moscow, another new experience awaited me. My canvas bag, containing clothing for the week, arrived dripping with honey. It wasn't just any honey, but the finest, purest honey from Altai, many jars of which Father Vladimir had brought as gifts for his fellow clergymen in Belaya. During the drive, bouncing over ruts that were more like pits in the road, the glass jars had cracked and the honey oozed out of his bag, which happened to be lying just on top of mine.

In Russia, accidents, mishaps, delays, and disappearances occur routinely. Travelers have ample opportunities to learn patience, dispassion and detachment. But this incident took me totally by surprise. Noticing my temporary paralysis, Lida picked up my bag along with hers and marched ahead into the hotel lobby. Natasha was there waiting for us, greeting each traveler with a rose, a kiss, and an urgent plea that we change our clothes quickly. The first event on the holiday program, a vesper service at the cathedral, was about to start.

Dreaming of a hot shower, a rest, and a change of clothes, I found myself facing the prospect of laundering honey-coated clothes in a sink barely large enough to wash a pair of socks. After chastising me for making much ado about nothing, Lida, my room-mate as well as interpreter, took things in hand, moving swiftly to investigate the damages. She wanted most of all to avoid making a scene, or angering Natasha, who would be waiting for us. As it turned out, the honey had not seeped inside the bag. With a tiny piece of soap, she quickly scrubbed the sticky surface, hung it up to dry, and we left.

Despite the honey ordeal, we managed to arrive at the cathedral, several blocks from the hotel, nearly on time. The structure had been magnificently restored and richly decorated for the holiday. Not only had Father Dmitry put all his energies and resources behind the events, but the regional Metropolitan, parallel to an archbishop, decided to play a leading role. Lavish ceremonies were underway by the time we entered the huge outer doors and furrowed a path through throngs of people, looking for a place to stand.

This was my first experience in a functioning Russian Orthodox church, as opposed to the churches that had been preserved as museums under communism. It was fascinating to observe, in practice, some of the unique Russian characteristics of church-going that I had read about, such as the absence of pews. It was an ancient custom to stand in the presence of God. Not even czars were exempt. They had had private places resembling three-sided gilded cages, reserved for them, but for standing only.

I had also heard about "the traffic problem" in Russian churches, the result of the standing rule combined with inordinately long services. Since few people can stand still for two hours, not to mention three or four on holidays, the rule was circumvented. Almost no one sat down, except the old and frail for whom there were usually benches in the rear. But there was constant motion during church services, comings and goings — to buy candles, to light them at particular candle stands, to say prayers in front of special icons.

That evening, inside the vast cathedral, there were several whirlpools of activity. In the front, clergy conducted vespers on the eve of the 600th anniversary of the Deliverance of Russia by the Mother of God. Their rites involved constant movement back and forth, in and out of "the gates of heaven" — doors in the icon screen symbolically separating heaven and earth. In the center of the church were worshippers who alternately stood still and moved about. In the rear were visitors, watching and whispering. Natasha's friends moved toward one another as space permitted, kissing three times on alternate cheeks, a Russian greeting derived from Orthodox custom.

I was very much the observer, awed by the spectacle, the beauty. I would have been happy to stand still and take it all in as I knew few of the out-of-town guests. Lida recognized virtually all of them, as Natasha led us, space permitting, on rounds of introductions. The group had begun meeting one another during *glasnost* at various conferences on metaphysical teachings. That evening was the first time they had come together in a sacred space.

Hours passed in this moving, flowing, pageant of people, ceremony, and mystery. It was a feast for the senses. Sublime music floated down from a place high overhead. A choir of heavenly voices bathed the huge cathedral in magnificent harmonies. The air was redolent with a mixture of incense and the fragrance of flowers. Flickering candlelight illumined hundreds of icons covering the walls and pillars. It was hard to imagine being enveloped by that profusion of beauty and not somehow be affected by it.

For Lida, and others like her, this turned out to be a pivotal moment. She was acutely aware of the contrast between meeting her fellow seekers in a lecture hall and meeting them there, under the dome of a great cathedral. The trappings of the ancient mystical religion created an inner openness which, she commented later, could never have been produced by ideas alone, no matter how inspiring.

Afterwards, as we walked back to the hotel, she seemed

electrified by the experience. It filled her with a new sense of possibility. She was aware of feeling a greater sense of kinship with the others than she had felt in the past, a stronger heart connection, and sensed the same from them. The gathering of souls in a sacred space had evoked a new dimension of spirituality in her, something she'd only read about previously. She likened it to *sobornost*, "cathedral-ness," the spiritual ideal of the 19th century Russian religious philosophers.

We both felt exhilarated when we arrived back in our room, though it had been a long and exhausting day which began at 6 AM in Moscow. We talked for hours, in the course of which Lida shared a vision that she had had of a spiritual "marriage" between East and West — between the spiritual teachings of the East regarding the evolution of the human soul, and the ceremonial religion of the West, Russian Orthodoxy in particular. Incredibly, she had formulated her own blueprint for the universal religion mentioned in the prophecies.

As she spoke, I could almost discern the outlines of the remote future, like cloud-covered mountain peaks way off in the distance. The puzzle I had long been playing with in my mind suddenly acquired important new pieces. I realized that the "marriage" Lida referred to had already begun taking place within the psyches of people like her and Natasha, and even some Orthodox priests, like Father Vladimir, in the depths of his soul.

I also realized, however, that recent Church developments made Lida's vision seem unimaginably far-off. The Church was again being charged with obscurantism, as in earlier times. Priests were either unable or unwilling to answer the questions of new parishioners who had grown up under communism. Rituals remained shrouded in mystery. Adults inquiring about baptism were often told to bring a towel and the requisite fee, nothing more. The history of obscuring rather than revealing meaning appeared to be on-going. Centuries earlier, most priests were uneducated — some unable to read the Gospels. Nowadays they were all literate, but frequently far less educated than their parishioners.

Father Vladimir represented a new breed of Orthodox priests, though they were a small minority and had been forced underground. They had entered the priesthood after a university education and a professional life. Some of those who began to attract the largest followings near the end of the "godless century" had previously been scientists and active seekers of truth. By the time they became ordained, they knew a great deal about religion and spirituality, a good deal more than they were officially "allowed" to know.

One of the problems facing the Russian Orthodox Church on the eve of the new millennium was the gap between what many people knew, and what the Church permitted them to know. This gap occurred, paradoxically, because of what the communist atheistic state had not wanted people to know. Above all, the Communists had sought to erase Orthodox Christianity from Russia's collective memory. It *was* possible, however, to explore other religions — under the rubric of "scientific study of culture." University students flocked to courses on oriental culture where they learned about Eastern religions. The result was described by a spiritual psychologist who knew hundreds of seekers like herself: "We learned about Hindu gods long before we could find out anything about Christ."

Thus the reemerging Russian Orthodox Church encountered generations of well-educated people with wide-ranging religious and metaphysical knowledge. The Anathema was its attempt to erase that knowledge, as the Communists had tried to erase all knowledge of Christianity, the "opiate of the masses." In essence, the Church was trying to compel people to forget what they knew, to unlearn what they had learned, or at least to recant what they believed to be true, as the price of taking part in the liturgy.

What ensued was yet another unintended consequence. Many educated people who wanted to go to church stopped speaking honestly about what they knew and believed. Some stopped going to confession or confessed to unrelated things. Only four years after the Orthodox Church repossessed its properties and regained a foothold in Russian life, it had extinguished all hope of truthfulness. The oldest institution in Russia, again the bedrock of life for the masses of people, remained riddled with totalitarian consciousness.

Some Russians I knew found this deeply troubling, as church was a place where they had gone to seek comfort when everything else was falling apart. Reconnecting with their Church, so deeply embedded in their culture and history, was important for them. Thus the Anathema created a harrowing struggle. This was difficult for me to comprehend, precisely because I shared their orientation to higher consciousness — to the cosmos, the spiritual kingdom, the human soul, the wisdom teachings, in general. I couldn't fathom how or why a church, any church, could have such a powerful effect on people that they would consider backing up into a wall of doctrine.

This lack of comprehension set me apart from my Russian friends. In a moment of candor, Natasha admitted that her main reason for wanting me to go to Belaya was to cure me of it. If I was going to write about the Russian soul, she admonished, it wasn't enough to have an intellectual grasp of things. She argued that it was the Russian Church, born when the people of ancient Rus were baptized in the Dnieper River a thousand years ago, which had kept alive the flame of the Russian soul. This was so despite its ignominious cooperation with Communist authorities, and despite widespread rejection of its dogma. That struck me as the mother of all paradoxes, in a country thoroughly mired in paradox.

Revelations

The first day of the holiday marked an unexpected milestone in my odyssey. Until then I had been mainly an observer of Russia, watching and recording what I saw and heard. I had often been touched and moved, sometimes shocked and dismayed, but always at some distance. Despite soul connections with a few individuals, some of them deep and suggestive of past origins, I had continued to see things through the lens of a foreigner.

The day began with a full-length, full-dress church service. The cathedral was packed. Thousands of people stood shoulder to shoulder, hampering the usual perpetual motion of parishioners. During the service, four hours long, I had to will myself to resist the urge to press through the crowd toward the benches in the back for the old people. They were the ones, ironically, who put me to shame. Nearly all women, *babushkas*, they had attended church throughout the "godless years" and had mastered the art of standing. With them as an example, and with constant instruction from Lida, I practiced mind over matter.

In the morning light streaming through the windows of the cathedral's great dome, the entire edifice was ablaze with color. Gold leaf glittered in the spiral mosaic designs of massive columns supporting the dome. Marble floors of intricate design shone like polished stone. A profusion of flowers and candles adorned icons of the Mother of God, Christ, and legions of saints, hundreds of icons in every conceivable setting. While this brilliant sea of color and light bathed the eye, otherworldly harmonies wafted down from an a cappella choir overhead, soothing every cell of one's being.

The clergy, in flowing robes of peacock blue trimmed with gold, conducted a long series of elaborate rituals. Over twenty strong, including Father Vladimir, they presented a kind of mystery play. Much of it was beyond my comprehension, ancient symbolic reenactments of things unknown and unexplained. After several hours, Father Dmitry, the head-priest, appeared alone, walking to the end of a long platform jutting out into the center of the church. The people gathered around, massing at the edges of the platform and gazing up at him. It was an almost biblical scene — a preacher surrounded by his flock, waiting expectantly to hear the word of God.

In this thoroughly unfamiliar setting, feeling rather like a cultural anthropologist, I was suddenly jarred by a very familiar-sounding message. Part of Father Dmitry's holiday sermon bore an uncanny resemblance to a talk I had prepared for a conference the following day. Instead of reciting ancient history, the story of the vicious conqueror who threatened to annihilate Russia six centuries earlier, he addressed Tamerlane as a symbol of darkness within the human soul. He called on his listeners to conquer their "inner Tamerlanes," with the help of the Mother of God, rather than blaming external forces, or "outer Tamerlanes," for Russia's woes.

As I listened to him, vestiges of my foreignness slipped away. It no longer felt strange to be standing in a Russian Orthodox cathedral, in a small backwater city on the other side of the globe, where the everyday language remained difficult — not to mention Church Slavonic, a lexicon foreign even to Russians. The priest was saying what I had come to know in the depths of my being: that if we want to create a better world, a better life, the place to begin is within the recesses of our own souls.

His message appeared to have a purity of intent, devoid of artifice. He chose not to couch it in terms that would comfort his listeners, including hundreds or even thousands of first-time visitors who were potential parishioners. Just the opposite. Resisting the Russian tendency to look for scapegoats, he urged people to look within, instead, for the source of Russia's problems. The simple truth of his words brought tears to my eyes.

Beyond the power of his words, the sound of his voice was mesmerizing. It had a deep, resonant timbre that reverberated throughout the grand cathedral, permeating every niche and alcove. After the ceremonial rites, when he preached from the Gospels, he stood like a pillar of fire. Spirit filled his being in such a way that one could almost sense an invisible presence overshadowing him. I had never known such a person.

The whole day was full of mystery and surprise. By the time the service finally ended, the morning sun had given way to an overcast sky. A procession of clergy (including a small cadre of nuns) carrying colorful banners and icons made its way outside through the cathedral's side doors. The huge body of churchgoers followed behind them. Within moments, as throngs of congregants were slowly squeezing through the narrow portals, the sky darkened. A fierce wind blew through the trees. When the rain came down, it fell horizontally.

A few people turned back for shelter, but most remained where they were, clustered together under the falling rain, craning their necks to see what was happening. The clergy were conducting a service beside a small, round chapel, shaped like a medieval helmet, just outside the cathedral's side doors. The chapel was dedicated to the martyrs of Belaya felled by Tamerlane in 1395 — before the Beautiful Maiden appeared in his dream and commanded the Mongol warrior to leave Russia.

The storm lasted about as long as the memorial service, no more than ten minutes. The sky cleared as quickly as it had darkened and the procession got underway. People looked upward as they began walking, shaking their heads in disbelief. A friend of Natasha suggested that the rain was heaven's lament for the soldiers who had given their lives, six centuries earlier, so that Russia might live. Many saw the meteorological event as a sign of divine participation in the anniversary celebrations. To those who knew what had come before, it was the second such sign.

Just prior to the holiday, there was a remarkable discovery of a holy icon, once the most sacred object in Belaya. People long believed that it had perished in the church desecrations following the Bolshevik Revolution. In fact, a devout believer had rescued it and had kept it hidden for decades. It was the original rendering of the Mother of God of Belaya, created in the 17th century, allegedly based on Tamerlane's vision as recorded by his scribes.

The reappearance of this icon was considered a miracle by many, a sign from the Holy Mother. Legend held that a sacred icon turned up on the eve of every new chapter of Russian history. This fanned the hope that a new era, a spiritual one, was truly about to begin. As the church procession slowly wended its way through the streets of Belaya, the icon was held aloft in the place of honor. The long stream of townspeople walking behind it chanted a doleful lament, as if atoning for the era just ended. They sang out, unceasingly, "Mother of God, save us, now and forever."

The procession continued for over an hour, following a circuitous route to an unannounced destination, stopping only briefly to bless two chapels under repair. It came to an end on the far side of town at yet another church still under reconstruction. People poured into this building en masse. Though the crowd had thinned along the way, the structure was small compared to the cathedral. To find a place to stand inside, one literally had to squeeze through the tight press of bodies.

This was the church dedicated to the Mother of God of Belaya exactly a hundred years earlier, on the 500th anniversary of Russia's deliverance from Tamerlane. By the time I found a space, the clergy were blessing the rediscovered icon and rededicating the church in her name. People stood in rapt attention, despite hours of standing and walking, during the Metropolitan's benedictions and sermon. Interestingly, while praising the work of restoring the town's sacred architecture, he made a point of downplaying the world of form. "We should pay less attention to the rebuilding of our churches," he admonished, "than to rebuilding the inner temples of our souls."

During the course of these ceremonies, little of which I could see or understand at the time, something extraordinary began to happen in the rear of the church where I was standing. It felt as though a cascade of spiritual energy had poured over the place, flooding it with Spirit. I felt a force washing over me, a purifying force that permeated my entire being. Tears began flowing from my eyes. When I looked up, I saw tears streaming down the faces of many people standing near me, nearly all of them women.

This was no ordinary sensation, like a tear welling up in one's eye. It felt more like a force of nature pouring through me in an act of watery purgation. The release of tears seemed to come from a place deep inside where old wounds were healed — in that instant. Afterward I had an inexplicable sense of peace, and joy. Curiously, not everyone shared this experience. Lida, for one, did not. But I could see from the tear-stained smiling faces of the women around me that many had been similarly affected.

This was something utterly new to me, and thoroughly baffling. I couldn't attribute it to the Metropolitan's words, as most of what he said was told to me afterward by Lida. Nor could it have been induced by the power of suggestion, since I had become aware of my own tears before realizing that many others were having the same experience. It was a mystery then, and remains a mystery to this day, one that changed me profoundly. From that moment on, I was no longer an objective observer, but increasingly a participant in the subject of my inquiry.

Afterward we walked back to the cathedral, where official guests had been invited to share the first meal of that day. By the time Lida and I arrived, my legs were practically numb. We were the last to show up, as Lida had missed the announcement that guests would be picked up and driven back for the dinner. Two seats remained on a bench in the rear of the main refectory. I collapsed into mine as congratulatory toasts were being made. There were glasses filled with wine and vodka at each place setting. In a state beyond exhaustion, it took only a sip to alter my consciousness.

It was a relief to be able to disappear into the crowd of a hundred guests. I sat quietly in the back of the hall, trying to assimilate my mysterious catharsis, when suddenly, jarringly, I heard my name called out. It was followed by the title "vice-president." Natasha had just finished making a toast, in her role as president of the

Belaya *Zemlyachestvo*. It evidently struck her fancy, in the spirit of the moment, to introduce the *Amerikanka* to the assembled clergy and out-of-town guests as the group's vice-president. Standing with her glass raised, on the other side of the large hall, she publicly called on me to do the same.

Barely recovering from one initiation into Russian life, I was thrust headlong into another. I'd heard virtually nothing about our fraternal society since its formation, over two years earlier. As far as I knew, it had never had a second meeting. Nor did it have any officers. In my understanding, it was mainly used by Natasha as a quasi-official umbrella for her varied activities in Belaya. Nevertheless, having been introduced as its vice-president, on that auspicious day, I was obliged to somehow respond.

Gripping the table with one hand for support, holding my glass in the other, I managed to stand. Lida stood with me, to translate. By then I already knew that factual information, dearly prized by Westerners, mattered little to most Russians. What seemed to really matter, especially at moments like this, was symbolism. I was an American, and one who was, as Natasha liked to tell others, "our American," by which I understood her to mean an American sympathetic to the Russian soul.

Having no idea what to say, and still reeling from the effects of what had transpired less than an hour earlier, I wasn't able to focus on anything but that. In a few sentences, I mentioned the sensation I had had while in the Church of the Icon of the Mother of God of Belaya, the powerful wave of Spirit that had washed over me. I said that it was new to me, I didn't yet understand it, but I took it to be an indication of Russia's spiritual potential. On the basis of that, I made a toast — to the future. Lida, with great aplomb, rearranged my stream of thoughts and concluded with appropriate words of holiday congratulations.

Power Shifts

It rained intermittently throughout our stay in Belaya, casting a gloomy spell at times, but the weather was of little concern. My gaze was largely fixed on the "program," as our week-long sojourn was called. It turned out that 1995 was a double jubilee year, and thus our program had a dual focus. The first was the 600th anniversary of a miracle alleged to have changed the course of Russian — and possibly European — history; the second was a birthday. It was the 125th anniversary of the birth of Ivan Bunin, the first Russian to win the Nobel Prize for literature.

The simple act of combining these two anniversaries revealed something about the Russian psyche. What united them was the town. Belaya was the place where the Mother of Christ had purportedly saved Russia by appearing in the dream of a Mongol invader, and where Bunin had gone to school as a boy. On the third day, the program abruptly switched gears, moving from the realm of religion to that of culture, with the start of a conference on Bunin. That gave it a more "scientific" character, in the Soviet vernacular, and brought comfort to local Communist Party officials, who in the end had given their support to the celebrations.

This support took many forms. The town administration provided a week's lodgings and meals at the hotel for over a hundred out-of-town guests: Natasha's spiritual network plus dozens of Bunin scholars from around the country. The mayor finally agreed to close the city's main arteries to traffic during the religious procession, something he had once vigorously opposed. Plus three tour buses — escorted by police vehicles with flashing blue lights — were provided for Bunin-related events that took place outside the town.

Making sense of things, logically, was a challenge. Bunin had fled Russia in protest against the Bolsheviks, forced by their revolution to abandon his beloved motherland, the inspiration for much of his writing. When he received the Nobel Prize in 1933, he was living in exile in France, condemned as a traitor by the Soviet Union. His works had been strictly banned until well after Stalin's death in 1953. Later on, *some* of his writings were available in limited quantities, but had never been allowed into the schools. Now, however, in a town still dominated by Communists, heirs of the Bolsheviks, Bunin was being repatriated, with great pride, as a native son.

A huge portrait of the writer, painted on cloth, was draped across the stage of the auditorium where the conference took place. Sitting on the dais, on opening day, was a curious mix of speakers. There were priests, including Father Dmitry of Belaya and Father Vladimir of Altai. There were politicians, including the mayor, and his boss, the regional administrator. There were academics, notably the head of the pedagogical institute, the town's highest institution of learning. And there were members of our *zemlyachestvo*: Natasha, another Moscow writer, and a Serbian poet. I was also a speaker, but chose to sit in the audience.

A few days before leaving home for this trip, Lida had sent me a warning that Natasha expected me to speak at "the conference." From prior experience I knew that refusing Natasha's requests was like swimming against a raging current. So I had prepared, hesitatingly, under the impression that the conference was about spirituality, since it was connected to the 600th Anniversary, which I understood to be connected, in Natasha's mind, with the spiritual regeneration of Russia. That was all I knew. No one had ever mentioned Bunin.

Trying to comprehend what was happening that morning was like trying to put together a jigsaw puzzle whose main pieces were missing. I would have been completely at a loss without Lida at my side, filling in gaps in my understanding and sharing, at times, my own amazement. The irony was classically Russian: inherent contradictions that evoke either despair or raucous laughter, depending on one's perspective. When my turn came, I gave my talk, as prepared, about spirituality. On a human level, realizing how out of synch I was with the actual event, I felt closer to despair. The humor came later.

Much of the week passed in that state, akin to living inside a bubble of surrealism. Everywhere, it seemed, there was a juxtaposition of opposites. And everything, it turned out, had been recorded — permanently preserved, on videotape. The camera's lens had captured bird's-eye views of all that transpired, magnifying details that had been impossible to see at the time. Toward the end of our stay in Belaya, a special screening was arranged at Natasha's request. The video crew was on the staff of the new historical-cultural society, a pet project of hers, i.e. of our *zemlyachestvo*, and they were more than happy to comply.

The video was riveting, starting with the first morning of the holiday at the cathedral. The two highest local officials, the Communist mayor and regional administrator, had been present, standing in places of honor near the main altar. What caught the cameraman's eye was the visual asymmetry between them and the clergy. The local chiefs, as they were called, faded into insignificance in their drab gray suits and dark ties, optically swallowed up by the peacock blue robes and colorful headgear of the clergy. The Metropolitan, a man of immense girth, wore a bejeweled, multi-tiered crown which made him tower over everyone else. The chiefs appeared small and alien by comparison.

As the scene continued, the chiefs, also called "the suits," appeared increasingly uncomfortable. Their expressions suggested they would have happily exited if there had been a way out. While standing in a place where they were easily observed by much of the congregation, a good slice of the local population, it was clear that neither had attended a church service before. They didn't know which gestures to make or when, and appeared confused about whether or not to make the sign of the cross, which was made with great frequency by Russian worshippers.

Father Dmitry tried to clue them in, whispering instructions in the ear of the mayor, who passed them on to the administrator. Still they fumbled a lot, bowing their heads and gesturing out of synch with everyone else. Much of the time they looked like wooden soldiers, standing ramrod straight and staring directly ahead. The mayor had the expression of an embarrassed school boy who hadn't done his homework. The administrator looked enraged, like a superior about to seek vengeance against the underling who put him there.

The screening room was quite small, barely large enough for three chairs belonging to the video staff members who worked there. Natasha, Lida and I occupied those chairs while the person handling the controls stood behind us. From the start, we laughed out loud. With each passing scene, peals of laughter erupted more frequently and raucously, soon drawing people from neighboring offices to come and discover the source. They arrived one by one, the last few pressed against the doorway, poking their heads in to see.

The humor came from the unmistakable awkwardness of the men in gray suits. Only a few years earlier, they had been totally in control. No one dreamed that the Communist Party would ever lose the power it held, absolute power backed by nuclear weapons that made them rulers of a super-power and an empire. In 1995, people were still skeptical about the *apparent* end of totalitarianism. They couldn't quite believe that the USSR, a seemingly impenetrable fortress, could dissolve so suddenly. There remained an underlying suspicion that somehow, some day, the authoritarian regime would resurrect itself.

In light of that, the continuous blundering of "the suits" was all the more hilarious. The video seemed to offer confirmation of their loosening grip on power. Under the old system, one of the pillars of absolute power was control of information. Communist Party officials were the ones "in the know." In the video, not only did they appear shrunken in size next to the clergy, but they were conspicuously *not* in the know. Maintaining a semblance of dignity depended on whispered cues from people, clergymen, completely outside their ken.

The laughter ebbed and flowed during hours of unedited tape. There were moments of almost uncontrollable hilarity. At the center of it all, laughing until she cried, frequently wiping tears from her cheeks, was Natasha. It was she who had arranged for the politicians to be honored in this way at the cathedral's 600th anniversary celebration. Their prominent positioning was the outcome of a deal she had brokered in the final hour to gain their cooperation. Until then, for well over a year, they had presented enormous obstacles. Watching them squirm, she revealed between bursts of laughter, was her "sweet revenge."

As the screening continued, something else leapt out at me, one of myriad details. I noticed an unsettling expression on the face of the "big boss," the regional administrator. There was a disconcerting hardness in his eyes. The mayor, by contrast, looked all the more like an innocent school boy. The big boss reminded me of the men in black hats who used to appear atop Lenin's mausoleum in Red Square on official Soviet holidays. Severe, unsmiling faces of Communist Party bosses formed my image of the Soviet Union from childhood. They were frightening then, and now.

What alarmed me about such faces was an icy coldness which bespoke the potential for brutality. There were no traces of softness, kindness, gentleness. It came as a surprise, somehow, to encounter such a face in Belaya, a place where people on the whole seemed open and welcoming. Even more surprising was what the big Party chief did while he was in Belaya, something which the video crew had recorded for posterity.

During the ceremonies at the Church of the Icon of the Mother of God, following the procession through the town, a new alliance had been born. At the time, I was standing too far back to observe it. In full view of the church-goers, the Party chief with the hard eyes knelt down before the Metropolitan, right next to the altar. The Metropolitan leaned over him, made the sign of the cross,

NANCY SEIFER

and planted a kiss on the top of his head. As the chief rose to his feet, the Metropolitan embraced him three times, as a brother in faith.

In the merriment overtaking the screening room, no one else seemed to notice. But as scenes of unintended humor kept unfolding, I began to have a sense of foreboding. The kiss on the head seemed to signal an unholy alliance of the kind filling newspapers at the time. Stories appeared regularly about priests blessing everything from mafia-run enterprises to new Mercedes Benzes, in exchange for rubles to fill empty church coffers. Could the regional chief have had a sudden conversion experience? Or was the Metropolitan, responsible for the same geographical region, selling his blessings?

In Russia, it is always hard to know whether to believe what you see. People are subject to sudden changes of heart and mind. It is common for a person to abruptly change course without notice or explanation. Moreover, Russians had been taught by centuries of suffering that it was safer to hide one's true feelings, to give the appearance of satisfying the will of "the authorities," to go with the prevailing winds. Assuming, however, that the chief had not experienced a genuine conversion, it seemed reasonable to conclude that Communist power, even in the provinces, was already feeling obliged to bow to the Church, at least for public consumption.

I couldn't help wondering where Christ was in all of this. It was impossible to know for certain, but there was at least the appearance of party politics in new garb. This raised new questions about the people who were trying to deepen my understanding of the Russian soul and its church. Was Father Dmitry, for example, really the man of God he appeared to be? Natasha, who constantly sang his praises, was by then working closely with him to realize the vision of Father Alexei, her spiritual father, who by reputation was almost saintly. Yet Father Dmitry was under the thumb of the Metropolitan, who increasingly resembled a venal politician.

Unraveling the hidden truth was beyond my ken. Plus, I reasoned, it was not necessarily germane to the story I would eventually tell. I had gone to Belaya to find more clues to the mystery of the Russian soul, to better understand the prophecies about the nation's destiny. I had come away with a new experience of the "workings" of Spirit and a clearer apprehension of things I had previously known about only from books. My focus was on long-term potentials, on the expression of a nation's soul in the distant future. The content of individual souls was outside my purview, or so I told myself at the time.

Toasts

During our week in Belaya, we made two day-long outings to nearby sites. One day was entirely devoted to Bunin. It began with places he had once lived — locales, actually, since barely a trace remained of the manor houses of the land-owning aristocracy to which he had been born. One site, marked only by a simple stone memorial to Bunin, was a wide stretch of undulating land where peasants were harvesting potatoes. Another, a small village where Bunin scholars hoped to erect a museum, contained a row of simple huts and fragments of stone foundations. The villagers sang and danced in colorful costumes to celebrate the writer's 125th birthday.

On the afternoon of that day, a banquet in honor of Bunin was held for the "visiting dignitaries," three busloads full. The site was a building literally in the middle of nowhere. No other structures were visible for miles around. The building's normal function was not clear, as no office fixtures or furnishings were readily apparent. On that day, it served as an enormous banquet hall for a meal the likes of which I had never seen. The extravagance was especially conspicuous since many Russians, at that time, were fighting starvation.

When we arrived, three long rows of tables with settings on both sides were covered with large platters of food. There were roast suckling pigs decorated with curlicues of butter, placed at short intervals along each table, plus trays overflowing with tropical fruits, a variety of salads, quiche-like cheese pies, meat pies, sausages. These were the appetizers. Two full courses followed, plus soup, before the cake to honor Bunin. Vodka bottles were frequently emptied and replaced, along with brandy, wine and beer.

Considering the quantities of alcohol imbibed, there was very little fracas. Aside from one rather dramatic incident, the diners were exceedingly quiet. By the end, some of the older men were actually asleep at their seats, heads slumped into their chests. This incident, however, was painful to watch. It involved Natasha's husband, Misha, a helpless alcoholic. His condition, which had worsened in the four years since I'd first met him, had recently forced him to relinquish his professorial post at a graduate school of drama.

Misha had a childlike nature. He often seemed more like a son to Natasha than a husband, though he was in his sixties by then. When inebriated, which he nearly always was, he became especially playful, rapping out tunes on the table with his fingers, singing loudly, uttering fragments of anecdotes. That day he was like a kid in a candy store. Alcohol was served by the bottle, bottles at a time, and he consumed all that was set before him. As the afternoon wore on, he began singing at the top of his lungs and muttering nonsense. People craned their necks to look.

Natasha was mortified. Her efforts to quiet him down were useless. Misha seemed completely oblivious. Exasperated, she called upon a close friend for help, a man sitting next to Misha who was very familiar with his condition. The friend removed the cluster of bottles in front of Misha, at which point Misha became livid. He let out a howl so loud that everyone in the room, well over a hundred people, including the local functionaries and Bunin scholars, turned to stare. It was a terrible moment.

A beautiful actress from Moscow saved the day, a compassionate soul who was there to perform in a tribute to Bunin. She had large blue eyes, sculpted blond hair that perfectly framed her round face, and an angelic smile. After Misha's howl, she stood up in the center of the hall, raised her glass, and announced that she wanted to make a toast — to Misha. Calling him a truly great director, she expressed her heartfelt gratitude to him for having given her, years earlier, her first big break in theater. Then she helped him to his feet, engaged him in a little jig, and raised his hand in hers in a sort of victory salute.

The tension in the room dissipated instantly. Misha dropped back into his seat with a faint smile on his face. People continued eating and drinking. Natasha was visibly relieved that a nightmare had been averted. But the joviality in the air at the start of the meal was gone. An unhappy fact of Natasha's life was now known in the provinces. People who visited her in Moscow were aware of Misha's condition; her close friends often helped him to bed. But this was a public event.

Shortly after the incident, the guests staggered outside in the late afternoon sun and boarded buses for the return trip to Belaya. Nearly everyone was inebriated and stuffed to the gills. The ride was about a half-hour long. An hour later, there came a knock on the door of our hotel room. Someone had come to tell Lida and me that Father Dmitry, unbeknownst to any of us, had been expecting Natasha's friends for dinner. Amazingly, most of the group, minus Misha, managed to rouse themselves. Neither Lida nor I could contemplate another meal, but in the end we decided to go.

For me, the main attraction of these dinners, which took place several times that week, was Father Dmitry himself. The genuineness that came across in his sermons was equally evident in the more relaxed, informal setting of his small refectory. He had a habit of speaking truth in a place where honest public speech was rare. And he seemed truly unconcerned about the consequences.

Curiously, it was the ritual of toast-making that created the arena for Father Dmitry's thoughts and opinions. There was a protocol for making toasts at these dinners, which lasted between two and three hours. At varying intervals during the evening, a guest who felt moved to do so would rise and face the head-priest, our host, raising his or her glass. Father Dmitry would recognize the person; he or she would propose a toast; everyone would raise a glass; and all would drink. While most male guests drank "to the bottom," Father Dmitry would take a small sip of wine. And then he would offer a response.

Given the nature of the holiday, the reason for the presence of Natasha's friends in Belaya, many toasts were proposed to Russia's spiritual revival, or to the rebirth of Russian Orthodoxy. Each time that happened, repeatedly throughout the week, Father Dmitry would immediately correct the speaker, like a teacher mildly scolding his pupils. He would say, "Russian spirituality has *not* been revived; we are only taking the first step," or "The Russian Orthodox Church has *not* been reborn; only the buildings are being restored. The rest depends on the content of people's souls."

At one of these dinners, several nights after the 600th anniversary, a completely different kind of interchange occurred between the priest and another actress from Moscow. The actress, named Alexandra, trembled slightly as she stood and raised her glass. Her "toast" was actually a personal statement that rambled a bit. It started with a prophecy made many years earlier by a clairvoyant believer, about Alexandra's new spiritual theater troupe, which had come true; it ended with her experience of being in Belaya, which mystified her. She said she had felt the presence of God while in church there more strongly than ever before, and that at various times and places she had found herself weeping, inexplicably.

Father Dmitry responded like a tender, loving parent, acknowledging and encouraging his child's development. He said to Alexandra, "If someone is able to weep in church, that means the bliss of God has entered the person's heart. I can *see* that you have experienced the presence of God, and that you are carrying the spirit of God with you now." Alexandra's eyes were filled with tears as she sat down. The atmosphere was rather solemn. Then Father Dmitry had an afterthought. In a lighthearted nod to new age jargon, he said, "I can see you've received a powerful impulse of energy — from the universe." Everyone burst out laughing.

Those evenings in Father Dmitry's small refectory, with groups of fifteen or twenty guests, offered rare glimpses of the possibilities of *sobornost*. One had the sense of being in the presence of someone who was in the presence of God, and who thus evoked the highest from everyone else. It wasn't a question of being on "good behavior" or currying favor with an authority figure, as Father Dmitry was not that for the guests who were there that week. Many would likely never return to Belaya or see him again. There was something else.

Many Russians have a finely honed sense of intuition. In a country where rules are made to be broken and rulers change their minds on a whim, intuition about whom to trust is a survival mechanism. The people attending those dinners seemed to trust Father Dmitry, and to respect him deeply. By the end of the week, some saw him as a spiritual teacher. He was able to stir their souls, rousing them to be better, more mindful of truth and goodness. He did that in part by confessing his own imperfections. Once, when talking about his health problems, he linked them to the Mother of God. He spoke of her as a loving mother who was helping him, through his physical weaknesses, to learn humility.

Intrigued by this man, I wanted to learn more about his origins. He granted me the first interview he had ever given, in part, no doubt, because I was *not* Russian. Priests were of little interest to the local intelligentsia, almost none of whom attended church — because they were atheists and because they believed the Church had forfeited any claim to moral authority during the Communist era. Moreover, the Church forbade priests to discuss anything personal. Father Dmitry had never spoken about his life to anyone outside his family, and did so with great reluctance.

The story of his early life revealed an interesting, little known side of 20th century Russia. He was born at the end of World War II in a small Siberian town. His father, a school teacher, had died when he was six and his mother was soon remarried to a man who drank heavily, and who was cruel and abusive to him. At eight he decided to leave home and live with his paternal grandmother, whom he dearly loved. She was a devout believer who took him to church, taught him how to pray, and gave him a crucifix to wear.

The crucifix placed him in serious jeopardy at school. It evoked angry taunts from other children, who were taught that Jesus Christ was an imaginary being, a fictional character, and that people who believed in him and his religion became slaves. The crucifix also aroused the fury of the principal, who warned the boy of dire consequences if he continued wearing it. He ignored the warnings. One day the principal ripped the chain from his neck and threatened him with expulsion.

The situation continued. The principal came close to killing him once. In a spasm of anger, he had picked up a desk and thrown it at the child. He survived, returned to school, and the cycle of violence resumed. Finally the police were called in and took him into custody. The boy, then nine years old, declared to the police that no matter what they did to him, he would never stop wearing his crucifix. Eventually they let him go, and the defeated principal left him alone.

Our interview was far shorter than I would have liked, but it offered some clues to the mystery of Father Dmitry's unusual moral courage, his steely determination to speak the truth. If I had had the time, as well as the nerve, I would have wanted to ask him whether it was true that the KGB had infiltrated *all* churches and whether, assuming he had refused to report the names of his parishioners, he had been personally threatened. I left with the strong impression that he would have faced them down, as well.

Paradoxically, the authorities who caused him the most trouble in his adult years were those in the Russian Orthodox Church. He had run afoul of them repeatedly, during the communist era, when the Church was under strict surveillance. His main transgression was speaking with parishioners who came to him with their troubles, many of which, naturally, were caused by the state. By offering words of counsel, or consolation, or doing anything beyond conducting officially sanctioned rites, Father Dmitry had knowingly put himself at risk. He was transferred, repeatedly, by superiors who deemed he was "too friendly" with parishioners.

By the time he appeared in Belaya, during the final months of Soviet rule, he had suffered many small crucifixions that might have broken a lesser man. But his faith appeared to have rendered him fearless, at least when it came to the wrath of human beings.

Four years into his tenure there, he had evidently aroused the enmity of his superior, the Metropolitan, nervous about Father Dmitry's connection with Natasha and, through her, members of Moscow's cultural élite. The Metropolitan, who had turned out to be a major political player, was irate about the dinners in the refectory for "outsiders"— despite their edifying toasts.

Toward the end of the holiday week, Father Dmitry was threatened with another transfer. Soon thereafter, he suffered a heart attack. I was amazed to find him still there the following year, appearing absolutely undaunted. One could see his courage in the simplest gestures, though he was thin and almost frail-looking in everyday clothes. In his clerical robes he looked regal. It was easy envision him as a monarch of an earlier age. He was a person who seemed to answer to no one, except his God.

Native Saints

Most of the roads leading out of Belaya to nearby towns and villages were unpaved. Some may once have been paved, but had not been for a long time. In a curious way, the poor condition of the roads turned trips of any length into adventures. There was always the chance of a mishap or breakdown along the way. When a vehicle arrived at its destination in one piece, with all the passengers in tact, there was a general sense of relief, even gratitude. Nothing in Russia could be taken for granted.

During that same week, in September '95, we made an outing to Zadonsk, a small town with the feel of a village. It was known for its monastery, and for the great soul who had spent the end of his life there. Tikhon of Zadonsk, called Tikhon Zadonsky, had died over two centuries earlier, and the monastery had been totally desecrated. Soviet authorities had used it as a prison labor camp, and an insane asylum, among other things. But it had once been a very holy place, due to miracles attributed to Tikhon, one of Russia's greatest saints.

Thanks to Dostoyevsky, the light of Tikhon's soul had radiated across the vast expanse of Russia, and ultimately around the world. Tikhon was the original model for the holy Elder in *The Brothers Karamazov*. The writer, having devoted much of his life to novels about social evils and personal pathologies, had become irresistibly drawn to the idea of depicting absolute goodness. He set for himself the challenge of portraying a "wholly good man" in the novel which he sensed, prophetically, would be his last.

Tikhon died nearly fifty years before Dostoyevsky was born, but had left a large body of writings. Before retiring to the life of a simple monk, a life he had fervently desired but was repeatedly denied by superiors, Tikhon had been rapidly promoted up the ranks of the Russian Orthodox hierarchy. In his thirties, he had become Bishop of Voronezh, where he encountered a morally and educationally impoverished clergy. He took it upon himself to instruct them in the basics of religion, and to educate the laity as well, through ecclesiastical texts and popular pamphlets on wide-ranging topics that included child-rearing in the spirit of Christ.

Tikhon's writings and sermons, which had filled a great void in 18th century Russia, were widely circulated. Dostoyevsky had been deeply touched by their wisdom, compassion, and moral courage. As Bishop, Tikhon had often used his sermons to condemn serfdom — both the institution which permitted "one soul to own another," and the unconscionable treatment of serfs by their landlords. He spoke of serfs as brothers in Christ, reminding his listeners, many of whom were wealthy landowners, of their shared humanity. When Tikhon died, tens of thousands of serfs traveled from all corners of Russia, in simple horse-drawn carts and on foot, to be present at his funeral in Zadonsk.

Near the end of Dostoyevsky's life, as he began work on *The Brothers Karamazov*, he actually met a wholly good man, a second model for his character. The encounter took place at the legendary monastery of Optina Pustyn, not far from Zadonsk. Dostoyevsky had journeyed there from St. Petersburg in the wake of the greatest personal tragedy in a life marked by suffering and sorrow. He had yearned to meet Optina's renowned Elders, but hadn't found a chance to make the difficult journey until the loss of his youngest son. Inconsolable over the death of his beloved child to epilepsy, inherited from him, he was finally persuaded to go there.

Optina Pustyn was the center of enlightened spirituality in mid-19th century Russia. Its Elders were men whose spiritual authority derived from a recognition, by their fellow monks, of their illumination. The role of the Elders had nothing to do with ecclesiastical rankings, though they were monks, and often priests as well. It was based solely on inner, spiritual attainment. One of the most important aspects of their role was "spiritual direction," a practice that depended heavily upon the gift of clairvoyance. They had the capacity to "read" a person's soul, to know his or her destined life path, and to offer appropriate guidance.

The Elder whom Dostoyevsky encountered at Optina was Amvrosy, considered the greatest of all the Elders. Though burdened by serious illness from youth, he followed an extraordinary regimen that included conducting formal prayers and rites, translating religious texts from Greek and other languages into Russian, providing spiritual direction to all who placed their souls in his care, and offering words of consolation to pilgrims — hundreds each day — who traveled long distances and waited for hours, even days, to see him. According to Dostoyevsky's wife, the writer returned home feeling consoled by Elder Amvrosy, and having acquired new material for his final work.

Tikhon and Amvrosy were both canonized, nearly a century after their deaths. Amvrosy was among the first newly declared Russian saints in the post-communist era. Miracles had been attributed to both men, during their lives and after their deaths. Like Elder Zosima in *The Brothers Karamazov*, the character largely drawn from them both, they had manifested the highest spirituality — offering glimpses of the superhuman kingdom while still on earth in human form. Such souls had always fascinated Russians. The lives of saints, the most popular reading material of earlier centuries, were again being widely read on the eve of the new millennium.

Our day in Zadonsk, from all appearances, was utterly blissful for the members of our group. It seemed especially so for Natasha, who had arranged it. She adored Tikhon, in the inimitable way in which Russians adore their saints. It appeared rather different from expressions of religious adoration in Catholic countries like Italy, for example, where the adoration of saints is also widespread.

Among Russian believers, I noticed an unusual mixture of worshipful devotion and personal affection — the kind of affection usually expressed in intimate friendships between equals.

That was how Natasha loved Tikhon. During a walk through a thickly wooded area on the monastery grounds, she led me to an old oak tree whose tall, leafy branches towered over a rushing stream. Legend had it that Tikhon used to lean against that very tree, watching the stream flow by, while composing his writings. Natasha approached the tree and placed the palms of her hands on its massive trunk. Holding them there, her eyes dancing with joy, she invited me to do the same, as if she were presenting me to a beloved old friend. Her gestures indicated that I, too, in this manner, could absorb some of his spirit.

A few yards away, the believers in our group were bathing in a holy spring with the same kind of zeal. The spring had been discovered by Tikhon during a time of severe drought and had long ago been deemed to have curative powers. The bathing took place inside a tiny wooden shed enclosing a small pool fed by the stream. As the pool was only large enough for one person at a time, a line formed outside. Despite gray skies and a chill in the air, and despite the fact that no one had a towel, most of my fellow travelers were eager to dowse themselves in the pool, three times, according to Orthodox custom.

They disrobed before submerging themselves, but might as well not have bothered since their dripping wet hair and bodies completely saturated the dry clothes they put on afterward. Yet as they stood around with their teeth chattering, trying with little success to wring the water from their hair and clothes, they looked utterly joyful. And they proceeded on to another shed where holy water was piped in for drinking. In a state of ecstasy, they drank it by the cupful, feeling purified and blessed, both inside and out, by Tikhon's spring.

Two young nuns with beautiful faces gave us a tour of the monastery, whose rehabilitation had been voluntarily undertaken by a corps of them. Remarkably, they had managed to restore an aura of purity and sanctity, removing all traces of the century's desecrations. They allowed us to enter the tiny monk's cell where Tikhon had spent his final years, while they stood guard at the door, eyes lowered in an attitude of reverence. It was a holy shrine now, simple and humble, in keeping with Tikhon's profound dislike of grandiosity and lavishness.

Some distance away, workers were busily, noisily reconstructing buildings next to the main church, which had already been restored. Designed by the master church architect of the 19th century, it was freshly painted an azure blue with white trim, dazzling to the eye. Pilgrims who had traveled to Zadonsk long after Tikhon's death, in hopes of receiving blessings and healings, had financed this church through their small offerings. Ironically Tikhon, who railed against ornate churches, often erected by wealthy merchants to impress others while God's children languished in poverty, would have found it far too grand and ostentatious.

Inside this church, in an alcove near the main altar, were Tikhon's remains. As a special concession to the visiting dignitaries, the priest had allowed the top of the sepulcher to be removed. Visitors were permitted to file by and touch the shroud covering the saint's corpse, which was said to be unusually well preserved. According to Orthodox tradition, this was a blessing of the highest order. Many of the Bunin scholars, presumed to be non-believers, availed themselves of it, along with the members of Natasha's contingent.

Standing back and observing, the thought crossed my mind, as it had on similar occasions, that the "godless era" had been largely an illusion. Our day at Zadonsk seemed to offer further proof that Marxism-Leninism and scientific materialism had only thinly, temporarily, masked the deeply religious soul of the nation. Academics in literature and history — all of whom were called "scientific" workers in Soviet times to stress the objective nature of their work — were visibly caught up that day in the unsolved mysteries of Spirit.

The whole day was about the mystical, the supernatural, everything the communists had tried to erase from the Russian psyche on the grounds that it was anti-scientific and thus regressive.

Now there were signs that the post-communist intelligentsia, at least a segment of it, might come to resemble the pre-Revolutionary one in certain ways. In this regard, Russia differed fundamentally from the West, where mysticism and science — spiritual experience and objective knowledge — remained strictly divorced.

It was interesting to contemplate what this could mean for Russia and Russians. Tikhon Zadonsky, a man who had become a saint, was alive in the minds and hearts of many visitors to Zadonsk that day. Speaking with some of them, I sensed they related to Tikhon as a person, a soul who had passed that way before, and who had demonstrated the Way. The literal meaning of the word for saint in Russian is "becoming like." Tikhon and other native saints had inspired Russian Godseekers, over the centuries, to try to become like them, as they had been inspired to become like Christ.

I found it hard to imagine what it might be like to grow up in a place where holy men and women had sprung from the same soil. In our secular culture, the word "saint" was mainly used as an epithet for a truly good, self-sacrificing person. The spiritual process of transfiguration, and the possibility that human beings *could* manifest divine attributes, were largely alien concepts to Americans, with notable exceptions. The wisdom teachings state, however, that such attributes become apparent near the end of every soul's evolutionary journey.

On first reflection, having native saints seemed to be a considerable "advantage" for Russian seekers. But then my mind flipped to the other pole of Russian life — the darkness that has characterized most of Russian history. The existence of innumerable holy people on Russian soil had apparently done little to counteract that darkness. Perhaps, I mused, extreme goodness manifested itself to counterbalance extreme evil. I began to see Russia as the stage of a cosmic dance, or mystery play, in which good and evil were continually at war. Sadly, at the end of every intense battle, they appeared to go their separate ways.

Gifts

Our last day in Belaya began with a tour of Father Dmitry's works-in-progress — the reconstruction of many of the town's churches. Only Natasha, Lida and I remained at that point; the rest of the out-of-towners had already gone home. Natasha had requested this tour, wanting us to see the incredible progress made by Father Dmitry. He had been nick-named "Father-Builder" by his parishioners, for undoing much of the century's damage with remarkable skill and speed. Most of the local churches that had survived the communist era were rotting hulks when he arrived.

He was passionate about this work, eager to remove the stain of the godless era and redeem all that he possibly could. While driving through the town, a wounded expression appeared on his face each time we passed a church still lying in ruins, and there were many for a town that size. Before the Revolution, Belaya had had close to forty houses of worship, including a Jewish synagogue. The town evidently had many wealthy merchants who sought to "glorify themselves," in the words of Saint Tikhon.

The newest of Father Dmitry's projects stood on the top of a hill in a quiet, residential area overlooking the town. Two lone workmen, one of whom was clearly inebriated by mid-morning, were beginning the awesome process of transforming an enormous, rubble-strewn lot into a sacred space. The head-priest appeared familiar with every inch of wall, floor and ceiling, having carefully studied what could be salvaged and what could not. It was up to him to find resources for all necessary replacements.

Clearing a path through mounds of rubble, skirting the edges of rough-hewn scaffolding made of raw timber fastened with rope, he led us to an alcove free of debris. On one wall, faint outlines of a fresco were visible. It appeared to be a large face. On closer inspection, one could discern an oval-shaped visage adorned with locks of hair in the style commonly used in Russian icons to depict Christ. Pointing to the area where the eyes had once been, a look of anguish flashed across Father Dmitry's face. There were two deep indentations in the wall, indicating that someone had gone to the trouble of gouging out the eyes.

At the end of the tour we were invited to lunch at Father Dmitry's new residence. Under orders from the Metropolitan, he and his wife and daughter had recently moved into a huge two-story building with a private chapel in the courtyard that was dubbed "the palace." Built by a philanthropic merchant not long before the Revolution, it had been intended as a home for orphans and the elderly. The building contained two large kitchens, one per floor, and countless rooms of varying sizes. "The Metropolitan's room," reserved for his official visits to Belaya, was large enough to have housed a dozen children.

Two months earlier, Father Dmitry's family had been moved out of its modest apartment and resettled there, as a kind of occupying force. "The palace" was part of the transfer of properties from state to church that got underway in 1990. The Orthodox hierarchy evidently feared that if left unoccupied, the building might be repossessed. Thus the head-priest of Belaya, used to living in simplicity, had been ordered to inhabit a setting elaborate enough for a 19th century nobleman's family, and intended as an institution.

The whole situation was filled with question marks and exclamation points. No one seemed to know quite what to make of it, including Father Dmitry. With a slightly bemused expression, he showed us through the facilities on both floors. Each time he opened the door to another room, the sense of irony grew stronger.

Not only was the size of the building preposterous for one family, but there was a clear if unspoken realization that the current occupants could be dismissed as readily as they had been summoned; that the lord of the manor was only temporary. In the meantime, however, for as long as he was there, this was home.

After a superb meal prepared and served by Father Dmitry's wife and daughter, who also kept up "the palace" and ran the cathedral's extraordinary choir, we moved to a sitting room. *Batushka*, the familiar form of "Father," had said that he wanted to give us "a few souvenirs" to take home. Natasha, Lida and I were seated on a divan in front of a long, low wooden table. *Batushka* went from one to another of the room's three large armoires, opening and closing the doors, carrying armfuls of things over to the table. This happened several times, until the table was overflowing. It was as though he could not stop himself from going back and bringing us more until there was no more space on the table to hold it.

There were so many gifts and some were so heavy that I wondered how we could possibly carry them to the train, and from the train to Natasha's apartment. Lying on the table were several large sacks of oranges, bags of kiwis, bottles of wine, boxes of chocolate, an assortment of beautiful books and photos of Belaya (featuring the cathedral), and finally, for each of us, a magnificent hand-painted lacquer box specially made for the historic 600th anniversary. It was a display of Russian generosity on a scale that dazzled and bewildered.

Questions arose, naturally — the kinds of questions that I dared not raise with Natasha for fear of offending her. In the scheme of things, the gifts may not have amounted to all that much but in Russia at that time an orange, just one orange, was a luxury for almost everyone. And local churches were increasingly under pressure to stand on their own financially, as the central Orthodox hierarchy had decided to cut off the money supply for restorations.

In fact, the hierarchy had recently turned the tables. An elderly priest whom Natasha had known for years had confided to her, in a state of despair, that the hierarchy had been pressuring local parish churches to send money to *them*. That pressure sent this priest into retirement after forty years in the priesthood. He could not in good conscience ask anything more of his poor parishioners, many of whom were pensioners, barely surviving, and already squeezing out their last kopecks for the church. From his point of view, the moral issues faced by priests at that time were even more compromising than during the communist era.

Nevertheless, as we bid farewell to Father Dmitry, sharing the weight of his gifts, we all felt joyful. It was the kind of joy I imagined that a well-loved child might experience at Christmastime. The pure delight produced by each successive gift accumulates to the point where it seems it can grow no more, yet it does. The stream of gifts expands until the child experiences what feels like an endless river of parental love. I could sense the elation of my friends, accompanied by a childlike sense of wonder, especially in light of the general impoverishment of those times. This was not the moment to inquire about "adult" things, such as where the gifts had come from.

On the train back to Moscow that evening the mood was subdued. Misha was in a drunken stupor, asleep in Natasha's compartment. Lida and I occupied our own compartment; the two other couchettes were empty. In those days fewer people could afford to travel by train and entire compartments often remained vacant. The most memorable event on the return trip was a stop at the station near Leo Tolstoy's estate. Natasha found an old woman selling large bags of apples for a pittance, just to buy some bread. She paid the woman twice what she had asked for and returned to the train in a rage, declaring she was ready to "go to the barricades" to protest against capitalism. It was, to her, a pure manifestation of evil.

Upon arriving in Moscow the next morning we faced a dilemma. It was physically impossible for us to transport all the parcels via the metro, yet taxi drivers had become highway robbers, which infuriated Natasha. Finally, the four of us, packed in tightly with Father Dmitry's gifts, took a taxi home to Natasha's apartment. It was also home to Lida, when she was in Moscow, and had become home to me as well. The last time I had stayed in a hotel I had been chastised, picked up and brought "home." Since then, the subject was not open for discussion.

That year, 1995, was the year after the death of Natasha's mother. I was given the room that had been hers. Next-door to this spacious room, filled with photos and momentos of the life of a high-level Soviet official, there lived one of the most unusual human beings I had ever met. She was called Baba Anya. *Baba*, the diminutive of *babushka*, grandmother, also means old woman. Baba Anya, then in her seventies, had never married. From the time she was eighteen, she had been a surrogate mother to Natasha, who was five years old at the time. Natasha's father had been declared an "enemy of the people" and dragged away by the police. Before setting out to find him, her mother had visited a nearby village to find someone to care for her daughter. She returned with Anya.

Baba Anya was nearly illiterate. She was born in a time when villagers were largely uneducated, learning only the rudiments of reading and writing. But she was wise in a way that few people are, though I've been told there are, or once were, many women like her in Russian villages. She had inner sight that could penetrate the outer veneer of any sophisticated "city person" and discern the quality of his or her soul. Hundreds of people passed through the household over the years. As soon as the visitors left, everyone turned to Baba Anya for her reading of them. Since she never forgot anyone she met, she also became the family's memory bank.

One of the great charms of Baba Anya was her capacity for pure, childlike delight. Funny little things made her laugh so hard that her eyes grew watery and tears spilled down her cheeks. Gifts also had this effect on her. If someone brought her a flower, or an apple, or a piece of candy, her eyes would grow wide with wonder. She would hold the object and turn it around in her hand, savoring it from all sides. Gradually, tears would well up in her eyes and she would let out a sigh. And then she would begin to giggle, making a sound so infectious that everyone around her roared with merriment.

Since the death of Natasha's mother, Baba Anya, whom Natasha considered her "second mother," had become the only one. But she herself was approaching eighty and had been considerably slowed down by a series of hip fractures. Though she was increasingly frail, this diminutive woman, who at times evoked the image of a small bird chirping merrily from up high in the branches of a tree, continued to keep the household running as she had done for sixty years. Despite her waning physical strength, her presence was needed ballast.

The morning we returned from Belaya, Baba Anya was in the kitchen waiting for us. Her deep blue eyes sparkled as she announced that she had prepared one of the family's favorite dishes. It was kasha, but not just any kasha. Baba Anya's kasha was part mystery. The heavy iron casserole in which she cooked it was removed from the oven, wrapped in wide strips of brown paper, then left to set at room temperature for several hours, before it was ceremoniously unwrapped and could finally be eaten. It was delicious.

After a hearty meal and a brief rest, Lida and I went out on a round of errands. The first was a stop at the US Embassy, where we went to learn how to obtain a visitor's visa for Lida. Visiting America was something she had long dreamed about and we were seriously discussing the possibility of her coming to stay at my home. On the way to the embassy, her mood visibly darkened. This sudden shift was an enigma, since I knew what the visit meant to her. She was upset about something, but refused to say what it was. I kept pressing her to talk about it, as the afternoon wore on, until finally she did.

It was a shocking piece of news about Father Dmitry. Having been with him only the day before, in the most convivial atmosphere, it shook the foundations of my sense of reality. Just as we were leaving Natasha's, Lida had learned that the Metropolitan made good on his threat to transfer Father Dmitry. Within hours after we had said goodbye, laden with his bountiful gifts, the last of the holiday visitors to leave Belaya, he had received the fatal call ordering him to pack up his family's belongings and prepare to move. Natasha was distraught. But soon there came the news of his heart attack. So instead of packing, he was being sent to a cardiac clinic in another city. Such were the vicissitudes of Russian life.

Original Sin

The transition to life at home was challenging. Shifting gears between Russian and American realities was always jarring, but never more so than that year. Two months before my departure for Russia, my husband and I had moved from New York City to a suburb of Washington, D.C. The setting was ideal for writing — trees, grass, and quiet. But after a month's immersion in Russian life the silence was almost deafening. Russia was chaotic, tumultuous, often incomprehensible and surreal. Yet while there I was engaged in the human drama in a way that I was not at home.

At the same time, I realized the illusory nature of that drama, in the Buddhist sense. Russian life seemed to involve constant turmoil and suffering. It did not lend itself to reflection *about* life. People were nearly always in the grip of a crisis, whether personal, collective, or both. Yet spiritual growth required the capacity to step back from life, to take the stance of the observer, to become dispassionate. The more I pondered this fact, the harder it was to envision how or when the prophesied future would materialize.

Moreover, as the century drew to a close, Russia's crises grew more menacing. Many people faced joblessness, homelessness, and starvation. Previously, until the final days of the communist era, there had always been a rudimentary level of security. Material crises were of a smaller magnitude. They often took the form of shortages, which meant waiting in long lines every day, or simply doing without. But not being able to buy sugar, or meat, even having to wait ten years for private living space, or a car, were not the same as being too poor to buy bread, or having no heat or electricity, or any shelter at all.

When the Soviet order collapsed, it was as if order *per se* had collapsed. Authoritarian rule had given way to the rule of money and brute force, often in combination. The mafia metastasized rapidly. Ordinary people were suddenly vulnerable to attack, as police were either unequipped to handle the exploding crime rate or bribed to turn their backs. A poet friend of Natasha's had been stabbed to death at her home in broad daylight. Natasha herself had barely escaped a hail of bullets in the metro, where rival gangs were conducting business one afternoon.

In such times, life seemed tragically expendable. Children were abandoned by parents who couldn't feed them. Orphanages overflowed. Cast-offs lived on the streets, surviving by begging, stealing, or worse. AIDS, tuberculosis and other infectious diseases spread like wildfire. Rates of alcoholism, drug addiction, and suicide skyrocketed. The average life span declined, and so did the birth rate, as many couples stopped having children. With every passing year of so-called freedom and democracy, the population of Russia was growing smaller and sicklier.

Life had become nightmarish. Even the robber barons, the so-called oligarchs who "privatized" the vast resources once belonging to "the people" and then stole their meager savings as well, lived in fear, traveling in thick clouds of body guards. "It is impossible to do honest business in Russia" was a constant refrain, yet business ruled everything, including government. It soon contaminated friendships, the milk and honey of Soviet life. Favors that friends had once done freely for one another had taken on monetary valuations. Time for friends became scarce. Everyone was desperate to "find enough money."

For the vast majority of Russians, life was unalleviated struggle. It had always been that way — from serfdom, to communist totalitarianism, to jungle capitalism. Yet the last time thinkers had reflected openly and honestly on social problems was well over a century ago, when the term "intelligentsia" first surfaced. It had been used to describe a group of people who lived for the sake of ideas and ideals. Fueled by the cry for "liberty, equality, and fraternity" of France's revolution, inspired by other social currents in Europe, many Russians had become caught up with the awful oppression of the masses — the serfs at the base of the social pyramid who served a tiny ruling class at the top.

Fatefully, over the course of the 19th and early 20th centuries, a split had occurred within the intelligentsia. One group increasingly turned away from ugly social realities in pursuit of higher knowledge for its own sake, becoming preoccupied with metaphysics, religious philosophy, mysticism, and varied forms of the occult. The other group grew increasingly political, radical and fanatical in response to the monarchy's imperviousness to cries for reform. Long after serfdom had legally ended, in 1861, the Russian masses continued to languish in abject poverty. Violence became inevitable. In the end, after a bloody civil war, the Bolsheviks imposed their version of equality and fraternity through the barrel of a gun.

And on it went into the 20th century. Violence was condoned as a necessary evil. Poor people were terrorized, "brainwashed" some said, into fighting, sometimes killing, rich people and other "enemies" of the new state, in the name of equality. If a neighbor was heard speaking ill of Stalin, the "Good Father struggling to create a happy life for his children," that person was branded an enemy of the people, deserving the severest punishment: imprisonment, torture, sometimes death. Lives were destroyed for telling a joke about Stalin. There was no recourse to justice, logic, and certainly not to truth.

What mattered in such a system was power. Survival depended upon compliance with power, however cruel and arbitrary. The rules were straightforward. Any deviation, however slight, could bring dire consequences. Compliance, on the other hand, meant the possibility of reward. The greatest rewards went to Communist Party members, a tiny fraction of the population represented as the most self-sacrificing and hardest-working members of the socialist state, the precursor of the communist utopia which would provide for everyone's needs, equally.

One had to wonder how such a wretched dictatorship could have resulted from such a noble impulse: to reform a society in which a small aristocracy lived off the unpaid labors of vast numbers of miserably poor souls. In the early 90s, Russians themselves wondered the same. There was a flood of ironic jokes and anecdotes, more tragic than funny, about how Russia perpetually suffered from the law of unintended consequences. The thread running through them was: "Whatever we do ends up the opposite of what was intended. We destroy whatever we touch. And we don't know why."

There was, in those years, a sense of being doomed to failure. The demise of communism exposed a profound inferiority complex — especially vis-à-vis the West, and most of all, America. Some Russians blamed themselves, as a people, for repeatedly fouling things up, yet were completely in the dark as to why. Bouts of self-flagellation were often followed by question marks. It was a pattern reminiscent of abused children who got into trouble, and realized they were to blame, yet didn't understand what made them do what they did.

It was not surprising to learn, then, that child abuse was widespread in Russia, both at home and in the larger society. It was often both physical and emotional. Most children had been negatively programmed in one way or another. Surely, I mused, this must have had something to do with serfdom, with the "horizontal hostility" often displayed by people of an oppressed class toward one another. Perhaps it even dated back as far as the Mongol Yoke. Yet under communism, I discovered, individual self-esteem had been *intentionally* negated in favor of the state. Children were raised to think they had no special inherent value. Parents, teachers, principals, nurses, coaches taught them, more often than not, that they were unworthy of love, praise, or approval.

This one fact, which I discovered belatedly, seemed to account for many inexplicable others. For one thing, it revealed why people generally treated each other so badly, and endured such miserable treatment themselves. Exacerbating the condition was the absence of psychological insight. Until *glasnost*, Soviet psychology was a primitive science focusing on behavioral change — making symptoms disappear. There was no exploration of the causes of problems. Any psychological or spiritual knowledge that could have fostered self-understanding — and thus undermined the catechism of the Communist state — was banned.

The only kind of self-esteem encouraged was collective, and derived from the glories of the state. Achievements in science, industry, education, space, the military, culture, and sports had helped make the suffering and hardship — which defined much of the 20th century — more bearable. To a greater or lesser degree, depending on their age, Russians shared the belief, and took pride in the notion, that the Soviet Union was paving the way for a new human civilization. The suffering masses were made to believe their personal sacrifices were on behalf of all humanity.

During *glasnost,* psychologists who began to receive training in the West were quick to realize that low self-esteem had suited the nefarious purposes of communist totalitarianism. The regime had survived, in part, by having people regard themselves as insignificant cogs in a machine so vast that it could lose many cogs and never even notice. Denying the value of the individual, ascribing no worth to him or her apart from the collective, made it all the easier to manipulate the masses into supporting the goals of the state.

It seemed an unusually cruel form of punishment to undermine self-worth on a national scale. Yet cruelty had been a feature of Russian life since long before the communist century. With sorrow in her eyes, a teacher of metaphysics once observed, "Russia is a place where souls are born who need to learn through suffering." If the earth was a schoolhouse for spiritual growth, and suffering was the main catalyst, then Russia was a hothouse. A 19th century philosopher had described his nation's history as a tale of "blood and mud." Yet Russia had also produced lofty dreams and noble ideals. Communism itself was the dream of creating a "heaven on earth."

Back at home in the States, with the distance of time and space, I found myself reflecting on this "Russian syndrome," coming back to it repeatedly. The juxtaposition of suffering and the pursuit of noble ideals had a familiar ring. I knew from personal experience that the pursuit of ideals could, at least temporarily, be a mask for suffering. In the heart of idealists everywhere lies the hope, conscious or not, that making the world a better place will ease *all* suffering.

But I also knew that outer circumstances mirrored, metaphysically, some aspect of the inner life of the soul. Suffering on the plane of objective reality has inner causes, initially unknown to the sufferer, who feels like a victim of circumstance. But those who suffer continually, or repeatedly, eventually face a crisis when the soul, in utter despair, cries out to a higher power: "What have I done to deserve this?" And a window opens. The realization dawns that one is somehow responsible, even if not conscious of how or why. There emerges a sense of cause and effect, of the past impinging on the present, whether understood as karma, the debt incurred from previous lives, or as "original sin."

In the fall of '95, there was little cause for optimism in regard to Russia, the country, but perhaps there was some, I thought, regarding the Russian soul. More important than the fact that millions of Russians were reading spiritual books, was the fact that many had taken note of the repetitive pattern of suffering in their history and had begun to ask why. Within this group, it seemed fair to assume that some would feel pressed to look for the answer and engage in a serious search for truth. And among those, at least a few, one could reasonably assume, would set their feet squarely on the spiritual path.

There was another related cause for optimism. I had discovered, from life experience and from spiritual studies, that the pursuit of idealistic causes is the stage in the life of a soul that precedes spiritual awakening. Having sensed the futility of idealistic projects aimed at changing "the world," the soul is finally led to the realization that *real* change begins within the individual. The question "What have *I* done?" becomes a turning point, an opening to transformation, which starts with a willingness to face one's inner demons. It seemed logical to think that Russia's current bout of suffering might well, ultimately, spur the awakening of her soul.

Synchronicity

L ida's dream of visiting America came true in the spring of
'96. She had no money whatsoever, but she had benefactors. Her
airfare was paid by a cultural organization linked to Russia that
had just received a bequest and whose director, the person who
originally told me about Lida, was happy to return her kindnesses
to him when he was in Moscow. Her lodging was provided by me
and my husband for a stay that turned into three and a half months.
And there was a great deal more to come.

The main purpose of Lida's long visit was to work on the newest
incarnation of my "book" (whose hidden objective I had not yet
realized). I had proposed that we become co-authors. It had
occurred to me that the weaving together of excerpts from our
letters might be an engaging way of portraying the Russian soul.
Our shared fascination had led us to explore a wide gamut of issues.
We had touched on everything from the genius of 19th century
religious philosophers, whose ideas foreshadowed 21st century
spirituality, to the lives of Russian women and the role of women
everywhere in the coming spiritual age.

We had also plumbed the depths of things, probing some of
the more perplexing questions about Russia, such as *how* a nation
of devout believers had been turned into a nation of so-called
atheists. Lida, who had an uncanny knack for turning up rare
documents, had come upon a detailed, eye-witness account from
the early 1920s describing the campaign of terror conducted by

Bolsheviks against believers in a Ukrainian town. This led us to the perennial question of means and ends, and the lengths to which human beings will go to convince themselves that good can result from unspeakable evil.

By the time she arrived, nearly four years of such letters had accumulated. They had resumed after our September '95 visit to Russia, when Lida returned to India and I returned home. But our free-ranging exchanges had begun to take on a new focus. We increasingly honed in on a specific location and cast of characters. Both of us were caught up in the vision, bequeathed by Father Alexei to Natasha, that Belaya could become a kind of experimental greenhouse for nurturing the Russian soul. Seeds had been planted; people were on hand to cultivate them. Time would tell.

Meanwhile, I continued living life as a journey, trusting my guidance. There were still moments when I lost faith, as well as focus, wondering if I should abandon my Russian quest and get a job in a bakery, anywhere, just to earn money. My husband periodically needled me about my lack of income, though he always maintained, in the end, that his own life choices would remain unchanged. That gave me solace, yet it still troubled me that we had no financial cushion because of *my* choices. And I was going to need money to return to Russia one more time, in the fall of '96, for another major historic event in Belaya.

To pay my way, I made one more attempt to obtain a grant. A new foundation had come into being with a worldview close to mine. After years of wandering in the desert with regard to grant-making institutions, this foundation appeared like an oasis. Finally I would be able to speak openly about who I was and what I sought to accomplish, without feeling obliged to disguise the true nature of my pursuit. Words like "spirit" and "soul" would not be automatic grounds for rejection. This in itself had the feel of philanthropy.

The application process was another story. Coming several years after the last of my unsuccessful attempts, I had to steel myself psychologically for another round of proposal-writing. The requirements, moreover, were unlike any I had previously encountered. They took me through a life review process that forced me to grapple with the awkward fact that I was applying for assistance to write a book nearly twenty years after my last published book. I had some nice clippings, but twenty years . . . .

There were days when I was convinced that I was spinning my wheels. By all outer measures of success, I was a failure. The way the facts lined up, according to prevailing standards of achievement, I had regressed. In terms of career status and income, there was a conspicuous downhill slide from a peak reached decades earlier. Plus five years had passed since my last regular, salaried employment, and those five years had produced virtually nothing to put on paper.

Adding to my woes, the foundation required that people applying as individuals, as opposed to organizations, provide a minimum of three letters of recommendation. This made me shudder. Initially, I couldn't conceive of asking anyone for such a letter. It was hard enough for me to confront my own lack of tangible accomplishments in recent years, despite all the learning and experience I had gained. How could I reasonably ask others to comprehend what they couldn't see and take a leap of faith on my behalf?

Gathering the courage to tackle this requirement provided another lesson in humility, one in a series of such lessons since I had left "the world." I made a list of five people whom I had known for years. Facing the prospect that all of them might decline for lack of anything concrete, of recent vintage, to write, I tried to narrow the scope of their task. I asked them to focus on the foundation's central question: Can this person be relied upon to complete the project she proposes to undertake? When all five gave me a vote of confidence, it was a tremendous boon.

My proposal to the foundation requested support for a book about the soul of Russia, based on my correspondence with Lida. She had lived there, she was of Slavic origin, and she knew the culture inside out. My own perspective — based on interviews, travels, and studies — was more broad than deep, but also more objective. Together, through our shared metaphysical understanding, we were creating a widening pool of insight. The grant, if awarded, would be shared between us.

Lida arrived in the US two days before the foundation's response. I hadn't told her about the application, not wanting to disappoint her if it didn't materialize. The response came in two parts. The foundation sent a formal letter along with a check. Its president sent a second check, her own, an additional sum to cover the total amount of my request. In a personal note, she wrote that she had studied music for many years with a Russian woman whose soul had deeply touched hers, and she was pleased to personally support the project.

As I read the letter, then the note, looked at both checks, and read everything over again, tears filled my eyes. The grant was not a huge amount of money but it was exactly what I had asked for and its arrival, as if by cosmic design, coincided exactly with Lida's. The Universe seemed to be sending a message that things were moving in the right direction. Finally, after all those years, there was some resonance between my inner voice and the outer world — a tangible sign of encouragement to proceed with my quest.

Until that moment, I had often felt I was on shaky ground. Living a spiritual life on the brink of the 21st century was stepping into unknown territory. One could have total faith in the journey itself, knowing that one's soul would undoubtedly grow, yet nothing was assured on the material plane. The goal in these times was the same as in ancient times: to obey the inner voice, to do God's will, as one perceived it. But the new challenge of our time was to do so while remaining in the material world, not retreating from it.

In attempting to discern the will of God, never easy for mortals, I was aided immeasurably by a working understanding of who and what God is. I had come to see God as a combination of Creator, the transcendent God of the West, and divine inner spark, the God immanent of the East. And I had begun to see the Path of Return as the road one travels to gain increasing alignment between the two: the spark of divinity, which initially registers as that "still, small voice within" and the God who orders our universe, and whose hierarchies of intelligence have infinite ways of communicating Divine Purpose to awakening souls.

I knew by then that there were many awakening souls on our planet. I was hardly alone. Though this collective awakening was largely hidden from view, unseen by the mainstream culture, I knew from the wisdom teachings that a Divine Purpose was quietly working out. This awakening coincided with growing chaos in our world, which further obscured it. But what appeared to be chaos was actually the breakdown of a world order that had become an obstacle to a fuller expression of Spirit. Outer changes were masking, for the time being, the breakthrough to a higher order of consciousness.

I also knew, from personal experience, that a divine intelligence was actively fostering this breakthrough in my own life. I conceived of it as a small strand of the greater Divine Intelligence. In retrospect, I realized that this intelligence had been patiently waiting for me to recognize it. Once that recognition occurred, it began to lead me to sources of knowledge about the evolutionary process occurring on our planet, and to guide me in ways that would allow me to contribute to this process.

With all that I had learned, however, there was much that remained beyond my mental comprehension. It was evident to me that invisible forces were at work in all our lives, arranging events in such a way that sooner or later we would take note of them. Their mission clearly involved helping us to realize that we live in a divinely ordered world. They accomplished this mission, at least in part, through phenomena that *we* call "cosmic coincidences," or "miracles," or "synchronicities"— phenomena that remain utterly, totally, mysterious.

One such synchronicity was the arrival of Lida, from Russia, at the same moment in time as the arrival of the foundation grant. Looking back, as if I were viewing the frames of a film in reverse, I saw that this particular frame was the last in a sequence that had begun even before I met Natasha in '91 — the pivotal event in a long chain of events that included my link to Lida. It was the year before, in 1990, during my second citizen diplomacy trip to the

USSR, that I first had the impulse to write a book about the Russian soul. One of my traveling companions on that trip was the person who had informed me, five years after that trip, about the new foundation, whose grant arrived along with Lida.

The more I pondered the sheer quantity of smaller events leading to the larger ones, and the intricate ways in which all these happenings were interrelated, the more mysterious it all became. For things to work out as they had, for numerous lives to converge as they had in time and space, it seemed that the entire chain of events had to have been "programmed" long in advance by an unfathomable, invisible mechanism, or consortium of invisible beings.

Glimpsing only the dimmest outlines of what might conceivably exist "behind the veil" to account for such synchronicities, the notion that we alone control our destinies, a notion to which I had subscribed for most of my life, seemed laughable. The particulars of Lida's coming to the US provided a glimpse into what must have been going on behind the scenes in order to bring her here. It was awesome to contemplate both the timing and scale of "arrangements."

Prior to the grant, I couldn't have afforded to pay her airfare. The person who did pay for it was the same person who had originally told me about her. He was "in place," as it were, before there was a clear purpose for her to come to the US, and before even he could have afforded to provide her airfare, though I knew that he was looking for an opportunity to repay her generosity to him. Just as she and I were wondering how to get her here, he told me that a bequest had been left to his organization in the will of a wealthy donor. The funds became available only a matter of weeks before Lida was free to travel.

A believer in a random universe would call it a matter of chance. That would mean that simply by chance, Lida was given an airplane ticket to the US, work to accomplish while she was here, and a grant for her efforts, simultaneously. A religious person would call it a miracle. I had come to understand it as an outer manifestation of the inner workings of an intelligent, loving, and purposeful universe. When multiple synchronicities occurred, it was like a neon sign flashing: "Pay attention. This is happening for a reason."

A Spider's Web

Having Lida stay with us was a pleasure, for the most part, and always a source of interest. She had intense reactions to the material aspects of American life, alternating between fascination and outrage. Deeming our super-market shopping carts large enough for a person, she threatened to jump inside one each time we went to the store. Washing machines and dryers were marvels, as Soviet washers were tiny and often dysfunctional; dryers were clotheslines in bathrooms or backstairs. Dishwashers did not exist, even on the plane of imagination. Speechless on first encountering one, Lida declared: "It can't possibly clean dishes as well as a person can."

She was an unusual combination of East and West. It seemed as though her Slavic soul, and her affinity for Indian culture, had been grafted onto a Western personality. She had never traveled further west than the old borders of Yugoslavia, until then. But she was highly competitive, striving to excel to the point that making mistakes in English — her third language — was painful to her. She was also extremely adept at practical problem-solving and enjoyed the challenge of it. Had she lived in the West and been predisposed to business, instead of philosophy, she could have easily broken through many glass ceilings.

Lida's presence radically changed my daily life. It was like having a daughter, sister and co-worker all in one. She depended on me totally for daily sustenance, as everything was unfamiliar. But when it came to work, another side of her personality surfaced, a directive side. She had arrived with a mission *besides* the book: instructions from Natasha to turn me into a fluent Russian speaker. Natasha, with whom I usually spoke in *Franglais*, a hybrid French-English, was unhappy that I couldn't communicate directly, on things that mattered, with other members of her spiritual family. And another trip to Belaya was coming up that September.

Thus, mornings with Lida began with Russian lessons, part of which I enjoyed immensely. She had brought along a tape of newly released songs by a Soviet-era pop star who had turned into a devout Orthodox believer. The music was hauntingly beautiful but the lyrics were exceedingly complex. Every morning, except for weekends, we went over the words of each new song until I understood and could pronounce them all. Then we turned on the tape and sang together, feeling as though we were breathing the most rarefied Russian air. Whether this practice helped my conversation skills at all remained an open question.

In the afternoons, we absorbed ourselves in Russian philosophy, as further preparation for our book. Several new philosophers had emerged during *glasnost* who had found inspiration from the luminous body of spiritual thought that pre-dated the Revolution, and co-existed with it in exile. Lida translated excerpts from a new book on "The Russian Idea," a compilation of writings by philosophers who had tried to articulate this "idea" — the eternal longing of the Russian soul to somehow merge, or bridge, heaven and earth. I went through a stack of papers delivered by Russian and American scholars on related themes from conferences I had attended.

Mulling over many inspired writings on this subject, we realized that our exchange of letters would not suffice as the basis for a book. I had gone through the letters prior to Lida's arrival, rereading hundreds of pages and creating a subject index to make it easy for us to find our way around in them. The more closely we looked at what we had, however, the clearer it became that a tapestry of our own thoughts would not do justice to our main subject. Reluctant as I was to admit it then, I began to recognize the wishful thinking on my part. In search of a new format for the book, I had talked myself, Lida, and the foundation, into it.

One day Lida asked if I had kept my notes from our stay in Belaya the previous year. I had in fact made reams of notes in '95, and later entered them into my computer along with transcripts of the year's interviews. The next morning, my husband and I went off to a conference, leaving Lida at home with a hundred and fifty pages to read. When we returned that evening, she held up the stack of pages and declared, "This is it!" In her mind, the story of the actual events in Belaya — with their living, breathing characters, featuring Natasha and her spiritual family — was the perfect vehicle for the book.

At first, I resisted. I was feeling dizzy by then, like a spinning top. Accepting Lida's idea would mean that my grant proposal had already become null and void, something I was not ready to acknowledge. But it was clear that I, and now we, were stymied. Once again, a different form would be needed. And the more I considered her idea, the more it made sense. Her suggestion was to tell a story about the Russian soul, a true story still in process of unfolding. We cooked up a kind of sandwich approach to living history: between the Belaya events of '95 and those to come in '96, we would insert a section on "The Russian Idea."

According to this scenario it was once again *my* book, with input from Lida in the middle section. That meant another inner adjustment on my part, all the more daunting because the basic cause of these constant readjustments was still veiled, and would remain so for several more years. There were many rows to hoe before I would realize that "my book" was actually the vehicle for my journey — the instrument for encountering my own soul, in addition to the soul of Russia. It gave me access to another reality — called Russia — another way of seeing, perceiving, and living on this earth, which helped me better discern my own.

But at the time that Lida first broached her idea, I had the extremely uncomfortable feeling that things were spinning out of control. My book, and by extension my life, were like a kaleidoscope whose elements were constantly rearranging themselves into new designs. Each time they came to rest, I hoped in vain that that would be the last time. I felt besieged by change. And yet I couldn't help acknowledging that the latest design held a certain, unanticipated, appeal.

The new approach to the book, which I gradually came to accept, revolved around people. From my first visit to the Soviet Union, in '86, it had been the people who attracted me. The ones I gravitated toward were genuine and spontaneous. They lived in and for the moment, but also had learned to "read the book of life." They had a way of seeing things from the inside out, looking for the inner meaning of outer happenings. The newest format would allow me to focus on the light of Russia's soul through such people, rather than ideas.

I was excited by the prospect, but also anxious. I had never written anything remotely like it. Lida reassured me, repeatedly, that it would be easy, that the material was already there, in my notes. All that was needed, in her opinion, was some weeding, as in a garden. She offered to be the gardener. In a matter of hours, she went through those hundred and fifty pages, culling the cast of characters, and the events and incidents, to be highlighted. And then we returned to our synthesis of "The Russian Idea."

Spring and early summer passed quickly and pleasantly. On weekends we took outings with my husband; on week days we thoroughly immersed ourselves in Russia. That was another eye-opening experience, all the more so with hindsight. In our quest to learn more about the Russian soul, we were simultaneously uncovering more about ourselves, though we weren't conscious of it at the time. On one occasion we devoted an entire day to cataloguing the extreme polarities within the Russian character, and proceeded to focus on the good and the beautiful, while virtually ignoring the rest.

Despite the obvious external differences between us, Lida and I had similar inclinations — to each other and to the Russian soul. We did not live entirely on this earth, or for the things of this earth, but mostly for higher ideals. Increasingly, as I got to know more about her early life, I wondered why this was. Was it because life had wounded us? Did people like us seek refuge in higher ideals as a form of escape from the pain of this world? Or was it the reverse? Did the wounds of childhood sensitize our souls, directing them away from the coarser aspects of life and toward the more refined? Perhaps it was some of both. It was hard to say.

The differences between us were significant. One was that Lida kept her childhood, scarred by brutality, deeply buried. Mine had been far more benign, yet I couldn't imagine life without the benefits of inner healing. She rejected psychotherapy out of hand, claiming it was unnecessary to the life of a soul on the spiritual path, and had almost convinced me that this was possible. Despite all her early suffering, she was charming, brilliant, and fun-loving. She appeared to be a strong, inner-directed thirty-year-old, anticipating marriage, motherhood, and a career in philosophy. For the first time I began to wonder whether it truly was necessary, in all cases, to reopen wounds of the past.

One of Lida's charms was a childlike capacity for fun. Within days of her arrival, she had me and my husband, Martin, wrapped around her little finger, like doting parents complying with her every wish. When the three of us were not working, Martin and I were at her disposal. It wasn't until after she had left that I realized the degree to which I had altered my normal daily rhythms to accommodate hers. We ate breakfast and lunch when she wanted to. The three of us spent most evenings as she wished. On weekends we visited places she wanted to see. She said that she had never been happier in her life.

Peace and harmony descended over the newest version of the book as well. It began to assume a function that I could never have anticipated. Increasingly, without my being fully conscious of it, the book took on the colors and textures of a family project. The family was that of the late Father Alexei of Belaya, his spiritual children and "grandchildren," of whom Lida was one. By some mysterious, alchemical process, I found myself becoming the narrator of a family story. Later I learned, to my astonishment, that Father Alexei had predicted that "someone would come from the West" to tell the world about Belaya.

Little by little it dawned on me that I was caught in a web, though I never suspected how intricately woven it was. At times I had the sensation of being in the middle of a plot, while it was thickening, without the benefit of knowing anything about its beginning or possible ending. Strangely, moreover, when I first caught a whiff of this web, I didn't really mind the entanglement. Perhaps, I mused, it was somehow predetermined for me to play that role. Tracing the threads that had led me there, the awesome convergence of people and events, it even seemed plausible that this was the purpose of it all.

Everything began to have the scent of destiny. It seemed clear that the major characters in our drama had been fated to meet. Natasha was at the center the "plot," the spider spinning the web. Slava, her closest spiritual brother, had been one of the first entrapped, when he went to meet Father Alexei twenty-five years earlier. A larger-than-life figure, Slava was an inspired professor who attracted legions of students to his Russian literature lectures. And he was a keeper of family secrets. One secret, which he shared with Lida and me, helped to place the unfolding events in context. In Father Alexei's eyes, Natasha had been blessed with personal magnetism *in order to* attract others to Belaya.

In fact, there was a time, in the 70s, when Natasha had attracted leading lights of the Soviet cultural intelligentsia to meet Father Alexei. Several had been secretly baptized by him. A few placed themselves under his spiritual direction. He offered guidance for their lives and, before his death, confided in them his vision of Russia's spiritual rebirth. Natasha, Slava and the others had kept that vision alive amongst themselves until the fall of the USSR, when it could gradually be revealed to a larger circle.

Lida had come along in 1990, five years after Father Alexei's death. A bond immediately developed between her and Natasha, cemented by Natasha's sense of a past life connection between them. She invited Lida into her household and became her spiritual mother. A year later I met them both, when I went to interview Natasha for the oral history book. Five years after that, Lida was part of my own household. Her presence subtly strengthened my link with the others. Whether by conscious design or not, her confiding of occasional fragments of "the plot" had the effect of reinforcing the part I was to play.

As a writer, I should have been disturbed by what I was hearing. Bells and whistles should have gone off in my head. Instantly, I should have realized that my objectivity would be compromised, jeopardizing the value of whatever book I would eventually write. By then, however, I felt connected to the characters in the story and began to see its telling as a kind of dharmic task, an act of service. Given all that had conspired to bring me to that place, the notion that my role was other than purely journalistic had a certain logic. Little did I know, however, that a grander scheme was unfolding.

Wandering Pilgrims

The leaves were turning color when we arrived in Belaya. The summer of '96 had been abruptly curtailed by an early frost. It was bitter cold and rainy for early September, with little relief indoors. Since the heat supply was centrally controlled, and the town was not officially required to turn it on until October, it was freezing virtually everywhere, even inside the hotel. There was one exception, however, and Lida and I were its beneficiaries.

Belaya's administration had recently built a new apartment compound for military men and their families. The buildings, only three years old, were already falling apart, inside and out. But within the compound was a special block of apartments reserved for retired officers from the Afghanistan war. Those apartments received heat, while the rest of the compound, and the rest of the town, did not. Natasha found lodging there for Lida and me.

Our hostess, an unhappy woman named Evgenia, had recently divorced her officer husband. She had nearly gone mad, literally, in Afghanistan. It was a ghastly war for everyone, including officers' families. Her husband's alcohol problem had become severe, as had his abuse of her. They had separated shortly after returning to Belaya, where Evgenia met Natasha, who became a kind of life-line for her. Whenever Natasha came to Belaya, Evgenia wanted to be around her, offering to help in any way she could. Thus, our toasty quarters, while Natasha herself stayed in an icy apartment.

That year was the 850th anniversary of Belaya, actually of its first mention in the ancient Russian chronicles. It was a gala celebration of history and culture for which the mayor had spared nothing. He admitted to having begged, borrowed, and stolen (largely from pensioners, who reportedly received no stipends for months) to create a spectacle that would resound in the collective memory for generations.

What took place surpassed all expectations for a small, provincial city. The festivities, lasting three days, included elaborate musical, dance, and dramatic productions of that extraordinary Russian artistry that takes one's breath away. Dancers as young as four performed like professionals on the concert hall stage, on the rain-soaked town square, and on the muddy field of the sports stadium. As warmly dressed spectators sat huddled under umbrellas, young ballerinas, jazz dancers, acrobats, folk dancers and martial artists — often bare-shouldered and shivering — gave flawless, enchanting performances.

The main event was an outdoor pageant chronicling Belaya's long and diverse history through music, dance, and dramatic readings. Historical highlights ranged from its role as a medieval fortress, protecting Russia from Tamerlane, to its prominence as a model of 19th century industry, for which the czar had traveled there to pay homage. It ended with a moving tribute, enhanced by colorful floats and clouds of balloons, to a squadron of Belaya's soldiers who had liberated the German Reichstag in Berlin at the close of World War II. There was no reference, whatsoever, to the communist era — an omission all the more glaring in light of the fact that the town's "chiefs" remained Party members.

Just before the grand finale of fireworks, the mayor addressed the tens of thousands of residents crowded into the stadium. They hadn't budged during the four-hour spectacle, despite intermittent downpours, and they cheered as he approached the podium. While appearing genuinely moved, he gave all the credit to the legions of townspeople who had taken part. Beyond the main concerts and pageants, there had been smaller concerts, athletic events, historical exhibits, crafts displays, and a spate of new publications. The mayor spoke of the town and its people with immense pride, especially notable because of its conspicuous absence in Russia at the time. He asked everyone to share in and savor that pride.

All around town were permanent reminders of the 850th anniversary, thanks to a massive campaign of painting and plastering. In a year's time, Belaya had undergone a dramatic face lift that helped offset the relentlessly gloomy weather. Jewels of 19th century architecture, long hidden under layers of dirt and crumbling cornices, had sprung back to life. Great bursts of pastel yellow, blue, green and rose, all with white trimmings, transformed the dreary-looking streets and plazas. A theater closed for decades, a deteriorating hulk right next to the hotel, was a stunning edifice of cinnamon-rose on its opening night.

Unexpectedly, our sojourn in Belaya expanded from one week into three. Natasha, who had personal reasons for staying longer, went out of her way to find reasons for me and Lida to remain as well. When the hoopla died down and things returned to normal, I had occasions to widen my acquaintance with the local people, several of whom Natasha wanted me to interview, and to further explore the surrounding region. Prime among the latter was a trip to Optina Pustyn, the fabled monastery, in a nearby area of central Russia.

The trip had been arranged by Father Dmitry, who appeared in remarkably good health a year after I'd last seen him, just before his heart attack, and who had managed to remain in Belaya despite the Metropolitan's attempts to have him transferred. The head-priest had organized a pilgrimage to Optina for parishioners in honor of the 601st anniversary of Russia's Deliverance from Tamerlane by the Mother of God of Belaya. Lida and I received permission to go along.

The distance from Belaya to Optina was not great, as the crow flies, but the journey was exceedingly long. Due to the paucity of paved roads in the provinces, the route was extremely circuitous. Our chartered bus left at 10 o'clock in the evening and was due to arrive just before dawn. Whatever sleep we would get had to be gotten on the bus. People were told to bring their own food, however Lida and I had not been informed. Observing that we had nothing to eat, our fellow travelers heaped large quantities of snacks upon us.

It was pitch black when the bus dropped us off at the monastery gates. The group leader, acting as if she knew exactly where she was going, made several false starts. Thirty groggy pilgrims followed behind her, stumbling along in the dark, repeatedly reversing course until finally we found the small church where morning prayers were being held. By the flickering light of thin tapers, we groped our way to an empty row of wooden benches. In the predawn darkness, only the silhouettes of monks conducting the service were dimly visible. The sound of their deep bass voices chanting hymns was otherworldly.

The dreamlike spell cast by candlelight was gradually broken by the dawn. Skies were overcast, but the rain had stopped. After matins, our officious leader, Tatiana, led the way to another church nearby. This was a large structure in which a major service led by many priests was underway. Worshippers had formed several long lines, patiently waiting to give confession, and to receive communion. This was why they traveled far and long, with no inns or stopping places along the way, to reach this holy shrine, as well as to collect bottles of holy water to take home.

During the long liturgy, I sat on a bench in the rear, closed my eyes, and discovered, to my great surprise, that it was possible to fall asleep sitting straight up if one were sufficiently tired. Lida, barely concealing her annoyance, poked me in the ribs to wake me and inform me that my behavior was highly disrespectful. Tatiana waited outside after communion, lining up the worshippers in her care for the second part of the mission. Marching briskly ahead, once again pretending to know precisely where she was going, she led us down a gravel path, through a thicket of trees, on a hike that was well over a mile long, perhaps two.

Our destination was a well near a holy spring, but on arriving at the clearing where Tatiana believed the well to be, we came upon a large drain pipe and a pool of fetid water. We were lost, and Tatiana looked confused. Some of the elderly women, totally exhausted and visibly disappointed, were ready to settle for *that* water to take home in the plastic containers they had brought with them. At least it was on holy ground. Dispirited, they refused to budge. They finally balked at Tatiana's blind meanderings, ignoring her urgings that they continue the quest. It would take all their remaining strength to simply walk all the way back to the bus.

I was younger than many of them by a decade or two, but could barely move my legs. Sleeping on the bus had been impossible for me. By that point, my exhaustion was such that I passed up an opportunity to sit down on a tree stump for fear that I might never stand up again. Lida, an athletic young person who *did* sleep on the bus, was determined to find the holy spring. She pleaded with me to join her, which meant returning over a mile in the direction of the churches and then setting off in a different direction. Like the older women, however, I had had it by then.

Besides, I hadn't come there to collect holy water. My reasons were different, though still rather obscure, even to me. The name "Optina Pustyn" had attracted me from the first time I had heard it, something I couldn't explain. Over time, I would discover that the monastery was sacred ground to some of Russia's most inspired writers and philosophers: Tolstoy, Dostoyevsky and Gogol; Kireevsky, Leontiev, and Solovyov. They had all journeyed there to meet the great Elders who penetrated the veil to the Kingdom of Souls. I found it especially interesting to learn that the last of their lineage, Nektary, expelled by the Bolsheviks in 1923, had been the spiritual father of Father Alexei, the spiritual father of Natasha.

But on the day we were there, I knew only a few of these facts. I was dimly aware that Optina Pustyn had once been a spiritual oasis, and I harbored vague hopes of seeing vestiges of that legacy. What I'd seen thus far, the perfectly restored church buildings, created a beautiful picture, but the monks and priests seemed somber, even severe. None of the faces that I observed reflected anything resembling the inner radiance of Elder Zosima, Dostoyevsky's character. Later I realized what the writer had prophetically intimated: that this was a new time, when spirituality was supposed to leave the monasteries and enter the world.

Standing near that pool of fetid water, where the elderly women had sat down on the cold ground, I was ready to call it a day. But Lida implored me to continue searching with her, assuring me that it wouldn't be in vain. I finally gave in, willing my body onward for one final lap. The two of us pressed ahead, back down the wrong path, then toward another forested area. It was like being on an expedition with no map or compass, and no clear destination. I felt like a wandering pilgrim, that breed of Russian seeker who searches everywhere for something that exists in no particular place.

Lida had remembered seeing a well when she was there six years before, but the grounds had been strewn with rubble at the time. She usually had a keen sense of direction, but almost nothing looked familiar to her this day. Walking through a dense pine forest, which she remembered, she had expected to find the well in a clearing there. But there was no well. Reassuring me continually that we were on the right path, she herself was showing signs of uncertainty. But then suddenly, finally, at the far edge of the forest, the well appeared. A few fellow pilgrims were already there, ladling water into their bottles and cups.

Tatiana, who was among them, chose that moment to announce, with the bearing of a commissar, that our bus would be departing for the return trip to Belaya in exactly twenty minutes. At that same moment, I turned around and saw, or sensed, the reason why I had come there. Behind us was a campus — a large, circular, beautifully sculpted, emerald green lawn dotted with magnificent flower beds. At the circle's edge were several white clapboard cottages and a few buildings, among them a church. It was the hermitage, the place where the Elders had once lived.

As the others walked back toward the bus, Lida and I entered the gates of the hermitage. It was undoubtedly against the rules, but there wasn't a soul in sight to grant permission and we had no time to look. We could stay only five minutes, as it would take fifteen minutes to return to the bus. Inside the gates there was absolute silence. The loudest sound was the buzzing of bees in a nearby flower bed. New energy suddenly coursed through my limbs. I darted around the campus snapping photos, until my eyes fell upon one of the white cottages.

I stood in front of it like a statue, unable to move. Lida, noticing the small building my gaze was fixed upon, mentioned that it was the "cell" once inhabited by Elder Amvrosy. I knew I'd seen the place before, in the literal sense of *déjà vu*, already seen. In fact, I sensed that what my soul had been searching for in Russia was associated with that cottage. But just as I stumbled upon it, time ran out. We could hear Tatiana hollering in the distance. Lida warned me, sternly, that Tatiana would not hold the bus for anyone.

On Strike

The evenings in Belaya that September reminded me, in a humorous vein, of a Chekhov play. Almost nothing happened, but some people came and went, and others waited in anticipation. We gathered at Father Alexei's place, Natasha's home away from home. It was also then called Lilia's, after its only full-time occupant. Lilia, who had spent her youth on a collective farm, had become the nanny of Father Alexei's grandchildren in her thirties. When Father Alexei became paralyzed, he asked to have Lilia at his side. She remained there for eight years, becoming one of his spiritual children.

When Father Alexei died, Lilia stayed on to take care of his widow, *Matushka* Marya. When *she* died, Lilia stayed on to take care of Natasha and other members of the spiritual family whenever they came to Belaya. The place was still permeated by Father Alexei's aura. Little had changed since his death in 1985. It remained a kind of shrine to "the Muscovites," as Lilia called them, and she lived in constant anticipation of their visits. It was her happiness to prepare their meals and wash their dishes. She seemed as gratified to be needed, as they were appreciative of being cared for by her.

During our visit of '96, we gathered at Lilia's for meals at least once a day, in the evening, and sometimes in the afternoon as well. The apartment not only lacked heat, but frequently electricity, and sometimes gas. Lilia prepared meals in a tiny kitchen with no window, often by the light of a few candles. Yet nothing seemed to interrupt the steady stream of laughter emanating from the kitchen. She joked with everyone who came through the door, while chopping, slicing, and peeling, almost in the dark.

Traffic through Father Alexei's apartment was fairly constant, just as it was at Natasha's apartment in Moscow. There were never any scheduled mealtimes; people were fed when they arrived. Lilia, who sat at the head of the table, on rare occasions when she finally did sit down, was almost constantly in motion — bringing a plate of hot food to the newest arrival, removing dishes, serving tea, and sweets. Though well into her sixties, she sprang into action like a youngster, all day long, nearly always in good cheer.

There were days when hours passed doing essentially nothing. Unlike Chekhov's plays, there were no philosophical ruminations or emotional diatribes. There was mostly banter, some of it humorous, some of it meaningless, like the dangling, disconnected phrases issuing from Misha after too much vodka. There was also singing. Misha loved to sing, everything from Soviet war songs to Gershwin, rapping out rhythms on the table with his index fingers. Lilia often joined him, both in drink and in song. She especially enjoyed sentimental ballads about unrequited love, at the end of which a tear sometimes spilled from her eye.

Natasha made several attempts to organize "my program," as she called it. She was very pleased about the new format of the book, with its focus on Belaya, and tried to arrange for me to interview local figures. She put in calls, and we waited. Misha read aloud from the local paper's 850th anniversary issue, which carried a long interview with Natasha, and a photo of her with Father Alexei. This article was the first public statement about her spiritual life, secret until then, and it generated crank calls. One caller refused to give even her name but seemed insulted when Natasha declined to share the details of her personal life.

For nearly a week, the air was filled with suspense. At issue was whether Yulia, a lovely TV newscaster, would find an apartment in Belaya before it was time for her to leave. She had fallen in love with the town and wanted to move there and work with Father Dmitry. To earn the money to buy a place of her own, she had taken a job at a TV station in a northern Siberian town that had recently struck oil, and where she was due to return almost immediately.

Every evening, Yulia returned to Lilia's with reports of the day's happenings. Her apartment search had begun inauspiciously, with several false starts. On one occasion she had come close to losing years of savings to a local con man, the kind of person who had suddenly appeared along with privatization, and who she was unprepared to find in Belaya. Miraculously, with only one day to go, Yulia found her place, and managed to get all the necessary permits and stamps that same day. Something had finally happened, and that in itself was cause for celebration.

Around that time, Lida had begun acting strangely toward me. A surly side of her character came to the surface, a side that I had noticed occasionally in her dealings with others, but had never encountered directly. I was aware that she was capable of rudeness, extreme rudeness at times, but not knowing the people involved or the possible provocations, I simply observed. Until then, she had generally been respectful and caring toward me.

The incident that sent up smoke signals took place on the theater's opening night. After the play, there was a supper at the hotel for the cast and guests of the town. Lida and I sat at a table with Irina, the actress whom we had first met three years earlier on the overnight train. Irina had admirers in Belaya, as throughout the former Soviet Union. Diners at nearby tables were ordering bottles of champagne to be sent over to her. One woman came over to introduce herself, saying that meeting Irina in person was one of the happiest moments of her life.

While all this was happening, Irina began to recall her visit to Hollywood, in the 60s. While treated royally there, she had found it unbearably artificial and materialistic. During these reminiscences, undoubtedly triggered by my presence, a waitress arrived with a gigantic box of Swiss chocolates sent by someone across the dining room who was conspicuously nouveau riche. It was the kind of package that no one, outside of the Politburo, had probably ever seen during the Soviet era. Irina stared at it for a few moments looking puzzled.

Finally she picked up the huge box, placed it on top of her head, and began tilting her head from side to side, as if the box were a game or toy with which to practice balance.

It was a poignant moment, a sign of the times — the encroachment of lavish personal wealth into Russia's provinces. Irina's reaction made it unforgettable. What made it all the more unforgettable for me was Lida's bizarre behavior. Irina began saying good-bye to us, while wrapping up a package of uneaten cold cuts in a napkin to give to the "key lady" on her floor. Preparing to return to Moscow early the next morning, she was sharing some departing words with me, as I was not likely to see her again that year. It was expected that Lida would translate, as she always had. My Russian was still not good enough to catch everything. But Lida became mute.

The change came out of the blue and left me stunned. I said nothing about it at first, but the silence lasted, even after returning to the apartment where we were staying. When I asked Lida what was wrong, she answered "nothing," but remained largely silent, leaving me totally in the dark as to why. I wasn't aware of having offended her, though I knew that it irritated her when I asked her to translate the same word more than once. Certain words were particularly difficult for me to remember and on that trip, for the first time, my asking her, rather than looking in a dictionary, seemed to make her surly. But I knew that that alone could not explain her silences.

The tension between us grew. At stake were both our personal relationship and our cooperative effort on the book. We had agreed to a work plan while Lida was still in the US, just before her departure for Russia, about a month before this incident occurred. At the end of each day in Belaya we were going to compare notes. She would help me by filling in whatever I had missed from significant speeches, sermons, or conversations; I would record my own impressions, as well as hers; together we'd shape the contents of the last part of the book.

We started out that way, and then abruptly, our nightly review of the day's happenings came to an end. Lida stonewalled, making it clear, nonverbally, that she was no longer participating. I was increasingly on my own, in terms of both the spoken word and its deeper implications. She had been invaluable as a cross-cultural bridge, translating not only people's words but their subtler meanings. Suddenly, without warning or explanation, she was only sporadically willing to help, making it clear that she felt no obligation. The person on whom I had come to rely totally, unreservedly, was someone who, it turned out, I did not really know.

Adding to the enigma was the fact that money had entered our relationship, for the first time, just prior to this trip. Her assistance over the years had always been completely voluntary, and always initiated by her. Aside from her travel expenses, which I naturally absorbed when she accompanied me, no money changed hands between us. Paying her a fee was never an option. In the Soviet culture, friends helped each other. To pay a friend for their services was unthinkable, though it was fully expected that favors would be returned.

Fate had arranged for me to return Lida's favors when she came to the US, through our hospitality, and then the foundation grant. I had been thrilled to share it with her, having anticipated that it would fulfill her fondest dream. She had wanted to buy an apartment in the town where she had lived as a child, ever since it became possible to purchase property in Russia. Her father had promised to give her $5,000, a *huge* sum in those days for people in the Eastern bloc, enough for a small apartment in a small city. But then he changed his mind, saying he needed the money himself.

Lida was crushed. She had been longing for a place of her own, to collect her belongings under one roof, hundreds of books and personal items strewn about Russia in the closets of friends. When the grant arrived and I told her that half was hers, and that it was $5,000, I thought she'd be jubilant. Instead, an inscrutable expression appeared on her face, as if some inner conflict was going on, a cross-current of emotions canceling each other out. Oddly, she never even thanked me, which she had always done in the past, when I'd given her gifts.

I had observed that not saying thank you was not unusual

among Russians, especially those one came to know well. Not being thanked on that scale, however, was something novel. At least I thought so, until a Russian émigrée psychologist informed me that it was "normal." This psychologist, after sending money to her sister in Russia for years, without being thanked, had finally stopped. When I asked her to explain the phenomenon, she hesitated, finally positing that it might be related to the recipient's envy of the one who was able to give so generously, or to the recipient's fear of what might be expected in return.

Lida, without acknowledging the grant money, knew exactly how she wanted to spend a chunk of it. Right away. Still doing her translation work in longhand, she had dreamed of having a portable lap-top computer. Martin and I were immediately put to work researching the best bargain, ordering it, setting it up, teaching her how to use it, and then shopping for accessories needed in India and Russia. Finally, when it was all set up, she expressed her unbounded joy.

What happened between that moment and her "strike" in Belaya was impossible for me to know. If Lida herself consciously knew, she refused to say. After snapping at me a few times for asking, repeatedly, the meaning of a word, she accused me of being overly sensitive when I grumbled about the way she had responded. But it turned out that she had simultaneously offended our hostess, Evgenia, who had complained to Natasha, who had her *own* bone to pick with Lida for being short-tempered and disrespectful. Lida's response to these accusations was denial. It wasn't her nature to look inside. She didn't believe in psychology.

Feeling that I no longer knew this person, and could no longer trust her, I naturally withdrew from her somewhat. This upset her further. While refusing to communicate with me about what was really bothering her, she told me that she didn't like it when I was "reserved." It began to seem preposterous, surreal, in the way that Russian life often was. Nothing made sense. After years of intense sharing through letters and travels, mutual inquiries and adventures, she had unilaterally changed the nature of our relationship and had then become angry that I was not the same.

As the ramifications of all this came into focus, I was quite upset. Lida was a kindred spirit, a coworker, and had been a source of comfort for several years of my Russian journey. She smoothed out many of the rough spots one invariably encounters while being there, going to great lengths to make things as agreeable as possible. She was always at my side, helping, protecting, supporting, encouraging. Suddenly she had turned into a stranger, one whose company I wanted to avoid. And there was still no telling why.

In my effort to probe the underlying reasons, only one possibility surfaced that made any sense to me. In the US, Lida had been the focus of my attention, and Martin's, when he was home. She was the central character in our lives, treated as an honored guest. She had called it the happiest time of her life. Then we went back to Russia where Lida, who had admitted to being extremely competitive, became a support player. People saw her mainly as my interpreter. She had chosen that role several years earlier and had always seemed to enjoy it. But this year was different.

To make matters worse, assuming my hypothesis was correct, I had also become something of a celebrity in Belaya — the only American who had been there in years, and one of the few to ever spend time there. People sought me out, often overlooking Lida except when they needed her to translate. Moreover, while there, my attention was focused largely on what we were seeing and experiencing, less on her. If this shift in attention was, in fact, the reason for her growing irascibility, it would have been understandable.

Whatever the *real* reason may have been, Lida wasn't talking. The sudden change in her behavior was bewildering and saddening. It felt like a personal betrayal at first, until I discovered, in a book that Natasha gave to me, a possible explanation. In this book, written by a spiritual brother of Natasha's, a prize-winning author, I learned that unpredictability was a trait that Russians secretly loved about themselves. I had also learned, from a politician I met, that this very trait, which drives foreigners to distraction, was considered a central reason for Russia's unconquerability in recent centuries.

In the book Natasha gave me, unpredictability was related to uncontrollability. It occurred to me that acting unpredictably might produce — in people who inhabited a universe defined by external control — a sense of having leverage, if not actual power. I began to wonder if Lida's intermittent refusals to translate, for which I had depended on her totally, were an attempt to gain leverage over me. Why she would want that leverage, I couldn't begin to fathom. Whether her behavior was even conscious, I couldn't know. If it was, it did not have the intended effect. Inwardly, I was saying goodbye to Lida, with much regret.

Part Four

———

Heading Home

Culture Clash

I returned to Russia one more time, in December '97. Having nearly completed a first draft of the book, I had facts to check and questions to ask. There were many things I wanted to clarify with Natasha before sending the manuscript to an agent, which I was hoping to do the following spring. Needing her full attention, and knowing how easily distracted she was, I decided that my best option was to bring the manuscript to her myself before the Russian winter set in.

The trip, made possible by frequent flyer miles, was to be for only a week. That left me five full days in Moscow. I expected early December to be a quiet time, since Russian Orthodox Christmas wasn't celebrated until January. My idea was to sit down with Natasha at her kitchen table for a few hours each day, and try to keep her focused. It would probably have taken only one full day of concentrated effort to answer all my questions, but I kept that to myself.

A few months beforehand, when the idea first occurred to me, I had called Natasha to ask how she felt about my coming to see her at that time. After thanking me profusely for not being "like all those journalists who write whatever they please," she had assured me that she would be available. On a more personal level, she had seemed genuinely glad that I would be coming, since I hadn't visited that year. She said she was going to "tell everyone," which made me wonder if she really understood that the purpose of my visit was to work on the book. Two weeks beforehand, I called to remind her why I was coming.

When my plane arrived in Moscow, Natasha was there waiting for me. I was surprised and rather touched, since she hated the airport chaos — inevitable flight delays, lost luggage, traffic jams. In the past, one or another of her friends had picked me up. As it turned out, however, there was a reason for her coming this time: a change of plans for which she wanted to prepare me. Due to a plumbing crisis in her apartment, which made it impossible to take a shower, she had arranged for me to stay at a friend's apartment.

This apartment was in the center of Moscow, just off Old Arbat, a pleasant, well-lit, pedestrian mall that was a fifteen-minute walk from Natasha's. It belonged to a woman named Valentina, whom I had met once in Belaya. Natasha came upstairs with me, to reacquaint me with Valentina and say hello. While they were chatting, I dug the manuscript out of my bag. Natasha's eyes lit up. Clasping it to her breast, she assured me that it would be safe in her apartment, where we would be working.

There was only one problem, however, regarding work. The following day her household would be engaged in a celebration. Katya, a young woman from Belaya then living there, was going to receive her Ph.D. After the official ceremony, there would be a reception at the university, and then Katya's friends and family were going back to Natasha's for another celebration. She pointed out that I wasn't obliged to attend, but that Katya, whom she knew I was fond of, would be disappointed if I didn't. At any rate, Natasha would not be available.

And so it went. Day two was the birthday of Slava, Natasha's spiritual brother, whom I was also fond of. After giving his morning lecture at the university, where his students showered him with gifts, he came to Natasha's with his wife, college-age daughter, and the gifts, which included a large bottle of brandy. During the afternoon, which passed with toasts, pleasant banter and bursts of laughter occasioned by Slava's wry wit, the brandy bottle was emptied. Slava passed out on the divan and remained there until he awoke refreshed, able to drive his family home.

The day before, Natasha had promised me that no matter what happened, we would do some work the following day. What remained, at that point, was the evening. Moments after Slava left, Natasha told me, with wide-eyed excitement, that the most wonderful, unexpected thing had happened. That very morning, someone had given her two tickets to a sold-out concert for that evening. We didn't have to go, she said, but everyone was raving about the performer, a female vocalist, and this was her Moscow début. With a gesture at sincerity, she told me that she would understand if *I* felt we had to work.

I was tired, still suffering from jet lag, and agreed to go to the concert. The singer was breathtaking, the kind of "Russian miracle," as she was called, who appeared from time to time. She had started singing as a child with her *babushka*, learning ancient folk songs as they worked in their Siberian garden. Her voice, like the purest crystal, reflected her soul. At the first eruption of applause, she asked the audience to please refrain from clapping. Her intent, she said, was simply to be present, to allow Spirit to flow between them. With that, the concert hall became a temple, her performance — a holy communion.

During the intermission, Natasha took me by the hand and led me on a round of introductions. She told various acquaintances — a music professor, a film director, a novelist — that I had written a "monumental" book about the Russian soul. She told the host of a TV interview show, who often called upon her to recommend guests, that I would gladly appear on his show the following year. After the concert, we went to meet the performer back-stage, where a TV crew was waiting for her. Natasha literally pushed me in front of the camera to say a few words about my book, in Russian . . .

I realized that I was fast losing control of the situation; my purpose for being there was getting lost. But Natasha had been disarming right from the start. The previous day, in the car on the way to Katya's graduation, she announced that she had read the manuscript from beginning to end, starting the morning I arrived and staying up all night. As if bursting with pride, she told everyone that it was "a masterpiece," a "brilliant work." Since she was, in effect, the book's main character, I couldn't help being pleased by her response. But being familiar with Russian hyperbole — exaggerated praise and its flip side, excessive criticism — I took her burst of enthusiasm in stride.

And I couldn't help wondering whether she really *had* read the entire manuscript. If so, I thought, perhaps that would speed things up; she might have already marked whatever inaccuracies she had come upon. But it was difficult to believe that Natasha had actually read several hundred pages, in English, in one day. It seemed absolutely implausible, except for the fact that she commented on things which appeared in several different chapters. Still, given the way the week was unfolding, I had reason to doubt. And I really needed her to focus on unanswered questions, especially those that only she could answer.

The book had evolved into a kind of spiritual travelogue through the Russian heartland, with a focus on Belaya and the people who lived and journeyed there. Most of the main characters were part of Natasha's spiritual family. The events of '95 and '96, which she had played a large part in organizing, became my doorways into history, literature, philosophy, religion, and spirituality. Passing back and forth through those doorways, I had woven together past and present, with an eye toward future predictions about the spiritual destiny of Russia.

On the morning of my third full day in Moscow, Natasha and I had an unambiguous agreement to begin working. After a pleasant breakfast conversation with Valentina, followed by a walk in the enchanting beauty of gently falling snow, I arrived at Natasha's full of optimism. It seemed that I *would* accomplish, after all, the task for which I had traveled thousands of miles. Katya, who spoke perfect English, was willing to be our translator for the day. That helped a lot, since Natasha's spoken English was as limited as my Russian, and our mongrelized *Franglais*, mingled with Russian, tended to lack precision.

Things began well. We were finally under one roof, with no countervailing pressures or distractions. Waiting for Natasha to appear, Katya and I chatted, catching up on news. We were seated at the large dining table in the main room, the place where

Transfiguration Day had been celebrated in August '91, during my first visit to the apartment. I associated a string of pleasant memories with that room, including my fiftieth birthday dinner, prepared under the supervision of Baba Anya.

When Natasha entered the room, however, a cold north wind blew in with her. It was as though a switch had been flipped during the night. The pendulum had swung completely to the other side. The day before was a distant memory. It wasn't the first time I'd observed such a dramatic change of mood in her, but this time I was thrown by it. For every word of ecstatic praise spoken earlier, there was now a stream of vitriolic criticism. Poison arrows came at me so fast and furiously that poor Katya, who made no secret of her discomfort, could not keep pace with the translation and eventually gave up trying.

Reeling from the initial shock, trying to regain my equilibrium, I had the odd sensation of being on trial and having no idea what the accusation was. What flashed through my mind were stories I'd heard about Communist Party meetings where grown men were made to cry, and worse. Some had heart attacks afterwards, some committed suicide, unable to recover from the emotional frenzy whipped up against them. Guilt or innocence was not necessarily established; nor was it really the issue. It was the accusation that mattered most, especially if it came from a Party chief.

I'd heard that Natasha was capable of unexpected outbursts of anger; Lida was often at the receiving end. But I could not have imagined the staggering impact until I experienced it myself. And yet, being wired differently than Russians, it didn't produce the same effect in me. Once she quieted down and I realized what was happening, I calmly told her that the wave of negative emotion she had unleashed made it impossible for me to hear the content of her criticisms, however valid they might be. Natasha appeared stunned. She looked at me as if to say "Who, me?" Katya, sitting out of her range of vision, was beaming. She later told me that she had never heard anyone speak to Natasha that way.

When the dust settled, a few issues came to light that might have triggered her explosion, though they alone could not have fully accounted for it. One of Natasha's concerns had to do with "sins of omission." I had neglected to mention certain key figures of the 20th century, such as the geologist Vladimir Vernadsky, a seminal global thinker whom Natasha idolized (though there was no organic place for him in my story). Another issue, no doubt more upsetting to her, was my description of her mother as a Central Committee member and loyal Party official for most of her life, which she was. Natasha wanted me to *understand* that her mother was also the descendant of a long lineage of priests, one of whom had had a renowned ecclesiastical and academic career.

She had several other such revisions, before we finally approached my list of factual corrections and some larger issues that were baffling to me. Of the latter, one had to do with the use of the word "culture." The word itself seemed to be a kind of tinderbox. It had been the cause of a recent upheaval in Belaya. The current mayor, an atheist, had tried to cancel a conference devoted to culture. Clearly "culture" had a wider, deeper meaning to Russians, beyond music, art, and ballet. It *appeared* to be linked to religion or spirituality.

I had hoped that Natasha, who herself seemed to use the word with a sort of reverence, would explain the subtler dimensions it conveyed to Russians. That day, when I finally had a chance to ask her, she gave me a blank look at first, then appeared annoyed, as if I were asking something obvious, or elementary. When I explained the background of my question, she calmed down, until I asked what was meant exactly by "restoring Russian culture" — a topic much talked about at the time. She said she would think about it and let me know, but was visibly irritated.

Things went on like that, more or less, for the next few days. Beneath the clashes, however, there was an abiding affection between Natasha and me, along with an unusual kind of soul recognition. It had been there from the start. During our first interview, on the day of the coup, she had referred to me as a spiritual sister. She was making the point that we were moving into an age when Spirit would transcend all barriers — when bonds between kindred souls would supersede all national, religious, and other man-made boundaries. Six years later I was there in her home, with a manuscript in which she figured prominently, because of the light of her soul.

Polar Extremes

My time in Moscow was drawing to a close with many questions outstanding. I began looking for other ways to find answers — possibly e-mail, to which Katya soon expected to have access at her office. I had grown weary of trying to swim upstream; the current was much too strong. And it occurred to me that perhaps I was taking things too seriously. I recalled the advice of a friend who told me, more than once, that I ought to "lighten up." By the morning of day five, my last full day, I decided to let things flow.

No sooner had I made that shift in consciousness than an extraordinary soul appeared. Dressed in a tattered raincoat and threadbare slacks, she arrived at Valentina's as we were finishing breakfast. After walking up the flight of stairs, she appeared extremely winded. I realized she must have been in her eighties. Once she sat down and began to catch her breath, she turned toward me, slowly, and looked straight into my eyes. Her own eyes, a piercing shade of blue, were like laser beams.

She was Anna, an almost mythical figure to me. Natasha had spoken of her with a feeling approaching reverence. The two women had shared a remarkable history dating back to the Great Patriotic War, as Russians called World War II, in which Anna had been a pilot. Her younger brother, Yuri, a heroic tank commander, had met and fallen in love with Natasha's mother, who was widowed during the war, and who herself was quite heroic. She had volunteered to remain in Moscow after the evacuation of the city, to help defend it from the Germans, prepared to withstand torture if it came to that. They had planned to marry after the war. Days before victory was declared, Yuri perished.

News of Yuri's death caused terrible anguish for Natasha's mother, and for Natasha. She loved him dearly and had begun to think of him as her father. In their grief, mother and daughter reached out to Yuri's family. His mother was a gifted musician and a psychic. She had foreseen the deaths of Yuri and two other children of hers in the war. Prepared for the outcome, she comforted everyone else. Natasha grew increasingly attached to her, and to her daughter, Anna, who remained in the military after the war, rising up the ranks to the Soviet High Command.

Twenty years after the war, Natasha decided to be baptized. Her mother went into shock, worried about her daughter's mental stability, fearing for their safety. But Natasha's mind was made up. For the baptism, Father Alexei asked her to choose someone to be her spiritual mother. She chose Anna. Anna showed up at the cathedral in Belaya in her military uniform, unthinkable at that time. Stunned, I asked Natasha how, and why? Wasn't Anna an atheist? She replied, thoughtfully, "I chose Anna because apart from Father Alexei, she was simply the best person I knew."

Thirty more years passed. I was in Moscow with my manuscript. Anna had heard that I was there. She had also heard, apparently from Valentina, her neighbor, that Natasha was distracting me. She had shown up that morning with a mission: to find out if I was upset and, if I was, to make amends on Natasha's behalf. She indicated, with a roll of her eyes, that she knew how incorrigible Natasha could be. Then she looked into my eyes to see how I felt. I tried to console her, insisting that all was well, but she didn't accept my words. She sat there, as if she were examining my soul, until she found the assurance she needed.

Anna was frail. She got around with the greatest difficulty in winter. It was cold and the sidewalks were icy, untreated by sand or salt, perilous for old people who frequently slipped and broke bones. She had no boots. She apparently couldn't afford them despite a life of service to her country. Her shoes were old and badly worn; her socks were of thin cotton. But she had one overriding concern: that I did not return to America feeling offended by *her* Natasha. And her visit was, in truth, a healing balm.

After Anna left, I went to Natasha's apartment. I had invited a lovely woman to meet me there, a journalist named Sveta whom I had known for years. Several pages in my book were devoted to her and to some of the fascinating stories she had dug up for me. I was hoping to check a few facts with her, as well as to see her again, if only briefly. It felt awkward to ask her to travel across Moscow to meet me for a very short time, but given the number of schedules that had to be juggled, it was the best I could do. Even that small plan, however, was foiled by Natasha.

Knowing full well about my plan with Sveta, and my remaining questions for her, Natasha nevertheless railroaded me, in my remaining hours in Moscow, into interviewing her son, Pavel. In all the times I had stayed there, I had caught sight of this enigmatic man only twice, both times on the run. He was visibly uncomfortable around his parents. Misha's drunkenness made him cringe; his relationship with Natasha seemed complicated. Out of the blue, the night before, she had informed me that Pavel was "willing to be interviewed" for my book. I had never asked for an interview with him, as there was no conspicuous linkage; spirituality didn't appear paramount in his life.

Sveta was one of the few Russians I knew who was always punctual. She arrived exactly on time that day along with her younger sister, Nadia, a lovely young woman studying to be an English teacher. They came bearing gifts and the news that Sveta had met the man she was going to marry, leaving little time to discuss the manuscript before Pavel was due to arrive. Since Sveta knew no English, Nadia translated the pages in question line by line, going as fast as she could, stopping only when Sveta had a correction to make. Still, despite everyone's best efforts, the process was aborted.

Pavel arrived early. And Pavel was not a person who could wait. A film director, he was accustomed to being in charge and having everyone around him fall in line. When Natasha entered the room to announce that Pavel was there, she glared at me, signaling that I was to wrap up my meeting immediately. Then she stood in the doorway waiting for us to conclude. I expressed my profound regrets to Sveta and Nadia, hoping they would understand, assuming they were familiar with such Russian personalities. But as soon as they left, something inside me snapped. I turned to Natasha and blurted out, "Thank God I am going home tomorrow."

I had an ironic smile on my face, but the remark undeniably sailed forth on a wave of anger, impossible to suppress by that time. Until then, I had seen Natasha as a kindred spirit. I was aware of her foibles, the more serious ones by hearsay only. During my previous visits, when Lida and others were around, she had always been warm and engaging. That week, with every passing day, she became increasingly dictatorial. Only later, with the passage of time, could I see that the problem had also been at least partially mine. My pronouncement about going home was, in essence, an admission of my inability to hold my ground with her.

Curiously, my remark seemed to barely graze her. She took it in stride, shrugged it off. Her main concern at that moment was getting me settled at the table with her even more demanding son (an interesting man who advised me never to trust a Russian). But later that day, I said something that clearly did give her pause. It slid off my tongue quite naturally, unselfconsciously, which left me all the more unprepared for its ramifications. To me, it seemed like a small pebble which made surprisingly wide ripples.

Slava had come over to say good-bye. We sat around the table eating, drinking, and chatting. I was finally competent enough in Russian to have an elementary conversation with him, though Katya poked her head in from time to time to help with vocabulary. By that point in the week, I was more than happy to sit and drink vodka with him. Natasha mostly busied herself in the kitchen, seeming unusually agitated, stopping by occasionally but never sitting down.

Eventually, the cause of her agitation surfaced. Slava broached it with great delicacy. It seemed that Natasha was upset about my mentioning reincarnation in the book. This came as a shock to me, as she herself had a stunning perspective on the continuity of lives, with clearer past-life memories than anyone I knew. The problem, I learned, had to do with the Moscow Patriarchate of the Russian Orthodox Church, with which she had established relations concerning Belaya. The Anathema had been worrying her.

I sat there dumbfounded. Of all the potential audiences I considered while writing that book, the Russian Orthodox Church hierarchy was never one. From the start, I had been impressed by the large numbers of Russians searching for truth and finding their way to the wisdom teachings. Among the pillars of those teachings were the spiritual laws of reincarnation and karma. In my mind, these laws held the key to planetary transformation. If people understood the true meaning of "As ye sow, ye shall reap" — not as an adage, but an inexorable law governing the consequences of our actions — it seemed to me that the world would inevitably change for the better.

Once the topic had been aired, Natasha took a seat. The table was long and oval-shaped. I was sitting at one end; she sat down at the other. Slava was in the middle, and did his best to mediate. Without having read the manuscript, he took the position that I could delete a few references to reincarnation and all would be well. I replied that there weren't very many references to start with. Natasha, who fully understood the nature of the book, had no practical solutions to offer. She just looked concerned.

For me, the issue seemed loaded with paradox. During the years when the Russian Orthodox Church was an institutional pariah, Natasha was translating writings on Eastern spirituality into Russian, writings based on the belief that the Law of Rebirth, and the accompanying Law of Karma, were the vehicles of the soul's ultimate perfection. This translation work was an extension of what she remembered doing in a previous life. Moreover, she had shown some of those writings, along with certain Agni Yoga books, to her spiritual teacher in this life, Father Alexei, who had recognized their truths and appreciated them enormously, in the privacy of his room.

By then, my perceptions of Natasha were thrown into doubt. One of the things I had valued most in her, and other Russians, was an apprehension of the true essence of things. I was under the impression that spiritual truth mattered to Russian seekers, perhaps more than to seekers elsewhere, in part because it had been forbidden for so long. In communist times, people took enormous personal risks, facing the prospect of terrible reprisals, in order to obtain knowledge that was there simply for the asking in the West.

What I hadn't foreseen, and could never have imagined, was the rapid replacement of one totalitarian belief system, and institution, by another. The emergence of Church hegemony was sudden and sweeping. The Anathema had had its intended effect. Even people like Natasha, and Slava, who rarely attended church, felt compelled to refrain from voicing their true beliefs. The openness of *glasnost* — which literally means voice-ness, or having a voice — was already becoming a memory.

The comment I made, which unwittingly cast a long shadow, had come in response to a remark from Slava. "We Russians always have to be careful of what we say," he said to me, as if I were a slightly wayward Russian child. This struck me as the height of irony since only a few days earlier he had, oddly I thought, complimented me on being true to myself, not feeling obliged to "try to be Russian." Thus when he spoke to me that day about being careful, as if I *were* Russian, I simply replied, "I am not Russian, I am American." Silence followed — a long, heavy, uncomfortable silence.

The following day was my departure. A car provided by Pavel's company arrived a few hours ahead of time to pick me up at Valentina's, with my baggage, and bring me to Natasha's for lunch before going to the airport. To my surprise, a large group of friendly faces was assembled around the table, including Irina, one of my best teachers anent the Russian soul, who had, sadly, been diagnosed with cancer. That kind of gathering was the last thing I expected, in light of the tensions of recent days.

The meal was superb, specially prepared by Katya's parents, in Moscow for her graduation. Naturally, there were toasts. At the end, Natasha made a toast to the book. She prefaced it by saying that it was "something none of *us* would ever have done." Then she let loose with a volley of hyperbole, calling it a "titanic work," a "masterpiece," and so on. That was for public consumption. Immediately afterward, another spiritual brother, evidently privy to some of her concerns, leaned over to offer advice for the final chapter, still unwritten. "Remember," he whispered, "the ending must be positive, uplifting."

When the driver came in to say it was time to leave for the airport, I said my goodbyes and was about to embrace Natasha when she announced that she was coming with me. I had been looking forward to that ride as the first leg of my journey home, a time to be alone and regain my equilibrium after a week of swirling emotions. Natasha chose that moment to share her feelings about those times. With a vulnerability I hadn't seen in her before, she said, "I've never been so confused in my life, or worried about the future." Perhaps that was her way of explaining her behavior, or apologizing. I couldn't help feeling compassion for her.

Dharma

Back home again, I continued working on the book in the same spirit in which I began. My task, as I perceived it, was to reveal a side of Russia that was virtually unknown in the West, and scarcely better known to Russians themselves after the 70-year blackout. I realized that I couldn't completely avoid the dark side of present-day life, but felt I didn't have to dwell on it either. Many pens were taken up with that. I had hoped to offer a different view, and provide a link between the reemergence of Russian spirituality and the dawn of global spirituality.

Several months after returning home, I received a call from a Russian woman named Lyuba who had recently moved to the Washington area with her family. My phone number had been given to her by a mutual acquaintance, a student of Agni Yoga, which Lyuba also was. Her accent was heavy and often difficult to understand, but her command of the English language was otherwise quite good. Our first conversation, unusually long, made it clear that she was eager to communicate, glad to connect with a kindred spirit relatively close to her new home.

Lyuba sounded like a thoughtful, intelligent person with a probing mind. She asked a stream of questions about my travels in Russia, my book, my view of Russian spirituality. When I finished responding, she commented that my perspective on Russia was unique in her experience. Before moving to D.C., she had spent two years pursuing a Master's in sociology at a Midwestern university, where faculty interested in the former Soviet Union were charting its political, social and economic demise. None were aware of the spiritual side.

When I finally met Lyuba, what struck me first were the pain and fear in her face. Given the upbeat tone of our telephone conversations, I was surprised to find a person who looked so troubled, so clearly agitated. Her eyes, deep blue like many Russian eyes, seemed to be nervously scanning my face, as if anticipating a negative reaction. After awhile, however, she loosened up. The more comfortable she became, the more she smiled and joked, revealing a fine, Russian sense of irony. I soon forgot about the dark cloud.

In time, however, I discovered that Lyuba was living in a roiling sea of anxiety. Her husband, a scientist, had come to Washington for a quasi-governmental job. On a modest salary, he was supporting his wife and daughter, who had special medical needs, and his parents, newly arrived in the US. Lyuba, who had a Master's Degree plus a Ph.D. from Moscow University in psychology, had been hunting for a job for months. Puzzled over why she had received no responses to her queries, she asked my advice. It was hard for me to know what the problem was: her qualifications, her English, her salary requirements, or the shifting tide of opinion toward Russian immigrants.

One day she called to let me know that an excellent job had come along. Sounding pleased, there was also a hint of tentativeness in her voice, as if it were too good to be true. She would be working for a publisher that had frequent dealings with the US government and needed someone to expedite contracts and payments. The woman in charge had hired Lyuba for her human relations skills, explaining that the obstacles in dealing with the government were often personality-related. Lyuba's job was to smooth the way through a thicket of personalities. Her salary was many times more than she had ever dreamed of earning.

Things began well for her. A few months later, however, she called me sounding depressed. She was on the verge of losing her job. The reason given was that her English was inadequate. I was perplexed, since I automatically assumed that the problem was her heavy accent, yet her boss had to have noticed that immediately. As the story unfolded, a larger problem was her correspondence — faxes and e-mails full of errors. I asked whether her boss had inquired about her writing skills before hiring her. She had, and Lyuba had given her a copy of her Master's thesis. What Lyuba had neglected to mention to her boss, or to me until much later, was that the entire thesis had been edited for her by a fellow student, an American.

At the same time that Lyuba was in despair over losing the only job that had come her way, I was entering a new phase with my book. I had begun sending the manuscript to agents, waiting weeks to hear back from each one before sending it to another. The initial responses were discouraging. Those who liked the book didn't know what to make of it, how to handle it, what category to place it in. Plus, the old story, I had no credentials related to Russia. And something new: my approach to Russian spirituality was highly unorthodox.

While these responses were slowly coming in, Lyuba was reading the manuscript. She raved about it, much the same as Natasha had. She said she'd been leery about reading it, afraid she wouldn't know what to say if it were dull or mediocre. She had faced that dilemma with faculty members at her university who had asked her to read papers they wrote on Russia. But she said my book inspired her in a way that no other contemporary writings about Russia had, and it taught her things about Russian culture and history that she had never found elsewhere.

In retrospect, what happened next seemed like a set-up. It was one of those situations in life where it feels as if we have no free will, where everything conspires to move us in a particular direction. All doors are closed except one. We walk through that door sensing it is pre-ordained and assuming, therefore, that the outcome will be good. It doesn't occur to us, at such moments, that the outcome may be just what we need in order to grow, yet not at all what we would have wished for. Pre-ordained, but not for our greater glory; rather, for a spiritual lesson, often a difficult one.

Lyuba was desperately in need of income, not only for her

family's living expenses, but also for monthly payments on a car she had purchased to commute to her job. It was her first car, and after living a Soviet life she was morose about having to give up her newfound sense of independence. Around the same time, I had begun thinking about having my book translated into Russian. It dawned on me that perhaps, without consciously realizing it, I had written it primarily for a Russian audience. Lyuba, like Natasha, had called it a "gift" to Russia. The impact on Russians was dramatically different than on Americans.

The "perfect solution" presented itself: Lyuba could be the book's translator. There were only two problems — I had no way to pay her, and she had no experience as a translator. The more I thought about the second problem, the more solvable it appeared to be. She was a self-styled poet as many Russians are, in love with the rich nuances of her native tongue, which she spoke with elegance. She was also extremely bright and picked things up quickly. Plus, she had a friend in Moscow who was one of the most respected English-Russian translators, and who presumably could be of help to Lyuba.

When I broached the translation idea to her, she was thrilled. As for money, she said she'd need very little. Her main concern was the car, her freedom. She and her family were used to living on almost nothing. It would be a dream come true for her, she said, to work on the translation of my book. Nothing would bring her greater satisfaction than to do such work "for Russia." Knowing that she was among those émigrés who felt some degree of guilt about abandoning the Motherland in a time of crisis, I took her at her word.

The question was how and where to find the money to pay her. Lyuba had ideas and energy. She felt we should approach Americans interested in Russia. In her travels, she had met quite a few, some with considerable wealth. She took it upon herself to write and ask them to contribute to the cost of translating the book, to make it available to Russians. Though I was loath to seek help again on this project, I did contact a couple of people I knew who were interested in Russia and who had financial resources.

By then, I was editing the book, at a stage in which I really needed the information that Natasha had promised to gather. Months had passed since our last conversation, the only one since my visit to Moscow. Natasha had promised, again, to send me the material as soon as Katya had access to e-mail. I decided to call Moscow again, and asked Lyuba to be there with me. She was excited about speaking with Natasha, whom she had gotten to know through the book. And she was sensitive to my dilemma. We agreed that I would make the call, introduce Lyuba, and that she would try another approach to obtain the missing information.

We called Natasha together on a Sunday afternoon in the summer of '98, after attending a conference on Russia in a Washington hotel. It was reassuring to hear the responsiveness in Natasha's voice. As always, her first question was, "When are you coming to Moscow again?' The fracas of my last visit already seemed long forgotten. An endearing quality of Russians is the ease with which they forget and forgive. It is part of their nature, or culture, to forgive one other, even for things that sometimes seemed unforgivable — especially without apology, remorse, or acknowledgement of wrong-doing.

I explained to Natasha that I had met Lyuba in Washington, that Lyuba was very interested in the book, and that she might become the translator. When I put Lyuba on the phone I had no idea what would happen. I knew that Russians tended to be highly suspicious of one another in such situations, until or unless they managed to strike a common chord. Once that happened, they would start to call each other by nicknames — diminutives of their given names that range from the relatively formal on one end of the spectrum, to the informal and intimate, on the other end.

Natasha, because of her age and social status, was called Natalya Stepanovna by people other than family and close friends. Natalya is the formal name for which Natasha is the common diminutive; Stepanovna is her "patronymic," the second or middle name, which for women and men alike is based on the name of the father — in her case, Stepan. Thus, while Lyuba first addressed her as Natalia Stepanovna, by the end of the conversation she was calling her

Natasha. Whereas Natasha, who started out using Lyuba, the common diminutive for Lyubov, closed with Lyubochka. It seemed they had established, in the mysterious way that Russians do, some common ground.

Afterward, as we walked around the flowering, landscaped area of Washington's embassy row, Lyuba appeared buoyant. Something had evidently transpired on the phone that had left her feeling elated. I discovered that it was Natasha's parting comment. "Lyubochka," she had said, "Russia really *needs* this book now." Lyuba had grown to admire Natasha as a kind of mythic character through the pages of the book. That character was now urging her to help make the book a reality. Lyuba's enthusiasm, already considerable, was redoubled.

Something else resulted from that conversation that came as a gift to me. I suddenly had the feeling of being part of a team. It was as if a great burden were being lifted from my shoulders. Lyuba could sense my exhaustion after all of those years of effort, and was aware of the frustrations of my last visit. A "take-charge" person by nature and an optimist, she told me not to worry about a thing. She had a friend in Moscow with access to e-mail and other resources. Somehow she would get hold of the missing information.

As time went on, Lyuba became increasingly involved with the book, the whole process of giving birth to it. It was as though destiny had chosen her to be its midwife, in and for Russia. She led me to believe that getting the book to Russian readers had become her *dharma*, her soul's task or purpose, much as I felt that writing it had been mine. It was not just a current interest for her, a momentary preoccupation, but a significant opportunity related to her own spiritual journey.

Things reached the point where Lyuba said she wanted to translate the book even if it meant giving up her car. She insisted that she could live on next to nothing. But she knew that I knew she had to have a car, and that her family had to eat. We talked about how much she would need per month until her car payments were completed, and how much thereafter. I approached a philanthropic soul who had helped me once before, and who came through with enough for the first few months. That was a good omen. Things seemed to be falling into place. We both believed the remaining resources would, somehow, appear.

An Experiment

During those early months, I worked overtime trying to read the tea leaves. Several lives were now involved in "the book," in addition to my own. By the time Lyuba came along, it had been eight years since my decision to write a book about the Russian soul. My husband's life had been directly affected all along, as we had no disposable income to speak of. Now there was Lyuba to consider, and her share of her family's living expenses.

From time to time I was haunted by the question of why it was such a struggle financially. The amount of money we needed was insignificant, at a time when Americans were swimming in money, throwing it away. By the late 90s, vast numbers of people had acquired unimaginable levels of wealth. Even the opulence of the middle class seemed staggering. It was common to see entire computers in the garbage, replaced by newer, faster models. So why was my path so financially challenging? Was there something out of alignment, something I couldn't see?

Possible answers were legion, ranging from the subject matter of the book, to its worldview, to its style. Of the Americans who read it, about a dozen in all, some found it difficult, saying it required a lot of concentration. One friend said she read at night to relax and the book was "hard work." Academics of a spiritual bent applauded it, commending its copious footnotes, but the personal style and some of the content made it inappropriate for academic presses. It was appreciated most of all by "new age" readers, whose response was closest to that of Russians.

Russian readers, including some living in the US, offered praise, adulation, and something totally unanticipated — gratitude. I was repeatedly thanked for my "gift to Russia and Russians." Since most Russians had no money, however, including Russian publishers, many of which had turned into printers-for-hire, I understood that the book would be "a gift" in all ways. Apart from appreciation, there would be no compensation. I was able to live with that, as long as the book fulfilled its purpose.

My exploration of the Russian soul had never been about money. It was sparked initially by an urge to learn, to grow, to transcend boundaries. I had already learned more than I ever could have anticipated. My own world had expanded exponentially, while the larger world had shrunk in due proportion. I had learned almost viscerally, by being in Russia, that in the realm of the soul, boundaries evaporated. Boundaries were products of the human personality, with all of its limitations, and thus readily transcended by souls, especially old souls.

Russia had produced many old and great souls. They appeared to thrive there despite the rocky soil, perhaps because of it. In a land of constantly dueling polarities, personal struggles often revolved around good and evil. Everyday life generated encounters between right and wrong, truth and lies — skirmishes in the larger battle over saving or losing one's soul. The cumulative effect was to separate the wheat from the chaff; the gold from the dross. Only those who were willing to go through the purifying fires survived with their souls in tact. And those who did became beacons of light.

Anna, the spiritual mother of Natasha, was such a soul. I had met several others and encountered many more in the pages of Russian literature. The cost of their salvation was high, in a material sense, but small when compared to the jewel-in-the-heart born of sacrifice. Part of what I had hoped to convey in my book was this "other Russia" that had helped make sense of the prophecies I had come across. Communicating this discovery to others seemed to be my dharma. It didn't really matter to me who my readers were, or whether they could afford to pay money for the book.

In the past, I had started some projects that remained unfinished. This time I had resolved not to let go until the end. I had become accustomed to living with uncertainty. There were periods of calm followed by storm clouds appearing on the horizon, but the clouds never burst and eventually they moved away, as if kept at bay by an invisible hand. Recognizing that pattern helped me to stay on track, as did my inner guidance. My guidance had never steered me wrong, though at times it took me on detours, or what I perceived as such. In the end, problems found resolutions. And so the work went on.

The work now included Lyuba, who needed a lot of help, especially at the beginning. At the same time, she was an unexpected source of help to me. She had a good eye when it came to editing, even in English. One of the most laborious, often painful, aspects of writing is editing one's own work. I had dreamed of finding help, ideally from an editor at an American publishing house. With every passing month, however, as that likelihood seemed increasingly remote, Lyuba's help became all the more valuable.

Lyuba seemed like a godsend, literally, as if she'd been sent from above when I most needed encouragement. She was contributing to the work in many ways I had not anticipated: thinking of new, untried avenues for finding publishers, American and Russian; investigating self-publishing, if it should come to that. And she had an uncanny sense of intuition. Many mornings I found a soothing, consoling e-mail message from Lyuba, reassuring me about precisely the concern I was privately mulling over at the moment.

In the beginning, having Lyuba in my life was a blessing. She herself seemed to be a validation of the course I was on. As weeks flowed into months, that sense of validation turned into a lifeline. Had it been broken, there were times when I might have lacked the courage to press on until the end. The silence of "the world," of various people to whom I sent the manuscript, was deafening. At times it was nearly paralyzing.

Eventually, despite Lyuba and all that she symbolized, the unthinkable wormed its way into my consciousness: what if no one wanted to publish my book? I'd nearly given up hope of finding a mainstream American publisher or earning an advance. But what if no publisher in the US, not even a small press, were interested? How would I cope? How would I make sense of it? How would I explain, even to myself, the previous eight (nearly nine) years? How would I get on with the rest of my life? And, most importantly, what would such an outcome say about my spiritual guidance?

Most of the time, such questions remained beneath the radar. When they threatened to surface, Lyuba stepped in. By then we were working as a team to present our "gift" to Russia. Perhaps, we reasoned, it was intended all along that the book see the light of day in Russia *first*. If Russians collectively reacted as Natasha, Lyuba and others had, that reaction might somehow spark the interest of American publishers. Who could tell? I tried to suppress such speculation in favor of immediate tasks: one thing at a time, one day at a time. I realized that I was being tested, though I still didn't know what the test involved.

From June of '98 until the following autumn, Lyuba and I worked on the translation. It became an experiment in cross-cultural immersion. Having written about another culture, I was now experiencing what I had written through the eyes of people from that culture, with whom I was also working. Lyuba involved other Russians in the translation process, becoming a sort of contractor. She decided how many chapters she herself could translate in a given timeframe (which kept expanding), and then "sub-contracted" the remaining chapters to friends of hers in Moscow.

The first was Yelena, another Ph.D. in psychology with no formal translation experience, another poet, and another mother who desperately needed money. The advent of e-mail, which Yelena already had, made our collaboration with her possible. Express Mail to Russia, once a reliable delivery system, had become like the regular mail once delivery was taken over by Russians. Envelopes from the States that appeared interesting were often opened, resealed, and eventually sent to the Russian addressee after contents of any value had been confiscated.

While e-mail overcame many such hurdles, it could not, of course, turn people living with a different sense of time into responsive communicators. With most Russians, even those who had e-mail, that remained a headache. But in the case of Yelena, the distance between Russia and America shrank to nothing. She finished translating her first chapter and had it back in a flash, faster than Lyuba. The only hitch was getting money to her for the work she had completed, as the unannounced change in Express Mail delivery had already cost me several hundred dollars. Eventually we found reliable couriers, friends of friends traveling to Moscow.

Just when it seemed that our experiment was working nicely, a fly appeared in the ointment. Tensions arose around finding a way to *continue* monthly payments to Lyuba. At the end of four months, by which time her car had been paid off, the funds I was able to raise were running out. None of the wealthy Americans to whom she wrote had responded. Of the book's ten lengthy chapters, she had completed drafts of four, and hoped to translate three more in as many months. Yelena had agreed to do the remaining three.

The problem with Lyuba, unforeseen by me, was that our arrangement involved paying her on the basis of time — a monthly fee keyed to American costs. Having begun our collaboration in the spirit of an experiment, and in the hope of finding other funding sources, we had left the question of duration open. Yelena, on the other hand, was being paid for each completed chapter, as recommended by Lyuba. And since dollars went quite far in Russia, Yelena's fee for three chapters was relatively small. My husband, who had become committed to seeing the book published in Russia, agreed that we should bite the bullet and pay Yelena from our disappearing savings. By then, we were taking comfort from the aphorism: "Give all, that all may be given."

Then the question of how to continue paying Lyuba surfaced and, with that, other questions: the old one, about why money was not flowing into this project, and a new one, about how Lyuba was spending her time. She and I had never spoken about her work schedule. Not only would it have seemed demeaning to question her, but I trusted her implicitly. I believed that we shared the same spiritual values, and she seemed sincerely dedicated to the book, willing to work for little money, just enough to cover her basic expenses.

We both worked at home and agreed that having freedom compensated for many things, including a small wage, in her case. On the heels of her last job, involving long hours in an office with extended commutes twice a day, she seemed exultant. Now she could work any hours she chose, day or evening, take breaks at will, pick up her daughter after school, buy groceries and do errands at her convenience. Each day was hers to create, to shape as she chose, carving out periods of work around family obligations. Never did it occur to me that she would betray my trust.

Obstacles

When Lyuba and Natasha spoke for the first time, on the day we called Moscow together from Washington, Lyuba had asked Natasha again for the missing information, along with a few documents in the original Russian which would expedite her work. Natasha, as on prior occasions, cheerfully reassured "Lyubochka" that she would send those things right away. As in the past, nothing came. Katya, who was still living in Natasha's apartment, had access to e-mail by then. She sent me many newsy messages, but nothing from Natasha.

This led to my discovery, here at home, of a prominent facet of Russian life that had largely escaped me during my visits there: idle speculation. It is an absorbing, time-consuming and ultimately futile form of conjecture about why people do what they do, something like watching isolated fragments of a silent film and guessing what the characters are thinking. You can see images, gestures, comings and goings, but you can never decipher their real meaning, as there are no clues about motivation.

Lyuba was a master speculator. She could engage in it for hours. At times it bordered on raw gossip, since the shortcomings or insecurities of a person were often viewed as possible causes for otherwise inscrutable behavior. Fundamentally, however, her speculation was closer to psychologizing, attempting to "psych out" the deeper, hidden, unconscious reasons why a person might be acting in a particular way. Lyuba, a Russian and a psychologist by training, increasingly laid bare to me the mysteries of the Russian psyche.

I came to realize that speculation was a substitute for action — or interaction — with the person or persons in question. It was more palatable to spend hours conjuring up reasons for incomprehensible behavior than to ask the individual, directly, what was going on. In part this was because of the hierarchy of power in Russian life. The higher one stood in a particular pecking order, however great or small, the less accountable one was to anyone for anything. Questions weren't asked; answers weren't offered. In place of communication, life often seemed to consist of parallel lines and circles. In Natasha's case, things were invariably circular, including the speculation about her. It never brought us any closer to the goal: obtaining the needed information.

There was, however, an unintended consequence to our speculation about Natasha's broken promises. Lyuba began to see the book's central character in a new, less favorable light, which made Natasha more real to her, someone she could relate to. The Natasha in the book had few warts or moles. Out of respect, I had largely omitted her less than stellar traits, while poking fun at some, like her being a self-described "boss" from youth. I had also omitted unhappy facts of her life, such as Misha's drinking problem. Lida had reacted vehemently to a small reference I made to that in an early draft. Having decided it wasn't germane to the message of the book, I agreed to leave it out.

Lyuba, however, was fascinated by this and related facts. During one of our "speculations" about why Natasha was not responding, I mentioned that when I was last in Moscow, the previous December, Natasha had appeared old to me for the first time. Her hair had turned noticeably grayer in the course of a year and she had lost several teeth. I wondered whether her heart condition had suddenly taken a toll. Lyuba wanted to know — i.e., wanted me to engage in speculation about — why Natasha's son, Pavel, who was wealthy enough to buy an American SUV, had not bought his mother a set of dentures.

Things spiraled downward from there. I found out more about the underbelly of Russian life than I had ever wanted to know. It was a curious development since Lyuba, drawn to my book for its light, saw fit to reveal its opposite. A collector of statistics, she went beyond familiar ones, such as the seventy per cent rate of alcoholism among Russian men. She told me, for example, that child abuse in Russian families was the rule, not the exception; that it was not uncommon for husbands to abandon their aging wives; that the elderly received little if any help from their children. She described a place where ideals, of any kind, seemed ever more like fairy tales.

Such digressions from our translation work were actually few. They occurred only on the telephone, and Lyuba and I communicated largely by e-mail. When we did speak, however, and when the subject of Natasha came up, I often found myself rehashing my next-to-last day in Moscow, recounting the conversation with Natasha and Slava when I had made my declaration of independence — stating that I was American, not Russian, thus implying that I was not bound by the same rules.

That seemed like a pivotal moment, all the more so in retrospect. It occurred to me later that Natasha's silence at the time was no doubt a sign of her discomfort about my statement. But would that alone have made her anxious enough to want to foil the book? At that point in my speculation, Lyuba would remind me how *needed* Natasha felt the book was, in Russia, and assure me that Natasha would, in the end, cooperate.

In my depths, I suspected that the problem might have to do with control. Another prominent polarity in Russian life is domination and submission — the psychological residue of master and slave. I had had a taste of it under the rule of my first translator, but fortunately had been able to extricate myself. Now I was in unknown territory. Natasha was accustomed to being in control. In this case, while she was vitally important to the book, the central figure in a way, she was not the author. Would her need to control become an insurmountable obstacle? Would it determine the fate of the book?

While such questions were percolating, the honeymoon period with Lyuba was also ending. Her work hours appeared to fluctuate wildly, along with her moods. She wasn't doing well in an unstructured situation. It took me awhile to notice, but when I asked her about her work schedule, though I tried to approach the matter gingerly, she took offense. I explained that in the West we had a different relationship to time, that the time-money equation was part of our culture. I also mentioned that funds for the translation — my husband's and my savings — were all used up. To continue paying her, we would have to take out a loan.

As the months went by, Lyuba sent me the chapters she completed, drafts of them, so I had at least some gauge of her progress. I understood that translation work was like writing in certain ways; it often took awhile to find just the right word or turn of phrase. I also knew that her aim was to make the language sound like music, something I appreciated deeply. Still her work seemed unaccountably slow. It hadn't occurred to me that the Soviet workers' motto — "They pretend to pay us and we pretend to work!" — might have migrated to America and infiltrated a project like ours.

Then there was another new development. Lyuba didn't trust herself to be the final arbiter of the translation and wanted to enlist, for pay, the help of another friend in Moscow, an older woman who had had a distinguished career as an English-to-Russian translator. Nina Pavlovna Mitusova, a descendant of Russian aristocracy, was described by Lyuba as a person of refined literary discrimination. She was then a pensioner, but still quite active, organizing programs to resurrect Russian culture in the wake of the Soviet era.

Nina Pavlovna, whom I called by her first name and patronymic, agreed to edit Lyuba's translation for a very small fee, by American standards. She also offered to find a publisher in Moscow. She loved the book and wanted every fact and every footnote, of which there were hundreds, to be absolutely correct. If she had the slightest doubt about anything, she went directly to the main library, often ending up doing ancillary research for hours. She was one of those Russian women who seemed to have boundless energy despite her years, and despite the immense hardships of her life.

Our e-mail link with Nina Pavlovna was provided by her son-in-law, Igor, who had a small computer company in Moscow. Igor was willing to help only because he once had a crush on Lyuba. He had serious conflicts with his mother-in-law over family matters and took revenge by treating her like an uneducated village woman from Central Asia, where he originally came from. He refused to teach her how to use the computer, maintaining that she was "too great a risk." Thus she had to endure Igor's ire whenever she wanted to communicate with us.

Despite the abuse she suffered, and the ongoing sorrows of her life, Nina Pavlovna had a wonderful, feisty spirit. She engaged in life as an adventurer, ever eager to take on new challenges. Her manner, however, could be downright brusque. She was accustomed to being chief translator in a totalitarian society. When she disagreed with something I had written, she didn't beat around the bush. She simply decided that I was wrong and at times, without consulting me, replaced my words or ideas with her own.

There was one particularly eye-opening experience that had to do with the version of revolutionary history served up in Soviet schools. One of the disputed issues concerned, paradoxically, the role of a band of young aristocrats during the early stages of the Revolution. I had made a statement about them based on the personal account of a woman named Catherine Breshkovsky, born to the 19th century land-holding aristocracy, who had become devoted to educating and liberating the peasantry. Her activities landed her in prison, where she suffered terribly for decades, largely in the frozen wilds of Siberia, yet she managed to get letters out to American supporters who later published them.

Dubbed "the little grandmother of the Russian Revolution," Catherine Breshkovsky had helped launch a movement called "going to the people." Thousands of educated, upper class youths who sympathized with the plight of Russian peasants had sacrificed their privileged lives and gone to live in remote villages, teaching literacy and other skills, and generally encouraging the newly liberated serfs to demand their rights. Something I had written about this movement did not jive with the history learned in school by Nina Pavlovna. She decided it must have been wrong, and simply deleted it. To have it restored, to my book, I had to provide her with my evidence.

On the whole, however, my communications with Nina Pavlovna proved instructive and beneficial. She went over every sentence with such a fine tooth comb that by the time she finished working on a chapter, I had total confidence that everything in it was verifiably correct. The book was charting new territory in some ways, so its accuracy seemed all the more important. Her extreme diligence left me assured that it stood on absolutely solid ground.

Nina Pavlovna's involvement bore other fruits as well. A person who pondered things deeply, she said that before reading the book, she had believed the only way to improve society was by ameliorating the physical conditions of people's lives. "Now," she wrote to me, "I see that the most important thing is for people to take responsibility for their own souls." Dostoyevsky's literary journey had helped me illustrate that point, but it was a central tenet of the ageless wisdom. Nina Pavlovna decided to include it in a new curriculum she was writing for school children.

Meanwhile, Natasha was still incommunicado. Lyuba had called her one more time, but again failed to elicit the desired response. The newest candidate to find the missing information, and the one most likely to succeed, was Nina Pavlovna. Not only did she and Natasha both live in Moscow, but Nina Pavlovna frequently visited the Lenin Library, a stone's throw from Natasha's apartment. And Nina Pavlovna had already decided, independently, that she "needed to sit with Natasha" to go over certain things in the book.

She called Natasha, several times, to arrange an appointment to meet with her. After making herself frustratingly scarce, Natasha eventually agreed to meet Nina Pavlovna, who came away from that encounter completely charmed. And it turned out that the two women had mutual acquaintances. Nina Pavlovna told us that when she entered the main room of Natasha's apartment, she immediately recognized the face in a large portrait hanging on the wall. It was Natasha's mother. Nina Pavlovna remembered seeing her often, some thirty years earlier, at the home of her girlfriend —

the daughter of the chief of culture, who was the friend of Natasha's mother.

The news of that first meeting seemed auspicious. It came as a great relief to Lyuba and me. The "Natasha problem" had apparently been solved. They had made arrangements to meet again several weeks hence. By that time, Nina Pavlovna was going to have several chapters ready to show Natasha. Her plan was to go over them with Natasha page by page, asking whatever questions she had, and extracting the missing information as they came upon the blank spaces I had left.

But when Nina Pavlovna appeared on the agreed upon date, Natasha was not home. No one knew where she was. Nina Pavlovna offered to wait, and did so for two hours, but Natasha never showed up. A few days later, Nina Pavlovna called and Natasha picked up the phone. Without offering an apology, she simply said that she was very busy, she had to go to Belaya, and didn't know when she would return. Nina Pavlovna, one of the most patient, long-suffering people in the world, e-mailed Lyuba: "This is unimaginable, given what Nancy wrote about Natasha. I assumed she was of the highest moral caliber." I began to wonder what I had wrought.

Hope

As serious doubts began to surface about this latest version of my book, an old friend reappeared. His name was Vasily. I had first met him when I was beginning my interviews in early '91. Though quite young at the time, not long out of university, he had already won accolades as a journalist. He was also, by then, a long-time student of spiritual truth. And he was one of the first Russians with whom I felt a soul connection.

I had met him in the offices of his Moscow newspaper, where I had gone to interview another journalist. Vasily happened to walk by the cubicle where we were sitting as she was searching for an English expression. She called him over, knowing he was fluent in English, and it quickly became evident that he was more interested in my subject than his colleague was. She was feeling despondent about the condition of her country, equally so about the Russian soul, and had become deeply cynical. Vasily, on the other hand, resonated strongly with the idea of a new era of spirituality.

That evening, I was scheduled to meet with a group of psychologists at an apartment on the outskirts of Moscow. Vasily asked if he could attend the gathering. Getting there involved transfers between three metro lines and a long walk at the end. When he didn't appear, I assumed the distance had discouraged him. Long after the meeting got underway, however, he showed up, dressed in a jacket and tie, oddly formal attire for Moscow, which made me wonder if he'd hoped to add a few years to his youthful appearance. He still looked conspicuously younger than everyone there, by many years, until he began to speak.

The group was discussing religion, among other things, when Vasily arrived. I had asked them what they thought, as psychologists, about the great resurgence of interest in religion and spirituality in Russia. The conversation was wide-ranging, as they all seemed to have picked up a smattering of knowledge about metaphysics while studying Jung and humanistic psychology. They appeared to be open to everything. In fact, one of the guests was a psychic who specialized in identifying the source of people's health problems from their past lives, and claimed to see into future incarnations as well.

Vasily listened intently for some time before deciding to speak. When he did, the chatter stopped. All eyes were focused on him. I was floored by what he had to say, since I was familiar with the sources he quoted and had had personal experience along the lines of what he was talking about. The main point I remember him making, with the greatest conviction, was: "The age of religious *belief* is over. We are entering the age of spiritual *knowledge*. The new era will be a time of spiritual experience. People will have direct knowledge of higher realities. That will change the very meaning of religion."

The room was silent for a few moments as people tried to assimilate what Vasily had said. Then the conversation resumed and the group seemed to forget about this stranger in their midst. Vasily quietly excused himself. Before leaving, he asked for my home address, saying that he planned to come to the States one day. Less than a year later, he showed up at my apartment in New York. Columbia University had given him a scholarship to study philosophy and translate ancient religious texts into Russian.

Ever since we met, Vasily and I had remained in touch. There were long periods when I didn't hear from him. He traveled a lot for his work and studies, often to remote places around the globe. But eventually he would turn up again — by phone, or e-mail, or in person. Though he was a generation younger, I never felt an age gap between us. As was the case with other Russians with whom I had a special kind of communion, I was mostly aware of his soul.

Clearly an old soul, he had found his way to a spiritual teacher in Moscow as a teenager. The woman held classes in her apartment dealing with the sacred truths at the core of the world's great religions and philosophies. Vasily had been reflecting on the concept of a new world religion, based on universal truths and diverse practices, long before we met. He had grown up in anticipation of the new era. It felt completely natural to speak of these things with him, and it seemed that we were destined to meet.

This sense of destiny was reinforced by an incident which took place about six months after our first encounter. It occurred in the Moscow metro on the evening of August 21, 1991, as the celebration of victory over the infamous coup was winding down. After three turbulent days, there was a mood of quiet jubilation in the streets and metros. I had just said good-bye to my friend Tanya, the journalist with whom I'd experienced the turning of the tide, and who had just told me that for the first time in her life she felt proud to be a Russian.

The metros were packed. As I waited for a train with enough room to squeeze on, a sea of smiling faces flashed through my mind. Some had kept vigil at the Russian "White House" for the entire three days, prepared to die for the sake of freedom. Their eyes, red and glazed from lack of sleep, conveyed the most profound joy, tinged with a sense of the miraculous. Everything felt unreal. Less than twenty-four hours earlier, the country had been under martial law. Now, it seemed, a new chapter of Russian history was beginning.

I finally boarded a train, standing with my back against the doors, the only vacant spot. Unaware of the expression on my face, I looked up to find a young man opposite me smiling in a way that suggested he thought I was smiling at him. As the train began to empty out, he came over to my side. He knew I was American, through a special kind of radar Russians have, and struck up a conversation by saying that his best friend had just left for America. A silly line, I thought, but in the spirit of that moment I asked where in America his friend was going. "To New York City," he said, "to Columbia University." For the heck of it I asked the name of his best friend. That was when I first learned that Vasily was already in New York.

Over the years, Vasily and I supported each others' Aquarian ideas and creative projects. He always encouraged me with my book, especially during the valley periods, saying he wanted to read it as soon as it was finished. When that moment arrived, he was in Rome, doing research at the Vatican. His time was at a premium as his library permit was about to expire, but he asked me to send him the first few chapters by e-mail. A few days later he wrote and asked me to send the rest.

And then, a few weeks later, he wrote that he had decided to return to Russia, instead of to the US, as originally planned. He said that seeing the Russian soul through my eyes had restored his hope, and strengthened his commitment to try to do something in his homeland, to make a contribution in the realm of spirituality. That was music to my ears. Vasily had tremendous potential and was connected to a network of younger, spiritually-oriented people.

His return to Russia also rekindled hope for my book. If anyone could solve the mystery of Natasha, I thought, it was Vasily. The latest news from Nina Pavlovna had been hair-raising. She had finally pinned down Natasha to discuss the translation. When they met, Nina Pavlovna brought along her only copy of the Russian manuscript, which contained all of her painstaking, pencilled-in editing changes, representing months of work. When the meeting ended, Natasha asked to keep the manuscript, promising to return it within two weeks. By the time Vasily was due to arrive in Moscow, two months had passed.

Lyuba, Nina Pavlovna and I were suddenly faced with a crisis the likes of which I could never have imagined. It had been triggered by several interrelated factors. First, Nina Pavlovna's generation was unfamiliar with xerox machines. The possibility of copying her work before giving it away to Natasha had never occurred to her. If it had, as a pensioner living on next to nothing, she would have instantly ruled it out because of cost. Plus, in spite of all that had occurred, she trusted Natasha. "In Nancy's book," she e-mailed Lyuba as we tried to sort things out, "nothing even remotely suggested that Natasha was not an honest person."

With the disappearance of the manuscript, all work on the translation had ground to a halt. Vasily seemed like the best hope, and the last, to cut through to the core of things, to find out what in the world was going on with Natasha. Why had she hijacked the only copy of the edited Russian manuscript? What was her motive? Was she really trying, consciously or not, to sabotage the publication of a book in which she was instrumental, in every way, and which she had repeatedly said was "needed" by Russia?

Naturally, I was concerned that I had failed to see who Natasha really was, on the personality level; that I had mistakenly overlooked her flaws, thinking they weren't central to the book. Natasha was, in my mind, a symbol of the hidden potential of the Russian soul — she herself, her spiritual family, and her far-flung network. Plus I could see that something truly unique was germinating in Belaya, at least in part, due to her. But as the months wore on, I began to have the cold and clammy feeling that I had created a character more fictional than real. And if that were true, then the value of the entire book was in question.

Shortly before Vasily reappeared, Lyuba had turned up some new and surprising clues to the mystery of Natasha. She had called Natasha twice on my behalf, while Natasha was holding the manuscript hostage, in an effort to get it back to Nina Pavlovna. During the first conversation, Natasha confided to Lyuba that she feared the portrait of her in the book was "too good" (which I had also begun to fear). Lyuba's interpretation was that Natasha was afraid of the Russian-style pummeling she would get from those who knew her well and were aware of her shortcomings.

About a month later, Lyuba called again and found Natasha in Belaya. During that second conversation, Natasha expressed new but unspecified fears concerning Father Dmitry, the head-priest. She was afraid the book could somehow harm him. But at the same time, Natasha had sounded elated. She had just returned from a day's work with the film crew at the historical-cultural society. They loved the book and were using it as the basis of a new video about Belaya. Natasha was thrilled that Lyuba had called precisely at that moment, saying what a wonderful synchronicity it was, and how beautifully things were working out.

Something else transpired during that conversation that I never fully understood. Lyuba seemed to have largely forgotten her "mission," which was to get the manuscript back to Nina Pavlovna. When she called me afterward, she was bubbling over with excitement about Natasha's joyfulness at the timing of her call, and the film they were making in Belaya. Plus, there was other news. Natasha, hoping to see the book published first in the US, to enhance its legitimacy in Russia, had told Lyuba that she was already thinking about coming to the US for a publicity tour. And Lyuba had invited Natasha to stay with her family in the house they were planning to buy.

It was Russian surrealism all over again. I felt as though I were watching children at play in a field of hopes, dreams and wishes. The person causing me endless grief over completing the book was planning a triumphal book tour of my country — now with the complicity of Lyuba. I struggled to suppress feelings of rage and outrage, fearing that if I gave into them, everything would instantly unravel. I felt like a long-distance runner approaching the finish line. If I hesitated at all, if I even thought about how I was feeling, I might not make it to the end. And if I didn't, then all those old, unthinkable questions would resurface, along with new ones.

Keeping my eye on the goal, without stopping to consider the alternative, I tried to piece things together. Before that second conversation between Lyuba and Natasha, I had been under the impression that Lyuba and I were on the same team. Our team's objective was clear: we needed to get the manuscript back to Nina Pavlovna, deal with the changes we all assumed Natasha would want to make, and finalize the translation. But after that conversation, Lyuba sounded different to me. Apart from forgetting her mission, something in her voice suggested that she had joined Natasha's team, or that she was playing a different game, one that eluded me.

As things spiraled downward, I looked for possible explanations. I knew there was a tendency among Russian painters, writers and other artists to sabotage their creative offspring; to destroy — rather than revise — a work deemed less than perfect. Only recently, Lyuba had commented on the tortuous struggles of her countrymen to bring things into manifestation. When I mentioned that it had been nearly nine years since I had begun work on "the book," she replied, "That's nothing. In Russia a book like this would probably take twenty years." And she added, "It might never be published at all."

Her words, chilling as they were, shed new light on the Russian "mythological consciousness." I understood better than ever why Russians were often dreamers, and why for some the dream was all there was. Earthly reality was not only less than perfect, it was often heartbreakingly sordid. Savoring the dream in pure form gave meaning to life, whereas any attempt to realize the dream was likely to suffer attacks, betrayals, deceptions, broken promises. If, by chance, the dream were ever realized, in spite of *all* the obstacles, it would surely be annihilated by some cruel force. Far better to simply dream.

Vasily returned to Moscow in the late spring of '99. Three years had passed since he had last been there and tremendous changes had taken place in the spheres that called to him: religion, spirituality, philosophy. While renewing contacts and exploring possible futures for himself, he periodically sent me messages of reassurance about the manuscript. He promised to do whatever it took to have it delivered to Nina Pavlovna, even if it meant traveling to Belaya, to get his hands on it and bring it back. He was also going to look for a publisher, since those Nina Pavlovna knew had all become printers-for-hire, charging authors to publish their books.

One day I received an e-mail from Vasily full of exclamation points. He had met a priest named Father Sergei whom he called "a truly holy man, a new breed of priest." His sermons about love and compassion were attracting thousands of worshippers, mostly young people with no prior religious experience. Father Sergei had established, somehow, his own Russian Orthodox church, independent of the Moscow hierarchy that controlled the Church. He was, in fact, an outspoken opponent of that hierarchy, for many reasons, including the fact that its current leaders had colluded with the KGB.

Vasily had been inspired to write an article about Father Sergei and his new church for a popular magazine. His article had produced what Vasily called "a miracle" for my book. Father Sergei had been so pleased with Vasily's article that he had offered to publish a novel that Vasily was writing, about the spiritual quest, on his church's newly acquired printing press. Vasily told Father Sergei that his novel was not finished, but that his "spiritual sister in America had just written a wonderful book about the Russian soul." Father Sergei took a moment to consult his inner guidance and replied to Vasily, "Yes, it is a fine book. We will publish it."

Shatterings

As the weeks flew by in the summer of '99, I waited for word from Vasily about my manuscript. But I waited in vain. His plans to rescue it never materialized. Just when he was about to buy a ticket for the overnight train to Belaya, where Natasha had remained for an extended period, Father Sergei had come into his life. Vasily began writing articles, got involved in the new church, and that was that. Finally, however, despite this setback, some promising news arrived in the early fall. Lyuba heard from Nina Pavlovna that Natasha was, at long last, "ready to return the manuscript."

Lyuba believed her this time. She said she had sensed a change in Natasha during their last conversation, when Natasha had spoken of visiting the US. I began to think that things might possibly get back on track. The Russian mantram, "everything will work out in the end," might actually prove to be true. By then, however, I had largely given up thinking. I realized that my mind, which used to be reliable in sorting out complex issues, was of little use to me now. Prayer seemed like the more viable tool. I had come to feel that only a higher power could unsnarl this tangled web and set things straight.

Meanwhile, I was polishing up the final chapters of the book and sending them on to Lyuba; Lyuba translated my changes and sent them on to Nina Pavlovna. I still held out the hope that some day the book would be published in its original form, i.e. in English, and had been making small editing changes in anticipation of that day. And now, according to Vasily, Father Sergei was waiting to receive the Russian version. Nina Pavlovna was overjoyed by the news. She couldn't wait to go and meet this priest and hand him the manuscript in person.

In October '99, for reasons that were to remain obscure to me, Natasha did in fact return the manuscript to Nina Pavlovna. Nina Pavlovna pencilled in all the recent changes, her son-in-law, Igor, inserted them into his computer and e-mailed the finished chapters to Lyuba. After looking them over, Lyuba e-mailed the chapters to me, one by one. When they arrived in my e-mail, I could hardly believe my eyes. After more than a year of foiled communications and wasted speculations, here they were. Miraculously, things *had*, in the end, worked themselves out.

But suddenly, while scanning the chapters, I realized that something was missing. Something important. I had asked Nina Pavlovna to place brackets around the changes that Natasha suggested. The brackets would make it easy for me to find those changes, since I still found it laborious to read Russian, and the book contained several hundred pages. Natasha had made it crystal clear that she had some objections. I hadn't a clue as to what they were, and while I was willing to meet her more than halfway, I still reserved the right, as the author, to approve the final contents of my book. The brackets were going to vastly facilitate this task, or so I hoped.

The text arrived without brackets. Having recently sent reminders about this to Nina Pavlovna, while she was making the final changes, it seemed impossible that her omission of them was purely an oversight. That would have meant that both Nina Pavlovna, and Lyuba, who was to have reminded her as well, had both simply forgotten. And I knew Lyuba well enough to rule out the prospect of mere forgetfulness.

My discovery of the missing brackets was a blow. A feather could have upset my equilibrium. This meant that I could no longer trust my co-workers, whom I had relied upon totally for the translation, and whom I was still paying for their work. And yet I still wasn't able to let go of the book. I needed to believe that nine years of effort had not been for naught. And I remained convinced that the book held meaning for Russians readers, especially at that time. The dismal present made prospects for the future, with its spiritual potentials, all the more vital.

Two new challenges now stared at me: the question of trust, and the simpler matter of discovering Natasha's changes. I knew there had to be a solution to the second problem. And I never felt so American as when I set out to find it. The typical Russian response to obstacles that appeared insurmountable was fatalism, as reflected in two constantly used expressions. One was a rhetorical question: "What to do?" or "What can be done?" The other was a palliative: "It doesn't matter" or "It's nothing." Combined, as they often were, the sense was: *There is nothing I can do about it so I'll somehow manage to adjust and life will go on.*

I was determined to find a way to uncover Natasha's changes on my own, as neither Lyuba nor Nina Pavlovna appeared willing to help. Despite the fact that I had written the original text, reading every word of it in Russian would have taken me months. The solution was a technological godsend: an ingenious new software program discovered by my husband. Designed for lawyers, to highlight changes in successive drafts of a document, it enabled me to compare Lyuba's next-to-last draft, based on my text, with Nina Pavlovna's final one, which included Natasha's changes. The alterations made by Nina Pavlovna showed up instantly. Everything I needed to see was right there, in bright red text.

Combing through the contents of my own book in this way made me feel strangely like a sleuth. It was even stranger to discover that the vast majority of changes, made by Nina Pavlovna, were merely stylistic. She had an elegant way with words and had immensely improved the translation. As for the changes in content, they were remarkably few — given all the *sturm und drang*. But they had been ruthlessly executed. Several paragraphs, or portions thereof, were simply lopped off in the style of Soviet-era censorship. Where a whole paragraph once existed, a single line or two remained.

In some cases there was nothing at all left, just a gaping hole on the page.

Given Natasha's centrality to the book, and my faith that her higher self would ultimately prevail, I struggled to comprehend why certain portions of the text had been surgically removed. I searched for threads of logic behind deletions that were clearly hers, going back over the concerns she had voiced to me or others. But the exercise proved futile. Paragraphs that I would have expected to find missing or altered remained in tact, whereas others, which seemed thoroughly innocuous, had been sliced up or chopped off.

One deletion, for example, concerned the visit of the "spiritual intelligentsia" to Belaya for the 600th Anniversary of Russia's Deliverance from Tamerlane. I had written that they had met there in a house of worship for the first time, that previously they had met only at conferences, and that for Lida and others there was a dramatically different feeling about the gathering. Natasha deleted this observation. At the same time, to my sheer amazement, given her earlier protestations, she did not touch my few remaining references to reincarnation.

Most nettlesome to Natasha, judging by the missing paragraphs, were my sketches of Belaya's politicians in church during the 1995 holiday. Evidently it was the politicians she had in mind when she voiced concern for Father Dmitry, not the Church and its anathema. But then why, I wondered, would an American's observations of politicians cause harm to the head-priest of Belaya? Was her real fear that Russian readers, including Belaya's politicians, would assume that my thinking was a reflection of hers? Did she feel personally jeopardized? Was that her underlying fear all along? Then what about the portrait of her, which she described as "too good," and which remained unchanged? And so it went, in my head, question upon unanswered question, like a guessing game with no one to say right or wrong.

The year 1999 was fast coming to an end. Vasily wrote that Father Sergei was still expecting to publish the book, and that appeared to be the only way it was likely to see the light of day in Russia. The only other option was to pay for its publication, which increasingly seemed beyond the pale. Thus I rushed to finalize the manuscript, trying to get it to Father Sergei before the widely predicted Y2K computer failures. According to news reports, Russia, alone among industrialized nations, had taken no precautions whatsoever.

While racing toward that deadline, however, I had recurring, nagging doubts. Despite the reassurances of Vasily, whom I had perceived as a person of sound judgment, it was hard to believe that anyone, no matter how clairvoyant, would publish a book sight unseen. I realized that I was swimming in a very strange sea. Father Sergei espoused radical views about some things, but was quite orthodox about others. Would he really publish a book containing "heresies" associated with Eastern religion? Had Vasily fallen pray to mystical thinking and surrendered his Western, rational side?

Telling myself it was better not to think too much, I delved into finalizing the Russian text on my own. Wherever I could grasp Natasha's reasoning, I left her deletions as they were, creating transitions to fill the gaping holes. In only a few instances, where nothing made sense to me, did I restore the original text. Despite all that had transpired, I was still following her lead, respecting her preferences. Moreover, by that point, almost nothing seemed worth arguing over. My paramount desire was to complete the task, see the book published, and move on with my life.

In late December I sent the manuscript to Father Sergei by e-mail. His response came within a few days. He had read the entire manuscript. As I suspected, he was not intending to publish it on the basis of guidance alone. His message was extremely warm and friendly. The opening was a gracious invitation to return to Russia, to visit his church, to experience a new kind of religion and get to know his parishioners. As for the book, his verdict was: "It is too kind to Russia." He declined to publish it.

Thus, the entire saga ended with a whimper: "Too kind to Russia." I had heard such words before. Natasha had said essentially the same thing to Lyuba, fearing that my portrayal of her was "too good." I had also heard it in other ways, but I hadn't been ready to really *hear*. Now I was forced to. At first I felt a hollow emptiness inside. Then a rumbling began, like an earthquake that seemed to come from the very bowels of the earth. When it was over, the last of my illusions lay shattered in a heap of jagged-edged fragments.

After a few days, I began to collect myself and ask how? and why? How did I miss the signs that appeared along the way? How had I allowed myself to ignore them all, even the ones that appeared in bold print? How could I have come this far in life and still be blinded by illusion? And why? Why, in spite of all I had lived through, did I continue to cling to the ideal over the real? Would I ever learn to live in this world and make my peace with it?

The problem was that I heard a distant drummer. I had always heard it, for as long as I could remember. By the time I first discovered Findhorn, the spiritual community in Scotland, and learned that a new age was about to dawn, I was ready to "live" there in my mind. The New Age was real to me in a way that nothing in my daily life was real. My soul was alive to another way of existing on this earth, a way which I'd learned of largely through books about the Aquarian Age. The soul of Russia was also resonant with this vision of the future. The unfortunate reality was that its persona obstructed the way.

The way had been outlined in the wisdom teachings updated to inaugurate the coming age — in the books of Alice Bailey and others. It involved a conscious return to God — through spiritual *knowledge* rather than mere belief. Russians like Vasily understood this profoundly. Individually, in the depths of their souls, he and others were struggling to clear away the psychic debris of the 20th century's crusade to "annihilate God." They had grotesque ironies to deal with, like the obliteration of millions of brothers under the banner of worldwide brotherhood. There was still a yawning chasm between the radiant future and the path laid out to reach it. Nevertheless, they persisted in their quest for the divine.

The Russians I knew best were stoic survivors. Having glimpsed the abyss during the godless era, a totalitarian darkness that threatened to extinguish any spark of humanity, it was easy for them to make the leap forward. They joyfully embraced the next stage of evolution, dreaming of a world where spiritual light would prevail, where divine intelligence would govern, where the soul of humanity would flower. In this coming world, Dostoyevsky's call for Russians to demonstrate "the force of brotherhood and brotherly striving toward the reunification of mankind" could finally be heard and responded to.

Paradoxically, while much of America was drowning in materialism, I had met countless Russians who were probing the mysteries of our universe, pondering the deeper purposes of life. I ascribed some of my own blind spots to the sheer exhilaration of finding kindred spirits amongst our former enemy, the very people Americans had grown up fearing the most. In my own defense, I also realized that so much of what I had encountered was unfamiliar, and unexpected, making it difficult to interpret things accurately. And yet, in the depths of my soul, I knew that the dilemma in which I found myself had other causes, deeper still.

Out of the Ashes

M y friend Slava once told me an anecdote, in response to a question I had posed to him about the Russian character. The anecdote concerned an old woman and a dog, the woman's dearest companion. One day she brought home six chickens for laying eggs. The first night, her dog killed one of the chickens and ate it. The woman swore and hollered, warning the dog to stay away from the chickens. The next night the dog killed another chicken; again the woman swore and hollered. The same thing happened every night until the last chicken was gone, at which point the woman picked up a shotgun, killed her beloved pet, and fell into a state of inconsolable grief.

At the end, Slava shrugged and said, "No one understands the Russian character, not even Russians." Yet I noticed something oddly familiar about this anecdote. Its essence reminded me of an episode in *Eugene Onegin*, the masterful verse novel by Pushkin. In this episode, Onegin becomes intensely irritated at his good friend over something utterly trivial, and decides to take revenge. Onegin publicly humiliates his friend by winning the favor of his friend's betrothed at a party. To defend his honor, the friend challenges Onegin to a duel. Onegin is obliged to accept the challenge, though he does so unwillingly, and ends up killing his friend. In the end, he is awash in *self*-pity, for having lost his closest friend.

It occurred to me that Onegin, an intellectual, was a slave to his emotions in much the same way that the woman in Slava's anecdote was, and in much the way that her dog was a slave to his instincts. Just as Onegin had seemed unconcerned with the consequences of his actions, having failed to consider how his friend might react to being publicly humiliated, the woman had ignored the consequences of her *in*action — failing to protect her chickens after realizing their fate if she continued to do nothing. Both were victims of uncontrolled emotion (Russia's age-old Achilles heel), the cohort of a lack of logical thinking.

The parallels between the old woman and Eugene Onegin helped me comprehend the fate of my own book, at least the Russian version. When all was said and done, it appeared to be another tale of self-inflicted wounds. After exulting over the book and embracing it as a gift to Russia, a boon to Father Alexei's vision for Belaya, Natasha had turned against it. Instead of communicating her fears about it, trying to address them rationally, she instigated a campaign of resistance that left it mortally wounded. In the end, the greatest victim of this emotional frenzy was the spirit of sisterhood, out of which that version of the book had been born.

Unbridled emotions had made a blur of everything. Before it was all over, even the book's authorship had been called into question. This issue suddenly bobbed up when I first discovered the "missing pieces" in the translation and confronted Lyuba about them, asking why she and Nina Pavlovna had failed to alert me. It seemed absurd to remind her that I was, after all, the author of the book, until I heard her response. "It is not only your book," Lyuba declared, "it's also Natasha's book, and my book, and Nina Pavlovna's book."

From this point, the cultural divide widened into a chasm that seemed increasingly unbridgeable. In the eyes of my Russian coworkers, we were dealing with communal property. Lyuba stated, in a tone of righteous indignation, that she had put a year and a half of her life into the book, and that Nina Pavlovna had invested many long months in it. As for Natasha . . . well, without Natasha's story, and the trips to Belaya, and the access that she offered me to her world, what would remain of the book?

The converse of this line of thinking also surfaced, as the storm broke over what I perceived as deception. Nina Pavlovna introduced the notion of collective responsibility — part of an effort at peacemaking. When I asked her why she had neglected to put brackets around Natasha's changes as we had agreed, she replied, several weeks later, that she did what she felt was necessary to placate Natasha. She was acting on the premise that it was better to have a book with some deletions than to have no book at all. "Besides," she wrote, "We are all equally guilty. For the sake of the book, we must forgive each other and move on."

I was speechless. Not because I felt entirely blameless; it was my nature to search my conscience with a fine tooth comb for mistakes I might have made in any given situation. More importantly, I knew that nothing of this magnitude could possibly happen without just cause. I had to have done something to bring about this state of affairs. Yet in this situation, in this lifetime, I could not fathom how I was "equally guilty." Search though I did, I came up empty-handed.

The only logical explanation, for me, was that I was reaping karma rooted in the past. Whatever wrongs I had committed must have originated in a previous lifetime, or lifetimes. It seemed beyond question that Natasha, and I, and Lida, and Lyuba, and Nina Pavlovna, and many others had known each other before, undoubtedly in Russia. The ties that once bound us were evidently powerful enough to bring us together again in this life, against all odds, considering the vast divides of geography, history, and culture.

These ties, however, seemed destined to be ephemeral this time around. It appeared that their purpose was to bring me back to an unfinished past, to somehow resolve it, and then to move on. My liberation came with Nina Pavlovna's attempt to tar us all with the same brush. The notion that we were "equally guilty" didn't wash with me. I found her attempt to keep us unified under the banner of collective guilt, to save the book, a curious sort of olive branch. It obscured any sense of individual responsibility or any true understanding of what had taken place.

By this point, even if publishers had come knocking at my door, I could not have gone forward with the book *as it was,* and I didn't have the stomach to go back to it and take another look. Mercifully, I was spared that dilemma when Father Sergei declined to publish it. Nina Pavlovna offered to look for other publishers, but I couldn't muster up any encouragement for her to do so. It seemed she and Lyuba had concluded that Natasha's way was the only way, but it wasn't my way. In the end, the book I had written took a back seat to the liberation of my soul.

I had no doubt that I had "earned" my plight, but it took time for me to understand how or why. As the dust was settling, I looked back over the most critical challenges I had faced in this lifetime. They all involved relationships with powerful people. A pattern emerged, starting in childhood with my mother, and ending, finally, with Natasha. The core issue, I realized, was the use and abuse of power: arbitrary authority, domination of the weak by the strong, the imposition of one person's will over another.

In the course of exploring Russian spirituality, my soul evidently had another priority. It had engaged me in a learning experience of another kind. The book was my teacher. Its chief lesson was about the destructive power of unchecked human will. Knowing how the laws of karma and reincarnation work, I could hardly doubt that I was suffering the consequences of past actions. In this light, the dénouement of my rendezvous with Russia was actually an encounter with a distorted aspect of myself, though largely inverted in this lifetime so that I could experience being on the receiving end. I came to see the characters in my Russian drama as mirrors of a part of myself in need of redemption. From there, it was only a small step to forgiveness.

Natasha, of course, was the toughest one to forgive. I could not have imagined that a friend would betray my trust as she had, or encourage others to do the same, in order to gain control of a situation that cried out for cooperation. But it appeared that her line of least resistance, her habitual mode of behavior, was to dictate the desired outcome of a given situation. Her actions reflected a distortion of will that was utterly incongruous with the sense of our being "spiritual sisters." In the end, I was left to conclude that she was acting on blind instinct, reminiscent of the woman and her beloved dog.

Natasha was, after all, the product of a culture where power was everything, where the powerful had no need to explain or to apologize, where individual rights did not exist, and thus the powerless were forced to submit, to swallow betrayals and humiliations and to go on, passing abuse down the chain to those still less powerful. At the same time, paradoxically, Natasha was an old soul, an old soul who remained the victim of her emotions. Unable to cope with conflicting feelings about seeing the book in print, she had fallen into an emotional morass, ultimately destroying the very thing she had sought to bring into manifestation.

At least she destroyed it for me. Despite my intense attachment to the book, after all those years of involvement with it, I was forced to let it go, to let it die. It became Natasha's book. In early 2001, I learned from Lida that Natasha "was ready" to publish it, and later I heard that it was being published by Belaya's historical-cultural society. For reasons as obscure as ever, Natasha evidently wanted to keep me abreast of things, though I never heard from her again, nor did I ever see a copy of the Russian version of my book. The "English version" was apparently never meant to be.

For a time I felt as if I had lost a child. I would joke with friends about the length of my "pregnancy." I had heard somewhere that the gestation period of an elephant was nine years, which wasn't true, but that was exactly how long it took to give birth to my volume on the soul of Russia. When it turned out to be stillborn, at first the pain of loss was nearly unbearable. So much of my own life had gone into it, only to see it die.

But with time I was able to perceive, from the stance of the soul, that in Russia, especially in Natasha, I had met a part of myself that needed to die. By letting go of the book, and by assimilating its spiritual lessons, I was able to release traces of a personality pattern that had accompanied my soul from past incarnations into this one. By the end of my Russian odyssey I sensed, in every fiber of my being, that old karmic debts had been repaid; that the scales of justice had been balanced. A reckoning had taken place.

With that reckoning came my freedom, true freedom. My soul felt completely unburdened, released from the past. I entered a state of existence different from any I had previously known, lighter in every sense of that word. The experience of death had stripped me of all remnants of personae, masks, false identities. Feeling as though I were standing naked before the world, I experienced an epiphany. My personality, my individuality, had nothing left to lose, and also nothing left to prove. Only my soul remained, shorn of unwanted baggage, and filled with indescribable joy.

That, it appears, was the Higher Purpose all along. Out of the ashes, a spark of creativity miraculously burst into flame. A new book began to write itself, the one you are now reading. It flowed into my mind from a higher place like a clear and uninterrupted stream. Its intent was to portray a life's journey from the vantage point of a soul. The writing of it, directed by my spiritual guides, helped me to interpret, chapter and verse, the meaning of my encounter with Russia — in this incarnation.

As for the past, details of my Russian sojourns remain largely buried in the mists of time. My soul memory was potent enough to stir recognition of people and places, but not the particulars of past lifetimes. Wise Ones say that this form of forgetting is a demonstration of divine mercy. Were we to know all there is to know about the journey of our souls through time, everything done in ignorance over the course of countless lifetimes, the burden would be too great for us to bear. Far better that we learn just enough of the past to glean its lessons.

As for Mother Russia, so much a part of my existence for well over a decade, she, too, has receded into the past. The unfinished business that swept me back into her orb exists no more. I can only guess how many lifetimes I spent on Russian soil, but it very likely was more than one. The small white cottage at Optina Pustyn that beckoned to me so powerfully was a very holy place. Surely it was somewhere else, at some other time, perhaps even in another country, that I incurred the debt that came due in this lifetime. At present, all that matters is that this entry in the Book of Life can now be marked "paid in full."

BVG